Helter Skelter

Clash of Beliefs   1177

Helter Skelter

Helter Skelter 2nd Edition (Colour)

'... or, if the Gods are not wilfully involved through jealousy or spite, they sit idly by while man wrecks himself through passion or heedlessness.'   On the Tragedies of Euripides.

This book is for my grandchildren
and all the children of the world

Copyright © 2018 Tom Law

ISBN 9780648226819

Published in Australia by:

Longership Publishing Australia

Swifts Creek Victoria 3896 AUSTRALIA

ABN 73446736413

email: longership@email.com

First published in Australia 2018

Copyright © Tom Law 2018

Cover design: Tom Law

The right of Tom Law to be identified as the Author of the Work has been asserted in accordance with the Copyright, Designs and Patents Act 1988.

Cover Photo: Ekaterina Kr by G.Boksteiner

Law, Tom

Helter Skelter 2nd Edition (Colour)

ISBN: 9780648226819

pp 304

Helter Skelter

Helter Skelter

tom law

LONGERSHIP

OCEANA

Longership Publishing Australia

Helter Skelter

Helter Skelter

Contents

Helter Skelter

Detail, Christ Carrying the Cross, Mathis Grünewald 1522

Then Jesus told them: "Before this night is over, you will fall to pieces because of what happens to me! There is a scripture that says:

I'll strike the shepherd;
helter-skelter the sheep will be scattered.

But after I am raised up, I, your Shepherd, will go ahead of you, leading the way to Galilee."

Matthew 26:31-32 The Message.

11

Helter Skelter

Helter Skelter

Forward

Many people will criticise and perhaps even feel disdain at the content of this book. To others it will cause anger and promulgate abuse as they throw it across the room or out of the window. Despite such reactions I guarantee that the reader will, possibly against her or his better judgement, crawl over the carpet or rush to the street below to retrieve the text and continue on to the last page. The problem that we all face is that when our preconceptions are challenged we pass through various states of emotion. Firstly, as predicted, anger and disbelief; then comes a period of rumination as we digest the confronting information and think on it; lastly comes the painful revelation as our consciousness accepts a paradigm shift in values and beliefs when we come to the realisation that we have been lied to and that deceit and treachery manifest themselves as blatant truth regarding the nature of the complex world of which we are all a part. A long time after we have been transformed and move along our personal timeline of everyday life we start to ask of ourselves the most basic question: "so what can I do about this reality?" This opens up a whole spectrum of action by us mostly powerless and feeble humans when wanting to challenge the Goliathan corporations that are doing the wrong thing. Most of us will do nothing, others will join political groups, join demonstrations, write protest letters to newspapers or place posts on social media whilst a miniscule percentage will choose direct action and travel down the road of terrorism. But terrorism is a convenient label for the powerful to use when describing the minute pinpricks against its colossal mass and hideous inertia. The individual intellect need discern, when viewing and dissecting a whole range of actions by the giants, .. must discern which actions are the greater evil? This is the dilemma of modern humans in the complexity of the machine termed global society!

To assist my readers before they are confronted by fake mirrors, reflections and refractions of language, oscillatory coordinates and place in space-time, let me warn that the storyline is interwoven with political outpourings, observations and graffiti ramblings. Sequence is a problem as factual narrative merges into drama, futuristic fantasy and prediction. So, as I said, be warned: the flow is deceptive as the text is driven into cataracts, over waterfalls and through chasms lined with sharp rocks and oblique boulders. The writing is at times confused, abstract and didactic.. in other words, unconventional!

Although the tome displays bucket loads of negativity and evil, the Coda titled "Of Course, It Doesn't Have to End This Way!" is a final escape route to the possibility of an alternative and possibly something better. Humankind is not innately wicked. The majority wish to follow happy and fulfilled lives that have meaning and purpose. The various kaleidoscopes of the media give us false hopes of perfection. Perfection in physical attributes, perfection in clothes, perfection in material possessions and the dream of excessive wealth. However, with just a bit of common sense we should all see through these games and trickery and identify the 'illywhacker' at the fairground with his ridiculous promises of the elixir of eternal youth for just ten dollars!

Family, close friends and a determination each day to make some contribution to your fellow beings, however small, is the true path to happiness. Avoid excess in anything, for excess is poison to the body and the spirit or inner you! Some choose comfort in their religion; it is not for any of us to judge for our existence is temporal and short when compared to the eternity of the stars. The message in the book is oft repeated; be patient and tolerant and you may get something of value from the words herein.   Tom Law, Mt Beauty Nov. 2017

This 2nd Edition is the colour version of original with minor editing.

Minus One **Minus One**

It was cold at 6 am on a Friday morning as the handsome young woman made her way to the central railway station in Amsterdam. She purchased a return ticket to Rotterdam then made her way to the platform, grabbing a long black coffee from a vending machine en route. Pigeons flapped above her head as she sat almost motionless on a long grey plastic bench. Her breath formed little clouds which mixed with the steam rising from the coffee. The styrene mug kept her hands warm. There were already many commuters on the platform which she assumed were going to work in the next big city. The journey would only take about twenty five minutes.

"Goedemorgen missen, waar ga je deze koude ochtend?" said an elderly woman taking her seat next to the younger woman. She was wearing a buttoned up gabardine full length coat and scarlet woollen scarf wrapped to cover her neck and mouth.

"I am very sorry, I do not speak Dutch"

"Ah you iz Englisch ya?"

"Australian actually.. so you can speak English?"

"Oh yes, I have been to London many times. I have a son working at the Great Ormond Street Hospital as a surgeon.. yes many times! So where you come from?"

"Well I was born in Jakarta, Indonesia. My father is Australian and I was brought up in Melbourne."

In fact the young woman grew up in the country, but that was too long a story to tell, far simpler to say Melbourne. After all she did live and attend a girl's secondary school there for several years.

Just then the high speed intercity slowed to a halt at the platform.

"This is your train? Better get on quickly, it rarely pauses for more than a couple of minutes.. always rush rush rush these days; take care now!"

The younger picked up her overnight bag and got onto the express and quickly found a seat. Before long the outskirts of Amsterdam were flashing past the broad carriage window. She flicked through a fashion magazine also purchased from a machine at the station and looked mainly at the pictures, guessing at the text. A few passengers were hidden behind newspapers but most were focussed on cell phones or pads, either reading text or just listening to music. After fifteen minutes she started to nod off for a quick respite. A narrow screen at the end of the carriage flashed the next station accompanied by a female voice describing the same.

"We naderen nu Rotterdam Centraal Station, We naderen nu Rotterdam Centraal Station" came the voice at last. The woman bustled into the aisle packed with commuters. It seemed as though all were intending to alight.

The large news-screen in the pavilion rattled off the latest world events, sports news and lastly the weather. It was still minus one degree Celsius this November morning in the city. The woman approached a fast-food restaurant, one of the Dutch chains recommended to her by her Aunt back in Amsterdam. She ordered an omelette and another coffee from the polite and efficient android at the counter. It was not quite 7 am yet. She had arranged to meet another student from Warwick, England at 7.30 on the main steps at the Northern exit. She had her pad with her if anything went wrong.

Sure enough the young man was there as she exited the pavilion. They shook hands and exchanged a cordial 'good morning'

"Well you made it. I wasn't sure.. thought maybe you would have second thoughts on the whole deal?"

"No, I said I would join you, and here I am!"

"I am staying in an apartment with sympathetic students about three K away so we'll take an ubbu."

"OK"

The pair got into the driverless cab, spoke their destination and settled back. The woman was keen to look at the buildings parks and gardens as they whisked along various streets through the city. They passed the Museumpark, the Museum Boijmans Van Beuningen and Erasmus Medical Centre affiliated with the University.

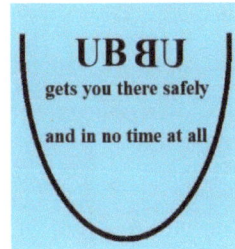

UB ᘔU
gets you there safely
and in no time at all

On arrival, the woman was introduced to two other students in a fairly spacious apartment. One was tall, lanky with long dark hair and an immature looking beard; he had a spotty face! The other young man was more handsome with moderately cut blond hair and an athletic physique. "This is Hans and Johann. They are lending us a room but will be away for the weekend so we'll have it to ourselves. I already have everything we need for the operation. Johann has been particularly helpful as he has many contacts. We should be safe here after it is done. I recommend that you don't return to Amsterdam until Monday morning at earliest to reduce the chance of being picked up!"

"That suits me fine. I plan to visit the Witte de With Centre for Contemporary Art on Sunday as well as wander about the CBD."

The plan had been hatched by the 'inner clique' of students at a meeting in 'The Ragged Staff' hotel in Warwick a few weeks before. This operation was to be of a violent nature against a Military Fair and Expo in the city and not a mere street demonstration. The organising company

'Bach-Trumpet' would be inviting Sheiks, Shahs , Military and Government leaders from around the world to attend a conference and exposé on all the latest military hardware at 'The Palace Concordia' in downtown Rotterdam. During the day there would be a huge assemblage of students, unionists and Labour Party (i.e Dutch equivalent) members protesting the fair from the street. The venue would be heavily guarded by armed police.

The plan for the pair however, was to plant a bomb on the roof of the building at 2 am in the morning. Immediately after the explosion, a couple of aging grenades were to be tossed into the rupture hole to do more damage at ground level. The aim was to avoid human casualties such as had happened at the London fair the month before; but at the same time perform enough physical damage to render the fair unworkable!

This was a complete turnaround for the young woman who had always despised and shunned any form of violence, preferring passive resistance. Why had she decided to go down this road.. it was so out of character? Perhaps the arrest of her boyfriend whom was involved in the London attack had persuaded her! Or rather, the knowledge that she was about to return home to Australia before Christmas due to the deteriorating world situation may have determined some false sense of security? Whatever the reason, she had committed herself and there was now no chance of turning back.

It was after midnight when the pair entered a gloomy apartment block adjacent to the Palace Concordia, the man carrying a haversack. Again it was extremely cold. They rang the bell at a door on the third floor and were immediately admitted by an elderly man seemingly in his sixties. No names were mentioned, in fact they were received by a mere nod and a grunt. No words were spoken. The old man's apartment was small but tidy with two walls covered with books from floor to ceiling on planks with bricks between as supports. A computer sat on an old wooden desk and was streaming world news in American English. The old man was obviously some kind of academic, maybe a university lecturer or a writer. He proffered some hot soup and bread followed by bakery cakes and coffee.

They sat in silence until about 1.30 am when the old man gesticulated with his hand pointing to the ceiling. Putting on balaclavas, they followed him up a short flight of stairs then out onto a level roof top where some washing still hung on a line; ancient metal boxes hummed with fans feeding the reverse cycle air conditioners of the apartment complex below.

The distance from the parapet to the adjacent building was about two metres which presented a problem, particularly for the woman. But the old man produced a plank some eight feet long which was carefully straddled across the gap. The fall to the cement paving below was around forty feet (12 metre). Apart from being below freezing, there was no wind; the city was bathed in an eerie silence and the stars shone down brightly. The young woman momentarily thought about the remote countryside in her native Australia; but here there was only the smell of diesel, no sweet aroma of eucalyptus and wattle blossom! The young man crossed first. Hesitant, it took the young woman a few minutes to pluck up courage to cross.

"Just don't look down" the professor whispered in husky tone.

Almost across, there rose a faint sound of footsteps from the narrow lane far below. The pair froze. A soldier lit up a cigarette, said something to his companion causing a guffaw; then the two proceeded on their way chatting in low pitched voices as they went.

About half way up the sloping roof, the young man took a bundle from the haversack and set it down. He passed a single grenade to the woman.

"I hope you have practiced with these" he whispered.

"Of course I have. Are they set to four seconds?" she responded.

"All's good, don't worry. Just try not to miss that's all!"

The woman felt the cold creeping in to her body and soul. She shook just a little from anxiety as well as the low temperature of the air.

"OK it's ready to fire. You get back across to the other wall and get down. I'll be right behind you."

A minute more passed when suddenly there was a deafening explosion with debris hurled high into the air then raining down where the two students crouched. The man suddenly stood up, pulled the pin of his grenade and threw it into the gaping hole. The woman followed suit. Her grenade hit the roof above the hole.

"Christ" retorted the man. But fortunately the grenade rolled down into the hole and dropped into the dark cavernous space below. Two more violent explosions were heard welling up out of the building. The pair quickly escaped back down the stair from off the roof and back into the old man's apartment.

The professor signalled for the couple to lie quietly. Time passed. Suddenly there were many heavy footsteps in the stair well and loud shouting. Armed soldiers were banging on every door and screaming for the occupants to open up. The sound of heavy boots reached the third floor and the door of the old man; the three lay as quiet as mice. Several more minutes passed. More orders shouted and more footsteps. Suddenly there was a crash and bright lights flooded the room. A sudden 'rat-at-tat-tat' was the last thing the woman heard as pain shot through her body.. excruciating and rapid pain as she had never experienced before.. then within seconds, all went black.

The following morning news burst all over the Western TV media of the terror attack in Rotterdam. Three terrorists were shot dead at the scene of the crime. Two were believed to be English and one to be a local of the Netherlands. A Major of the Dutch Special Anti-Terror Squad was interviewed. He seemed to relish the success of his men and could not desist from a cruel smile on his countenance in front of the cameras and reporters. He praised his men for a job well done! There were no other casualties.

Later in the day the news reports had subtly changed the story: "It is now reported that this was an Islamic terrorist attack in Rotterdam.. Islam Khilafah has claimed responsibility!"

A small group of students huddled in a corner of the bar of 'The Ragged Staff' in Warwick, England ruminating on the news. They were glad of the success of the venture but saddened by the loss of two of their colleagues.. a heavy price to pay!

"IK played no part in this.. typical of the fricking establishment and the media.. they never get it right!" said one in muffled tones.

"Oh you are quite wrong there old chap; they feed the masses with the story they want us all to believe.. they're not stupid! Never miss an opportunity to twist it their way. Who's up for another pint?"

Helter Skelter

Zero   **Early Daze**

Jumping Back Some Fifty Years Earlier: It had rained during the night and all was wet. Sun rays burst through the tree clad crest of the opposite hill to give narrow shafts of light through the rising mist. A black wallaby foraged close by as the boy pushed through the long wet grass, fern, nettle and thistle, flicking back sprays of jewels as their heads and stems sprang to their former upright positions. Broken black bark peeled from dead wattle. The lush and shady leaves of the tight foliage of blackwoods still provided an eerie shade twixt night and day. The creek gurgled and sang as it meandered between rounded boulders. The boy wore rubber boots and his blue raincoat. He pressed against some dogwood and stumbled up a slippery pathway a few metres until he stood on a verdant river flat of just an acre or so. Turquoise, verte, olive, ochre.. every hue and shade of blue and green enveloped the boy. The gullies on distant hills still shrouded with fogs lay dark and black as they creased the spectre of hill folded behind hill and onward down the tight valley. The mingled verse of lorikeet, thrush, blue wren and bellbird played on his ears. Startled and perceiving a change he moved forward with evoked inquisitiveness. There were neatly piled stacks of timber covered in black plastic the skirts of which flapped about in the soft breeze. Low stone walls appeared forming a rectangle with a half finished chimney standing clear at one end. Three large boxes of blue-grey slates randomly lay on the ground tilting this way and that. Each bore the label 'Devonian Quarries, Marysville'. Tethered, a large black goat stood aloft one of the boxes and gave a gentle bleat. A few tools lay scattered about such as hammers, shovels and steel wedges all bathed in a film of dew not yet dried.

The sun made more effort now, breaking the puffy clouds above and revealing an expanse of blue sky promising a fine day. Kookaburras laughed in unison in a gay chorus to welcome the morn. Many other birds were hopping hither, flying thither and filling the air with sweet melodies. The boy was taken aback at the new scene since his last visit to this cranny some months before. Suddenly the newcomer emerged from the doorway of a large steel shed tucked in close to the hill. Tall and slender grey box and apple box trees lurched menacingly above threatening its imminent destruction. Cascades of mistletoe, its fake leaves glittering red-orange reflecting the sunlight from their oily surfaces hung overhead. The newcomer wore a white grubby jumper with roll-neck and wine coloured chord jeans frayed at the knees. His long main was of pure gold and his beard red and profuse as a pirate's. He stretched and yawned then his gaze fell upon the boy.

"Morning me lad, what's your game then so early?"

The boy was rooted and dumbfounded, not able to form words at all. In fear of the newcomer's countenance he just stared at the ground in front of him. In a gentler tone

"Where did you come from? Did you walk all the way from town?" The newcomer seemed friendly enough and the boy stammered

"I often comes this way mister, for fishin' eels in the creek. I likes to poke about the dumps jest looking fer things you know".

"I see" said the newcomer "but it's so early in the day for a lad to be wandering the bush alone- you know these parts then?"

"Oh yes sir, I've been many times with me dad. But now I comes by meself mainly as dad is always busy workin'".

A robin flew onto the cement mixer, poised, looked about then flew down to pick up a grub then immediately flew away again. Picking up courage and surveying the scene the boy said

"What are you doing here mister, building someint?"

"Yeah, it's a long project but I am building a house here. I hope you don't mind?"

At this the boy shuffled his boots and looked down at the ground again. Without eye contact he just whispered

"It's OK mister".

"Call by any time then" said the newcomer as he started to shovel gravel and sand into the gaping mouth of the mixer. The boy gave a bit of a smile then retraced his steps back to the creek. The newcomer leant on his shovel watching the blue of the boy's coat as it merged with the surrounding plants and trees until it disappeared altogether. A group of black cockatoos screeched as they swooped overhead, settling in the higher branches of the tall river gums. "Omen of storms" thought the stranger at his self constructed myth. "They've flown from the Dargo no doubts".

The lad of hardly a baker dozen years or more slipped away along the stream, dazed as a sleepwalker. Then 'cross pebble and brook investigating every corner for colour and living things to please his mind and tender his soul in harmony. 'Twas here he belonged; this his playground of nature's gifts bestowed by that unseen cosmic hand for boy and man to wander or therein build his home at leisure; to explore, to engage and supplement the yearning inner soul.

He was certain that the boy was close at hand on many occasions after that. The newcomer sensed his presence in some way. But the boy, guarded, always kept his distance as he passed the building site so that the newcomer did not catch a glimpse of him again. However, on inquiring at the general store the newcomer gleaned a little of this solitary personage. He was the son of a mill hand.

"You know, the bloke who lost his arm a while back.. that's his eldest boy. He's a MacIntyre!"

The newcomer also sensed that he had ventured into the boy's world of escape on purchasing this wild three acre block adjacent to the old mine workings upon which to build a home for his young family. But the land was large and there was enough space for the boy to wander and fossick to his heart's content. The newcomer hoped the boy would remain happy and share without malice this small area of his playground.

Later that morning the newcomer and his young family were scouring hills and dales for the gifts of nature; namely mushrooms, mint and wild asparagus. Later in the season they will collect blackberries and later again, rosehips. But the most tedious of their efforts is the collecting of rocks and river stones for the walls of the new abode. Schist, granite and the occasional white quartz were all to be had close at hand. The miner's middens from their excavations in search of gold-bearing quartz reefs were everywhere and although often covered in moss and lichen, made easy pickings. The elder boy lets out a scream as he is bitten by a jumping jack and his mother comforts him with the immediate application of a soothing cream to the skin.

"You can continue alone now, we will return to the shed and I will prepare some lunch."

The young man with his shoulder length locks continues to place rocks into the small trailer pulled by a red super-bug (German VW car). He flicks off any unwanted ants, spiders or scorpions with a robotic dextrous swift movement of his hand. He has done such collecting so many times before it is now a natural rhythm and regimented process. When satisfied that the trailer is reasonably full, he drives back to the house-site and deposits the rocks on a growing pile.

The occasional copper head, black snake or large brown may be seen. There are no tiger snakes down here but plenty up in the higher country. A large blue tongue lizard lazily sleeps in the sun not caring on the activity close at hand. It is hot now and the cicadas drum to a deafening music in the trees above. It is a relief to enter the shed for respite of the day's heat and to peck at some delicacies prepared by the loving hand of his wife.

"Cold roast lamb, tomato and green chutney, sangers.. would you like tea of coffee?"

"I think I'll take a glass of milk.. might have a nap after lunch, too bloody hot to go out there!"

"Oh I forgot to mention that Guy Italiano is down the block unloading some hives. He said that you'd already OK'd it with him."

"Yeah, he promised to give us some honey. I'll stroll down as soon as I've finished eating."

"Oooh can I come too dad?" piped in young Bill.

"Well as long as you keep well clear and run home as soon as I tell you OK?"

"Great dad.. I will"

Although only a three year old, Bill would never wish to miss an opportunity of accompanying his dad on a stroll through the bush; and to see the bee-man at work was an extra bonus. Guy had travelled up from Romano Island on the Gippsland Lakes. He was familiar with the best places in the forested hinterland to place his bees and cautiously followed the seasonal burst of flowers from field, water course and gum tree to maximise the yield.

There was always such a variety of fair in the country kitchen. Quince jelly, rabbit pie, homemade bread with the addition of walnuts, chestnuts, almonds and hazel nuts when in season. Guy's clover and wattle blossom honey was as clear as a mountain stream with the most delicate and fragrant aroma and taste.. an elixir of the Gods! With the arrival of the first frost, the sweet texture of the perfumed persimmon was a breakfast favourite. The newcomer liked to make cider, blackberry nip, beers and other concoctions from the fruit at hand. A favourite was rosehip mead; tedious to make but a rewarding drink.

Heavy rain brought the Bogong moths from the ground. They flapped everywhere day and night for several days leaving their powdery trails over clothes and furniture, pillows and towels. The writer will regale with his story about a local farming lad that was called up to Geelong for a classy wedding of a former school chum. Retrieving his mothballed suite from the wardrobe, off he went to the salubrious occasion, stuffing his prepared speech into his breast pocket. At the quintessential moment he stood with glass raised and pulled his sheet from the pocket. To the amazement and mirth of the guests, a giant Bogong moth emerged from same pocket and flapped over table among the now hysterical revellers.

"Well Bruce" retorted the groom spontaneously, "you've certainly brought the Snowy Mountains to Geelong!"

The newcomer was very busy over the next week preparing for the 'raising'. There were twelve massive messmate beams lying close to the stone walls of lounge and kitchen, now completed to ten feet or so from the ground. Each beam was about sixteen feet in length and six inches by twelve inches in cross-section. These must be raised to straddle the stone walls and being several hundred weight each, some thought and careful planning on the operation was necessary.

After playing with his son's Fischertechnik, the newcomer devised a hoist in the form of two parallelogram structures pivoted on large bolts acting as axils. With the aid of steel cable, block pulleys and a friend's 4-wheel drive vehicle, the beams could be lifted horizontally and slid across the walls into position. The big day arrived and a dozen friends assembled to assist with lifting and cheering. Remarkably the job was completed in less than two hours. Glazed Dave exclaimed

"I just wish my father was here to see this!"

Soon after, wives and children joined for a picnic and celebration with much food, wines and beers and homemade lemon cordial. The story swapping on the progress of each of the other owner-builders was intense. Then topics such as brewing, tree-planting and vegetable growing were taken up with keen interest. Seed savers were discussed as well as different approaches to tilling and preparing the soil for various crops. The scene reminded one of the Christian Germanic Amish people of America. This was a community effort extraordinaire and much appreciated by the newcomer and his family. The way was now prepared for the raising of ridge and rafters which the newcomer would do mainly by his self with a little assistance from the Russian.

Later that evening there was to be a 'Bush Dance' at the Mechanics Institute in Rushing Creek. Most representatives of the new influx of owner builders and their families were there along with many local families. The band 'The Rollickin Bushwhackers' up from Stratford way included a variety of traditional instruments including Gaelic tabors, bodhrans and flutes. The mix of music was of Celtic renaissance, traditional Australian and American country folk. The Pride of Erin and many progressive square dances were taught to the novices by the eloquent gestures and guidance of the band's compare and leader, one Max Guilgrig.

It was a wonderful evening of ancient pageantry where adults and children mixed freely on the dance floor to pass away the evening having immense fun. It mattered not if you were novice or expert. Everyone passed a delightful and friendly evening to the beat of simple and uncomplicated music. The band members were shared among the guests for free lodging. In one case, the music continued at home to the wee small hours accompanied by non-conservative quantities of liqueurs and rolled tobacco.

The night demonstrated a welcomed tolerance of the established country folk to the idealistic young invaders from the city. At last one could detect a melding of the two with meaningful dialogue and learning on both sides. There were no extreme puritanical stances but an appreciation to the views of each. For the country folk, some of their long held views were challenged. For the idealists from the big smoke, the recognition that country life is not so simple or easy came as a shock. But they were hardy stock and took each blow in their stride and loved every moment of their chosen pathways. All had slightly different approaches, but all made up a beautiful patchwork of a new society with recognisable common values; to strive and survive as best one could with limited resources and, when possible, to enjoy one's life to the full in a healthy and creative way.

Whether it was the natural spores of the trees and grasses dissolved in the cool night air, or a slight excess of oxygen when compared to the phlogiston of the dirty town; or perhaps even the slight elevation of the local topography? .. but it is unarguable fact that one slumbered deeply and contentedly through the night in this haven of havens!

Helter Skelter

Another morning. There are stone walls and heavy beams straddling the walls. Windows and doors are the vacant eyes of a building under construction. The newcomer has decided to raise the ridge plank first before hoisting the rafters one at a time. He has a tower structure of crude timbers, blocks and steel rope. Using his car he will pull the rope to hoist the ridge beam. Pausing for a rest and a drink of water the newcomer took in the panorama of hills and forest about him. Only nature filled his view with no sign of a habitation anywhere on the landscape before him. A gentle breeze wafted and blew the high branches of river gums back and forth in a gentle rhythm. The sun reflected from thousands of individual leaves in a sparkly display like Christmas tinsel, delighting the heart and soul of the builder. He paused to reflect about his plans and life in this haven of stream, hill and tree far from the bustle of his own childhood. He dwelt on his beautiful wife with her fair skin, blue eyes and long dark hair. He gazed down on his two small sons Bill and Jonas, with their rosy cheeks and golden hair, playing in the sand pile. Pausing for those few moments he experienced the ultimate sensation of joy and happiness with his life, his luck and fortune, in his creation and that of his maker. It passed entirely through his being as a wave bringing a tremor to both his body and soul. Carl Jacobs was indeed a most fortunate man wanting for nought!

This chapter was adapted from 'Boy in Blue Raincoat' by Tom Law

One   **Enough is Enough**

We have moved on some forty years with Carl being remarried and recently returned home after many years living and working in Indonesia and China. Once again he has two young children, this time a girl and a boy. Read on:

No longer the 'newcomer' and with much water having flowed down the Rapid River, Carl Jacobs looked out his lounge room window over a frosted stretch of grass towards a thin dirt road adjoining the main thoroughfare some seventy metres away. A collection of mailboxes roughly attached to wooden poles stood huddled together at various angles to each other, bearing rust or flaking paint of differing colours. Two magpies clung overhead to the power line. A boy and a girl stood close by to the mailboxes throwing pebbles to the road and occasionally at each other as they waited for the arrival of the school bus. It was a ten kilometre ride into Rushing Creek, a small hamlet of some four hundred souls.

A pub, a bakery, a corner store and a post office were its main commercial services to this community which was also served by a timber mill and government Lands Department office. A Bush Nursing Centre provided daily health care and where a locum doctor presented one day each week. Cattle and sheep grazed lazily on the surrounding hillsides. This was the hinterland of Eastern Victoria, Australia. It was pretty; it was for the most part relaxed and the community thrived. Despite being only about four hundred persons in all, it boasted three churches; however congregations were normally just a handful of people, sometimes as few as just three or four attendees.

Carl had returned from a teaching job in China and his Indonesian wife

Tina was studying online for a Masters degree in Secondary Teaching. Her main subject was Computers which she had taught in international schools in her native Indonesia and later in China. Their two children, Charlotte (Charly) and Jason (Jay) were almost fluent in Chinese as each had attended a Government Primary school in Nanjing, Jiangsu Province. In fact Jay had been born in China. After returning to Australia, the children had missed their apartment, extravagant trips to Shanghai to shop, travelling on the Metro and visits to the Zoo and museums. The Australian bush was at first alien to them after their previous cosmopolitan way of life. However they soon made new friends and began to enjoy the freedom, clean air and the birds and animals around their home as well as playing in the cool waters of the creek on a hot summer' day. Carl had purchased an antiquated Disco (Landrover) which added to their exploration of the forests and mountains in this nook of Victoria.

A black snake or occasional brown snake invaded the chicken house and surrounding garden but generally these kept out of the way of humans. Parrots, kookaburras, blue wrens, blackbirds, thrushes, wedge tail eagles, bower birds and honey eaters were all visitors. The buzzing of a frogmouth or coo coo sound of an owl competing with the 'kark kark' of a fox lulled them to sleep at night.

There were no restaurants; neither kaki-limas nor travelling salesmen came to disturb them; it was a haven of peace and tranquillity splashed with the olives, greens and browns of eucalyptus and acacias over feminine curves of surrounding hills. On a breathless evening one could just discern the chatter chatter of the creek as it journeyed towards the mighty Rapid River. Morning mists cloaking the surrounding hills reminded them of Chinese or Japanese scenes they had experienced in the Changzhou Art Gallery.

Actually, just a hundred years before, these same hills rang to the voices, tunes and thumps of Chinese gold diggers that had come to seek their fortune (coins with the familiar central square hole might still be found with a metal detector). Most had returned home but a few stayed, now lying in the local bush cemetery in unmarked graves. It would have been a very hard existence in these remote valleys and gullies during the nineteenth century.

This was Carl's second marriage. He had built a stone house here years before having raised two fine strong sons Bill and Jonas, each now a professional man with a family of their own living in far away Melbourne. Why had he returned to this remote haven? Well for the same reasons he chose to live here some thirty years before: to live a life at a slower pace and enjoy the products of his own labour, as close to self-sufficiency as is humanly possible. He had always loved these mountains from his student days. But the thought of some final catastrophic war had also nagged at the inner recesses of his mind; he did not wish to be part of a big city. He recognised that if such a war ever came, his family would stand a better chance of survival living in a small community in a remote location blessed with natural gifts of clean air, water, soil and forest.

Carl's new family seemed to readily adapt to this environment and soon came to enjoy and appreciate all it had to offer. The children were reasonably versed in three languages at such a young age: Indonesian, Mandarin and English. Their mother was Muslim but not conservative. Her parents lived and worked in Bogor on Java Island as Agricultural research scientists that had already interacted with Australians from CSIRO as well as from Monash University in Melbourne. They were quite liberal and vastly different from those Muslims of the Middle East or even the more conservative neighbour, Malaysia! However, Rushing Creek was a remote rural community of mainly Anglo-Celtic stock with a smattering of Irish, German and Dutch. It was a little conservative itself and Muslims at this point in time were not quite the flavour of the year! The community had however experienced an Egyptian doctor in recent years. Tina met a minimal of prejudice from the miniscule ignorant, but on the whole was readily accepted. As an outgoing woman with copious energy, she did not find it difficult to accumulate a circle of close friends.

But this story is more about Charly than the rest of the family and there is little description about her other than her linguistic abilities. Charly was perhaps more than a little hyperactive as a child. She loved books, drawing, painting and music. She was a highly skilled communicator with a strong mindset, always knowing what she wanted and where she was headed. It should be mentioned that she understood a smattering of Arabic as well.. at least the characters and prayer words of the archaic language of her mother's religion which she whole heartily embraced. Prayer was just a dutiful thing that one did. Apart from that, the family did not spend hours reading the al Quran or discussing religion. Charly loved science, animals and experimentation. She was inquisitive and learned fast. Her father, having been a science teacher, liked to formulate chemical concoctions including stink bombs and fireworks. In hindsight, this may have led her in later life into close encounters with Mr Plod and the law! She had learned the recorder at an early age and later graduated to the flute. Towards teenage years, ipads, ipods and the internet were becoming a distraction which Carl and Tina worried about!

Jason was becoming a typical country lad. He loved the outdoor environment, playing footy and riding his bike. He restricted his friendships however to just a handful of boys his own age with a singular 'special' friend. At school he might mention his religious habits and the various religious days as they came around. It took him a little while to realise that in fact none of the other children shared his experiences and had no understanding of Islam. It would take him a while to adjust to the fact that he was unique in the community on this basis! Soon a new environment and a new school would bring new friends, the trombone and cub scouts. His every waking moment would be full of challenges with much to learn.

After a spell of four years, Carl and his family were now in another town, Fowler, on the other side of the Divide. His Indonesian wife Tina was a new teacher at the local Secondary College. It was a smart little town of some three thousand people nestled at the top of a broad fertile valley with rolling tree covered hills at each side. From their new house, the family could espy Mt Fowler, a hill of some 2600 metre above sea level. In winter it was capped in snow like the head of a bald man watching guard over all below.

One day Carl wandered in to the College to give a brief note to his spouse.. actually a telephone number that she would need to negotiate the purchase of a new car. The bell had rung and the corridor swelled with students as he made his way towards Tina's staffroom and desk. "Excuse me" a very tall male teacher called. "Ah, what do you want, can I help you?" The man in his early forties towered over Carl.

"I'm looking for Tina to give her a message.. "

"Please report to the office, it is this way" he directed in a rather unfriendly manner.

"Thankyou" replied Carl (followed by 'wanker' muttered imperceptibly under his breath!) Carl was not yet known to many of the teaching staff. But he felt uneasy and thought the teacher's manner more than a little presumptuous, bordering on sanctimony. Carl understood that this was an era of protectionism, secretiveness and boy-scout watchfulness! The whole nation had entered the 'age of fear'. He wasn't carrying a bomb nor had the intention of raping one of the grade 12 girls but felt a little humiliated as if the man had said: "what the hell are you doing wandering about this school, peasant?" Fortunately Carl was rescued by a most pleasant lady who smiled and looked for Tina who was about to commence her class. A quick word and all was well.

Walking home in his heavy navy overcoat was pleasant though the wintry day still rather cool. Carl sidled past the mirror-like lake and along quiet streets to the edge of the township. A radio controlled model plane was somersaulting and skimming just above the water. Most of the houses were of timber and of similar simple design from an earlier period when it was a government settlement for the building of hydroelectric dams. The newer occupants had cleverly manicured and shaped their gardens to give uniqueness to their homes. At the last intersection where horses played in a field on one side and cattle ruminated on the other, a police car appeared from the oncoming direction. After passing Carl it abruptly performed a U-turn and ventured back.

"So what's going on?" the officer called. Carl strolled to the window of the car.

"Good afternoon officer, how can I be of assistance?"

"Just wish to know who you are and what you are up to!" - a second confrontation in the one day, but Carl remained calm!

"My name is Carl Jacobs and I am the husband of the new Indonesian teacher at the Secondary College. We are renting number 31.. are you carrying a gun?" Carl could not prevent himself from asking the question.

"Yes, it's something one needs these days".

"Ah yes, sad times. Mind you I do not envy you your job; it's getting harder I understand. You don't think the reintroduction of the rope might deter a would-be criminal from killing a cop?" One could see that the local policeman already had had enough of Carl and judged that he was no threat to society.

"I don't believe so. Well I must get going, you take care now."

"Same to you and I will see you around".

Two native ducks and a mob of Galahs scavenged in the grass at the edge of the road as Carl plodded the last one hundred metres or so to the small white timber house. Caged ducks quacked and a rooster crowed; magpies chortled expectantly.

The children Charly and Jay arrived home a little after four. Carl loved his children very much although he was a bit of a disciplinarian and pestered the children about homework as well as extra 'daddy school' which they endured at weekends. Carl would read to them every night as they nodded off to sleep. Tina took care of their religious duties. Carl was a non-dedicated C of E Christian but had married a much younger Muslim lady. He worried about the future of his children, particularly in a period of radicalisation and the interjections of 'youtube' content into the household.

"If we maintain our values of family life, love and tolerance I'm certain they will grow up as fine citizens doing useful work and earning respect of friends and colleagues!" Tina and Carl always felt this. Tina would only wear a head-scarf to a Mosque if she were home on holiday with her middle class parents in Indonesia. As mentioned earlier, both had been scientists at an agricultural research station but were now retired. Naturally they worried about their eldest daughter living in a western country with the current trends and political drift. But they were not extreme in their views.

"Don't worry mum, it's mainly the media beating up stories of violence. Most people are normal and just want to get on with their lives. It is no more dangerous living in Australia than in Indonesia!"

Carl loved to visit Java Island. In particular he loved the range of foods, fruits and vegetables. For our pathetic range of two or so types of mango or banana, Indonesia boasts dozens of varieties! Arum manis, pisang raja .. sumptuous! And street food such as martabak, sate or a Padang restaurant, he drooled at the mere thought! One could always find street food in Jakarta at any time of day or night. Yum!

Bali bombers, Jakarta mall bombers and hotel bombers, Australian embassy bombers had come and gone. But at the close of the war on IS in Syria and Iraq unfortunately resulted in Islamic warriors returning home the world over. It was once more an unsafe time where bomb manufacture and infantile suicide soldiers inflicted there evil work on society. Stabbings of westerners also became more common. One had to tread carefully and be constantly wary of such threats from 'lone wolf' fundamentalists with murder in their heads. It had become a sad indictment on a normally peaceful religion, especially in Indonesia with a population rushing towards three hundred million and where poverty was still a profound problem.

The TV brought the news of Madrid, Paris, Westminster, Manchester and then Central London attacks, all by Islamic extremists. With the

Charlie Hebdo attack the French Airforce suddenly found additional targets in Iraq. The Mayor of London (being a Muslim himself) echoed the words of the prime minister: "We shall never be cowered, we shall never be defeated!" Fine and noble words as they were at the time, the whole of the British people felt that they had entered a new epoch and that there were to be rocky times ahead. The 'White Right' were assembling and planning their responses.. responses that would bring a new wave of intolerance and violence to the nation. Their catch phrase was simply: "enough is enough!" Sadly, such extreme responses were not unique to the UK alone, a similar disease was sweeping Western Europe and America! But that great country also had its own unique problems with guns freely available and the occasional nutter randomly murdering just for the sake of it. Large assemblies of crowds became particularly vulnerable to the copycat terrorist.

Charlotte wended her way through primary school and secondary school with ease, taking Mandarin, English Literature, Mathematics and Science in her final year. She did extraordinarily well and won a scholarship to attend university in Warwick, UK. But this presented problems both financial and of a worrying nature to Carl and Tina. The financial was eased by a temporary loan which Tina was able to procure being a well paid teacher with permanent tenure. Carl had published some of his writings, including poetry but had not struck gold! Their main worry was the rise in the political right and the reported violence that had occurred in various parts of the country. The fact that Charly was a Muslim

UNIVERSITY

WARWICKSHIRE

girl also worried her parents as there had been continual attacks on Muslims and mosques for some years now. Having said this, Charly

rarely ever wore a headscarf and seemed to blend in with jeans and casual-smart clothes just like any other young woman of her age (in fact, like her mum, she only wore the head scarf when holidaying in Indonesia and attending mosque with her grandparents). Carl had relatives in England and Scotland that she might fall back on in any emergency. After long deliberation balancing the pro et contra, the decision was eventually made that she would go to Warwick.

"If any major problem occurs, like widespread civil conflict or any other threat of danger, you must promise me that you will fly home immediately.. OK?"

"Yes Dad, I promise"

"That's my good girl!"

The scenes described were lightyears away from the spacious park in Greenwich, London. It was a Sunday and many families strolled about or rested on blankets for a picnic on this warm June day. A gentle breeze played through the hair of children running and tossing a ball to each other. One particular group gaily clad in colourful dress, sat on rugs sharing out a variety of foodstuffs from a basket. All were chattering and laughing. There were seven adults (which included two grandparents) plus five children from the age of twelve down to just a few months. The sun was creeping down behind the head of General James Wolfe and the Octagon Room of Flamsteed House, the old Royal Observatory.

Suddenly, running down the grassy knoll there appeared a team of five men dressed in what appeared to be Arabic clothing and black balaclavas yelling out "Aulla Akbar" wielding bayonets and swords. They were soon upon the seated group followed by a frenzy of slashing and stabbing. Then in just a few more seconds they ran down the children and quickly dealt with them in similar manner. Distant onlookers imagined some sort of game or perhaps a filming of some bizarre episode for television. The five continued on down towards the Maritime Museum, past the old Admiralty building and then they were quickly out of sight. This macabre scene of brutal killings was over in less than two minutes. The summer grass reflected the afternoon's golden rays from the copious blood oozing from throats and body wounds.

This was an extended Pakistani family that lived locally in Blackheath Village; they were well known and well liked in the local community. They lived above their grocery shop business close to the railway station, selling both local produce and some Asian foodstuffs. The street was named Tranquil Vale, but tranquillity had now been broken; it was a dark beginning to something more terrible as we shall meet.

Later on that day a posting appeared on social media: "Today the Holy Knights and Defenders of England have dealt another blow to the whores and vermin of Islam. Let them be aware that all terrorist acts will be responded to in a ratio of ten for one. Blood for Blood!"

This was now the beginning of a new period in history. More innocent lives were being taken as a consequence of the actions of the minority of the deranged Islamic terrorists. The HKDE were basically a group of young thugs that no longer had trust in the police force or the government and had decided to take direct action themselves. Acts of terror by radicalised Muslims had been going on for two decades now with spurious killings at nightspots, sports events, concerts and any place where the public was likely to be assembled in large crowds. The Defenders had decided that an 'eye for an eye' was

43

insufficient. Their way was to take the lives of as many of the Muslim faithful as possible until all terrorist attacks ceased. Unfortunately terror did not cease. In fact it only got worse with more frequent attacks and greater numbers of victims. Britain was sliding into chaos and unabated 'Holy War'. This all seemed bizarre, especially when one considered the very low attendance at Sunday services in Christian churches.

On the eve of the second referendum for Scottish Independence, it was clear that this time the SNP had won the day by a considerable margin. Jim was sauntering home from his workplace 'Highvale Armaments Works' on the West side of Glasgow. As the people on the streets were in a cheery mood he decided to drop into his favourite pub for a pint of heavy ale and a chat with friends. The pub was more busy than usual; there was even a group of students in a corner singing folk songs and other tunes Jim was not familiar with.. probably top ten ditties he guessed. He recognised 'Flowers of Scotland' though!

"How ye fairing Jim?" called a mate.

"Awe ye know, makin' ends meet". There was a small TV screen hanging precariously high on the main wall where statistics and voting results were being screened along with continuous commentary and interviews with politicians. Of course Mrs Cod and Mr Salmon were there, hardly containing their joyous smiles at the success of the referendum.

"It's a new Scotland.. the people of Scotland haf finelly chosen freedom and self determination.. etc etc." Jim himself wasn't that moved by the result, being more of a pragmatist.

"Aye, well, let's hope it doesnay bring poverty te all an' sundry!" he remarked slowly.

After just two drinks he made his way through the dense crowd and out the door to the street. It was cold and dark with a fog descending as he plodded the familiar road to his home. This was a medium sized council apartment which he shared with his wife Mary. They had just the one child, Lizzy whom was now in her early twenties and working and living in Birmingham, England.

"How are ye hen? What's fer tay?" he greeted his wife as he entered.

"Just sausages an' chips me dear. Did ye have a good day at the works?"

"Oh aye.. jest the same as usual"

They sat later at the dining table chatting. Jim presently worked on the high explosive floor where bombs of various capacities were assembled. His job was inspecting the final assembly of the deadly pieces and ensuring they were safe and up to an exacting standard. The current batch was destined for various overseas buyers, mainly rich Arabian states in the Middle East such as Saudi or Emirates.

It was almost time to view one of their favourite evening programmes on the telly and the couple were quickly finishing clearing the table when Mary remarked:

"Where's yer wedding ring Jim.. did you need to tak it off at yer work today?" Jim looked down at his left hand with a puzzled expression.

"Well damn me.. you know I hadne noticed. Musta slipped off at the factory, but I dunna remember it luv! No doot it'll turn up the morrow so dunny fret!" They settled down, Mary with a cup of cocoa and Jim with a large bottle of his favourite local stout. Their program was interrupted by the news of the Greenwich murders by White extremists.

"Ach look at that.. them thugs will be the ruin o' the nation soon enuff.. mark ma words lassie!"

It wasn't long before similar violent groups arose in France, Germany Holland and other European nations. These were no longer sedate protest groups shouting and holding placards aloft. These were thugs causing havoc and mayhem not seen since the 1930s during the final Hitler years before the commencement of WWII! In America there were some spurious violent crimes against innocent Muslims with virtually none in Canada. Australia had experienced a little of such behaviour but again to a far less extent than in Europe. The newspapers coined the phrase '*Helter Skelter*' as a great wave of horror brought darkness once more to the civilisations of Western Europe.

The movement spread to teenagers in secondary schools. They held meetings, devised various ranks and a code of honour. Initiates were sworn in, making a promise to uphold Christianity and defend the various group' perceptions of values. Strangely, many adherents had never shown any adherence to Christianity before (apart from Easter eggs and traditional Christmas celebrations with all the paraphernalia and the exchange of presents). In fact their tenets were more in line with 'White Supremacy', hating *all* other races and religions as well as the Muslims! It was more about symbolism and herd instinct against a perceived enemy! Within a couple of years, vast rallies were being held at sports stadiums with electrifying speakers broadcasting simple, repetitive commandments and always with the one major tenet:

"Islam and Muslims is the enemy to our culture and way of life. They must be driven out or killed until none remain." But not all adhered to this vile rhetoric. Many stood up and protested the extremists. But as their numbers grew, fear crept over the society such that protesting voices grew less as beatings and violence gained its hold. Whole suburbs now became barricaded as the nation split between the righteous thugs of the HKDE and normal citizens. Other old hatreds began to stir also. Jews were beaten openly on the streets of some areas-their homes and businesses smashed. Some Protestants and Roman Catholics formed apartheid societies within the greater society. This was not true everywhere but particularly noticeable in the larger cities of the North and the Midlands. For a nation where church attendance was down to just one percent (and even less in many cases) it seemed ironic that people accepted labels of where they belonged in the strata of society. Freedom of movement was now hampered by the badge one wore. It was dangerous to walk openly in an area where you were seen as belonging to the minority and as a possible enemy. These enforced artificial dislocations brought many problems such as transport, food distribution and health care. The government had no choice but to proceed to emergency protocols with more or less the whole of the army deployed on the streets to try and maintain law and order with regular night time curfews. But this too began to break down as individuals gravitated to those groups that they perceived to owe some allegiance to, rather than to serve the nation as a whole. Finally the Prime Minister and remnants of her cabinet had no other resort but to call upon the assistance of the great ally- America.

And so, on July 15th, Britain signed over her sovereignty to the United States with the arrival of 750 000 Marines and other forces to help quell the various rebel groups and remodel a semblance of a total ordered society. Britain had become a servant and broken into four new states of that greater union. For a few months all seemed as though it might work until the Afro-American uprising. The unrest brought disquiet and a consequential slide into civil war in that great nation of America.

Helter Skelter

Two   The 'Kalif Inquisition' and the God Thingi

The struggle of each of the major religions has been going on for
thousands of years. Modern people fail to realise that the relation
between themselves and their religious beliefs has its cultural roots
going back at least 500000 years and probably more than this. The
reason basically is the dilemma of awareness of the human brain (the
self) and its struggle to comprehend any meaning to one's life or
existence. Humans and their ancestors before them (as with animals),
developed cognitive powers through basic necessities: the need to eat to
live, find shelter and survive; thus they slowly developed an awareness
of their immediate environment and what was of use to them to these
ends. As humans learned to live in small communities, environmental
factors led them to learn how to manage fire for warmth and cooking,
craft basic tools, make clothing for warmth and manufacture simple
weapons for hunting and protection. All this progress was for survival
alone. But the great tragedy of death and an end to life bore down on the
inner consciousness and thoughts of these early thinkers. For comfort at
the loss of a loved one, it was assumed that the inner ghost or spirit of
the person went on into an unseen afterlife where all was good and
perfect. Alternatively, one's spirit became a twinkling star in the
heavens, forever to shine down on future generations. The concept of a
creator or God came later.

The sun was the primal choice as life through the seasons for all things,
plants and animals, depended on this recognised provider of warmth and
its cycle across the sky. But then animism sprang up where it was
accepted that there must be many Gods; a God for each of the
recognised and named elements of nature: sun, moon, stars, water, fire,
earth, wind, clouds, forest.. in fact everything that affected their daily

lives and their very survival. Ceremony developed to celebrate the good seasons; sacrifice became necessary to appease the Gods after bad seasons or protect against them. It appears that even the remotest of primitive human societies developed similar ceremonies and beliefs independently!

Modern man has not lost this fear and incomprehension of the meaning of death and struggles with the concept no less than primitive man of half a million years ago. Most of us try not to dwell upon the inevitable: our final demise. We know at an early age of our development from daily experience that all living things eventually die. Flowers, trees, elephants, cats, dogs and our pet goldfish; all eventually die and rot and become part of the ground again. Ashes to ashes and dust to dust.

The ancient Pharaohs were embalmed and wrapped in bandages. In their tombs they were accompanied by artefacts and personal possessions to aid them on their journey in the afterlife. An important person such as a chieftain of the tribe was buried with personal artefacts such as jewellery or weapons. It is not uncommon in modern times for friends and family to place music recordings and various other personal things alongside the body of a deceased person inside the coffin to go into the ground. Hopefully the battery has been removed from the cell phone!

Different cultures in different geographical locations around the world developed their own religions or ways to communicate with an all powerful God or collection of Gods. Prayer, praise and sacrifice all became part of rituals and ceremonies forming a pattern of behaviour shared by the group. When different groups came into contact then new ideas were taken up. Contrary to this, violence would also occur as conflicting ideas challenged each other for supremacy. A famous

Pharaoh at one time had all the old Gods removed and he decreed that all his subjects must follow just the one new God. All statues and references to the old Gods were removed and destroyed. But soon after his death, the high priests and successor, a new boy Pharaoh, declared that the people must revert to praying and giving offerings to all the former Gods. This demonstrated that it is nigh impossible to replace an accepted religion in a short period of time.

Religious people feel comfortable with what they know and have been brought up with. It is part of their inner sacrosanct values and character. When such values are disturbed or challenged, humans pass through various stages of bewilderment, disbelief, anger then a final acceptance or rejection of what is new and different. It is the same when we are suddenly confronted with new scientific evidence that challenges ideas that we cherish and have always held to be true and incontrovertible. We have deniers of Climate Change, deniers of the benefits of fluoridation of public water, deniers of the Holocaust, and deniers of aspects of modern medicine such as child inoculations to preventable diseases. The list goes on.

[The author recommends you peruse Alex Berezow's book: The Little Black Book of Junk Science].

Racing ahead now to the 21st century, we again (or are still) witnessing conflict between religious doctrines and even between various factions and schisms inside those broader religious blocks in global society.

But this has always been. Priests in Rome have always discussed and argued the finer points of their doctrine and flavour of Christianity. At the beginning of this century the incumbent Pope decreed that Eastern Orthodoxy was but a wound in the Christian faith but at the same time insinuated that Protestantism was a not a true religion (Perhaps he would have preferred to have written the word 'heresy' but he did not go that far!) The Jewish faith has for centuries maintained various orders from the more extreme to the more liberal in its teachings. Likewise, Islam has two major branches, the Shia and the Sunni where one holds the belief that its leaders necessarily must trace their lineage back to Mohammad whilst the other permits its leaders to be selected based on wisdom and merit.

Violence and evil have accompanied all the major religions at various points in history. The Spanish drove out the Moors in the 14th century with many being put to death. The Inquisitors traipsed around Western Europe punishing and executing by burning those they considered devils or heretics. The French murdered thousands of the early Protestants, namely the Huguenots that were forced to flee to England and Holland.

Primitive religions found in ancient Europe, the Pacific Isles and South America included the ritual of human sacrifice. This generally dates back thousands and thousands of years where it was accepted that human sacrifice would appease and please the gods to ensure a good harvest. If there was not a good harvest then obviously they had either sacrificed the wrong people or there needed to be considerably more sacrifices. The story of Isaac in the bible makes reference to the practice.

God himself is said to have sacrificed all of humanity due to their iniquities and sinful lives by means of a great flood, sparing only Noah and his family. There is also the story of the destruction of Sodom and Gomorrah. It is likely that the biblical reference to the great flood refers to the end of the last iceage where in fact much of the low lying land was slowly inundated by rising seas, albeit over thousands of years. Is it possible that there was in fact a sudden burst of water from the Atlantic into the Mediterranean at the Straits of Gibraltar?

In the al Quran we see the words "take not the Christian or Jew as your friend for if you do then you are one of them!" and other references about the non-believers or infidels: "you must strike them at their

necks". During the decades at the close of the 20th century and beginning of the 21st century the world endured the revival of the concept of the Khilafah or Caliphate in Islam. This was started by a small hard core of Muslims following a dream of a pan-Islamic Caliphate whose inhabitants are to be Muslims only. In order to accomplish this, there must be Jihad or Holy War against all the infidels in the world. Due to the all-pervasive connectivity of the Internet, many disillusioned and gullible young men and women were/are attracted to the idea of Holy War. They made their way from many parts of the world to support the formation of the Khilafah. I will not name this army by its common name as I think it is an insult to all Muslims and Islam per se. I will call it 'The Army of the Kalif's Inquisition' for it was/is a type of inquisition where Muslims are judged and if they don't match the stringent criteria, they are killed!

Some families went to join and took their children along with them. The area they chose was a vast stretch of land across eastern Syria and Northern Iraq. The majority of the world's 1.3 billion Muslims were not interested in this Jihadist group of murderers and much preferred to stay in their own countries. But the story and picture is not so simplistic and the way it was told in the Western media produced consequences that were to be of momentous proportion and unforeseen!

If innocents were murdered in Paris, New York, London, Berlin or Barcelona by the 'Khilafah Inquisitors' using bombs, trucks or simply knives, there followed outrage and emotional outpouring on the Western media. One appreciates this, particularly as these were always labelled terrorists and the enemies of freedom and democracy.

But each and every day for years the West as well as Russia and their various agents such as Iran and Saudi Arabia along with others, were firing missiles and dropping bombs on Arab cities killing thousands, including women, children and generally innocent civilians. Even Israel occasionally joined in to bomb selected targets in Syria! Over the years this figure would run to millions in what is militarily described as 'collateral damage'. Not a lot of this ever reached the comfortable living rooms of those living in the West! For each child killed by so called terrorism, a hundred would die in the Middle East or Afghanistan under a rain of weapons made in America, Britain, France, Russia, China and many other countries, including those not involved in these wars. And successive American President's, whatever their political flavour, would condone further 'sales of armaments' and 'further increases of troops and combatants'. It is always told to us that 'we are the armies of righteousness'. But when one analyses what we have achieved and perpetrated, then perhaps we need to question this, question our methodology, and definitely question what our major media outlets tell us. There seems to be ALWAYS considered filters and selectivity on what is dished out to us. It is not good enough!

The author read a sample of the 'supposedly' IS propaganda magazine DABIQ, issue 15 circa early 2016. I say supposedly for it reminded me a little of the 'Watchtower' circulated by the Jehovahs, but more slick and colourful! Various articles pointed to the value of making it to the Khilafah and escaping the vile and evil Western democracies with all their iniquities. A particular article by one Umm Khalid al-Finlandiyyah described her upbringing in Finland, a failed marriage and child-confusion on the tenets of Christianity. Remarried as a Muslim convert she was ecstatic to make 'hijrah' (i.e escape our cruel world for the Khilafah) with her children and new husband. It even gave her joy later for her young son to be martyred! She had determined Islam as 'the truth'.

"Allah.. his law is just and all other laws are plagued with imperfection and oppression". The author looks at this later and states that ALL the 'one God' religions are an approximate to God's intentions and we must be cautious in our criticism.

".. and whoever desires other than Islam as religion, he in the Hereafter will be among the losers".

There was an article on 'WHY we hate you and why we fight you' where both Jews and Christians are described as disbelievers (kufr) and further that these do not recognise or appreciate the gifts of the natural environment. All Muslims must wage war on the kufr!

But, as with Christendom, the Khilafah is NOT a place or piece of land.. it is in the heart and mind of humans!

DABIQ* spewed hatred and graphically wallowed in 'death and destruction' of its enemies, which included many Muslims!

Having read this document most carefully and analytically, as with the 'Protocols of Zion' that was obviously written by a French Monk at the

[* see extract in Appendicitis at end of this book]

Vatican sometime in the late 17th century, the author of this tome concludes that "DABIQ IS A SIMILAR FRAUD CLEVERLY WRITTEN IN ONE OF: NEW YORK, TEL AVIV, MOSCOW, BEIJING OR ONCE AGAIN, THE VATICAN!".. take your pick! Its prime function is to engender "HATRED, MURDER AND DISTABILISATION!"

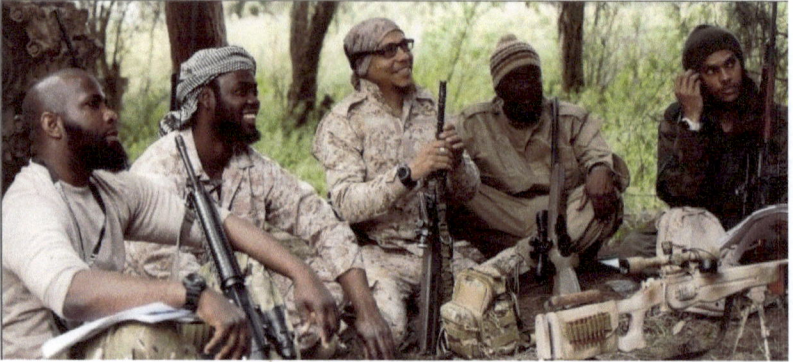

jihadis

Similarly one can download al Qaida's magazine *'Inspire'* from the internet. It also has the questionable tone and flashiness of a forgery or scam document probably manufactured in the same office as Dabiq! How else would they be permitted to exist freely on the internet?

It is expedient for some 'politique' to maintain such sparks between the two major sects of Islam and indeed from 1979 to 2017 we have seen some *eight million* Muslims killed in various wars from the Middle East to Afghanistan. This makes the Russian deaths in Afghanistan* plus the victims of 9/11 plus the victims in Europe, Africa and Asia from terrorist acts pale to insignificance. By January 2018, Muslim refugees numbered well in excess of forty million!

History witnessed the expulsion and ethnic cleansing of Muslims from

[* there are suspicions regarding 9/11 and this great Russian loss in Afghanistan!]

Spain in the 14th century. We saw it again in Myanmar in the 21st century with the Rohingya! The world witnessed the murder and ethnic cleansing of European Jews in the 20th century from civilised(?) European countries! Racial tensions and pogroms have blighted the African continent since the end of WWII.

The Kalif Inquisitors continue to target the Shia sect of Muslims even with suicide bombers. One might ask: "from whom did these fighters receive their finance and weapons?" One might point to those nations where prominent wealthy Sunni Muslims abide such as ..

The arrival of the true Mahdi will be universally recognised by his words and will alone, accompanied by genuine tears for all the suffering of humanity. According to Islamic tradition, the Mahdi's tenure will coincide with the Second Coming of Jesus Christ (*Isa*), who is to assist the *Mahdi* against the *Masih ad-Dajjal* (literally, the "false Messiah" or Antichrist).

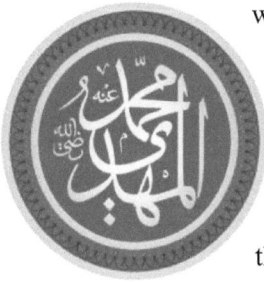

Murder of Muslims by Muslims cannot be tolerated. Those that are guilty face eternal nothingness and shall reap no reward and no afterlife! The murderer of any human of any faith shall suffer the same extinction and is to be pitied whilst alive!

There have always been wars and skirmishes in the Middle East since Mohammad's time. Ataturk created the Turkish Empire over much of present day Iran and Iraq. The European colonial powers squabbled over boundaries of their respective Oil Empires through the 19th and early 20th centuries. During the two World Wars, various Arab states aligned themselves with one or other of the European combatants. There were several problems, the major issue being that the nomadic Arabs were forced to accept the boundaries of countries imposed on them by the colonial powers and later the precursor to the United Nations.. the League of Nations. Oil and gas had been discovered in the early 19th century which had now become the essential fuel driving industries of Western economies, as well as being essential in times of war. Colonial powers set up oil companies and by bribery and the use of military force started to plunder the liquid gold. The handsome profits from this hardly trickled down to the peoples of the various Arab states to improve their lives. Not surprisingly, in the period following the Second World War (a war in which European states decided to tear each other apart), many independence movements sprang up followed by the nationalisation of foreign oil companies. This enabled some to build exotic techno cities and create sophisticated armed forces, purchasing weapons with their oil dollars. But others stagnated and made little progress other than the accumulation of extreme wealth by ruling families with little care for the people under them. Jealousies occurred and wars prevailed, the worst of which was the protracted war between Iran and Iraq where some five million were killed over twenty years.

The Kurds in the Middle East have suffered enormously for hundreds of years and when the colonialists were drawing up national boundaries, this group was overlooked. Collectively they share an area that overlaps North East Iraq, Turkey and Iran. The Kurds played a significant role in defeating the Kalif Inquisitors (IS) and deserve a small independent nation of their own. But the three countries mentioned are reluctant to officially cede any of their lands to this end and no doubt will experience continuing aggression.

Underlying this was the perennial problem of the schism of Islam into its two factions that, not infrequently, displayed animosity to each other. Lastly was the creation of the state of Israel by illegally ceding Palestinian Arab lands to a new nation of displaced Jews. Israel was formally declared a country and sovereign nation and recognised by the League of Nations in the 1940s. Palestine had to wait until the third decade of the 21st century before the United Nations gave it official recognition as a sovereign state! If there was a single factor that on occasion united all the Muslims of the world, it was the perceived unfairness in the treatment of the Palestinians. Israel might have had its cake and eaten it had it been more careful and mindful of the Palestinian people. But that was never to be!

As mentioned in the book 'Return to Animalia' **several major things need to materialize:**

(i)   A heavy handed approach to Israel on its land grabbing and excessive military response to its adversaries.

(ii)   The creation of the Palestinian State (or States if Gaza is to remain separate)

(iii)   The creation of a Kurdish state

(iv)   The annexation of Jerusalem as a universal UN governed separate State

(v)   The immediate end to weapons supplies to Middle East adversaries by the West, Russia and Eastern bloc countries.. possibility of tighter UN licensing laws for arms sales!

(vi)   Evaporation of current personal gun ownership in America and elsewhere.. more stringent laws on ownership and registration

(vii)   Extreme reduction in gun manufacture and supply worldwide by corporations in the arms business

(viii)   Liquidation and/or heavy laws against white supremacists in Western countries

(ix)   Return to détente and dialogue between Russia and the West

(x)   A sincere effort to raise the standard of living across all the third world

(xi)   Recognition by neighbouring states that they have a shared responsibility to eliminate religious and political extremism.

Afghanistan:

When did this Russian-US antipathy have its genesis? We could go back to the cold war and the nuclear arms race where Russia earned many gold medals for its testing and production of Thermo-nuclear bombs. However in more recent times I think the mistrust and pathological animosity commenced after the Russian invasion of Afghanistan in 1979.

The Russians suffered some 14500 deaths and around 54000 wounded. The Mujahedeen suffered around 80000 killed and a similar figure wounded. But ... wait for it... in excess of 1500000 civilians were killed, 3 million wounded with another 5 million leaving the country as refugees to Pakistan and Iran. **And all this my reader BEFORE the US, NATO and its allies arrived on the scene!**

The material losses of the Russian forces were astronomical, running into the billions of dollars.

The Soviet war in Afghanistan lasted over nine years from December 1979 to February 1989. Part of the Cold War, it was fought between Soviet-led Afghan against multi-national insurgent groups called the Mujahedeen, mostly composed of two alliances – the Peshawar Seven and the Tehran Eight.

The Peshawar Seven insurgents received military training in neighbouring Pakistan and China, as well as weapons and billions of dollars mainly from the United States, United Kingdom and Saudi Arabia. The Shia groups of the Tehran Eight alliance received support from the Islamic Republic of Iran. Early in the rule of the PDPA government, the Maoist Afghan Liberation Organization also played a significant role in opposition, but its major force was defeated by late 1979, prior to the Soviet intervention.

So why did they go there? Since 1947, Afghanistan had been under the influence of the Soviet government and received large amounts of aid, economic assistance, military equipment training and military hardware. They were lulled into Afghanistan by a government that had failed utterly to control the country, having had tens of thousands of dissidents executed at the notorious Pul-e-Charkhi prison, including many village mullahs and headmen (.. a similarity we later saw with the al Assad regime in Syria!) As well as the Western supported Mujahedeen, over ten years the Russians faced contingents of foreign fighters who wished to wage jihad against the atheist communists. Notable among them was a young Saudi Arabian named Osama bin Laden, whose Arab group eventually evolved into al Qaeda (the Base).

The West was finding it hard to meet their balance of payments with the newly independent oil producing Arab states. Hotels, retail outlets and other real estate in London, Paris and New York were gobbled up by rich Arab investors to help ease this problem. But it was never going to be enough. Solution? **Sell them more armaments and military hardware and covertly exasperate petty jealousies and hatreds to initiate more wars from which profits might be made.** Wrong analysis you say.. history will bear this out! After all, things have not changed until today. A conspiracy theory you claim? NO.. not theory, fact!

The military engines of the West as well as those of Eastern bloc countries were, and have ever since, been making squillions of dollars immorally by selling armaments to get back their oil dollars. The net result? The destruction of cities and social infrastructures across the Middle East, Afghanistan and elsewhere, with the death of millions of innocents and the movement of somewhere between fifty and one hundred million refugees worldwide, predominantly during the first two decades of the 21st century.

There was of course likely to be one and only one eventual outcome.. retribution! That retribution would be slow at first but would grow without stopping. Its momentum and inertia would grow as the peoples of the world become educated to the evil, contemptuous and uncaring attitude of the moguls of human destruction. Let it be understood, this simple but truthful concept: **'Money Is Always Behind Wars!'**

But what will be the final struggle? How will it play out?.. as the death knell of the International Armament Corporations is seen and approached? World War and World Destruction! Why you ask? Because it is the only thing they understand: **'Profit Above Morality!'**

The 'Khilafah Inquisition' is still active in South East Asia and Africa with the intention of forming separate Caliphates. The war against them will go on for some time. It would be nice for the Big Ugly Giants to 'come clean' and provide information as to exactly where they (the Kalif Inquisition) enjoy finance and exactly from whom they acquire their weapons. That information seems to be forever ignored by our news media!

This chapter has been a weak and thin history lesson and the reader must check facts and seek references if she or he wishes to know more. As humans we are limited by time and resources and the capacity of our brains to assimilate all the detail of history. Our lives are also short in the greater scheme of things. Perhaps this is another major reason why we are susceptible to error, failure and liable to fall into the pit of repeated mistakes of history. However, it is worth taking time to search and discover what drives the machine called the global community. If we can discover our major blunders and failures then, and only then, do we have a slim chance of seeking new roads to avert disaster on a grand scale. As Edward de Bono described, we need to 'put on our green hats' to discover creative ways to save humanity and the planet!

Helter Skelter

Three   **Mamoud of Syria**

The predawn morning was cold, very cold. Mamoud, his wife Halime
and their three small children huddled close in their basement apartment
in the south eastern suburbs of Damascus, Syria. The night had been
quiet with only a most faint rumble of bombs from some distant action,
sounding like the thunder peal approach of a storm. Both the Syrian
Government and Russian war planes had been targeting rebel groups at
Homs and other towns but this small suburb of the capital was known to
contain a few dozen insurgents with weapons supplied by the Americans
and their allies. (Coalition bombs on IS positions in Iraq were described
as 'low collateral weapons' in an attempt to reduce civilian casualties..
but there were always civilian casualties!) However, today it would be
their turn to feel the force of modern weaponry upon the houses. Sure
enough a missile rained down just on sunrise. The three storey building
that Mamoud's family were staying in was hit at the rear. The noise was
excruciating soon followed by heat and dust and flying debris. Mamoud
himself had no weapon and had not participated in any of the fighting,
although he had been outspoken and critical of President Assad on one
or two occasions.

"Halime, Halime, are the children alright?"

"Yes, they are fine, just coughing a little from the smoke. And are you
OK my husband?"

"Yes, just a very small cut to my right arm.. nothing more!"

Suddenly there were more bombs falling from the sky as jets swept by
overhead with a deafening roar. One two three.. Mamoud counted six
explosions in all in the space of ten seconds. The buildings across the
street were reduced to small irregular pyramids of concrete blocks and
bricks. Screams arose from the dust and smoke, horror screams of the

seriously injured and dying. A man lay prostrate in the middle of the street with no legs and blood rapidly pumping out of the stumps where his knees once were. There was much confusion with people running into the street calling to God, calling for help as dazed children walked aimlessly about, some crying for their mothers, others stunned into silence. It was more than thirty minutes before the honking of fire engines and a single small ambulance appeared. Bodies, both dead and alive were lifted into the back of an old utility which promptly sped away to the hospital. Mamoud and his family were in the corner of their below ground apartment with debris all around and just a slither of light piercing through from the street above. It would take most of the day to dig a way out and tidy a small living space in the remnant

building. But they were lucky. All five had escaped unhurt. Many of their neighbours lay dead interspersed among the piles of stone and rubble where houses once stood. It would be a tedious job searching for the bodies of friends and loved ones. Mamoud was in such a state of shock that he could make no effort to curse the regime for the damage it had poured on this small community. However he made a firm decision then and there at that moment that would dramatically change the life of his family. He would commence a journey to the South eventually to cross into Jordan and join the lines of refugees. From there, hopefully, they would make their way to Europe.

Yarmouk

And so the journey south began. Mostly, they would walk! This was extremely hazardous for Mamoud, his wife and three young children. They would need food and water as well as be on constant alert for the various fighting bands of men and women against the Government forces. The first night they arrived at a small village where they were warned that both government troops and a more extreme rebel group had passed through just days before. Fortunately the villagers were sympathetic to their plight and they received shelter for the night.

Mamoud always sat with the elders at each village, absorbing as much information as possible about the movements of the various fighters. It took the family thirty three days to reach the border with Jordan. It took another ten days before being transported to a UN refugee camp, Zaatari. They were to stay in this camp for almost two years along with more than sixty thousand others before making a decision to move on again, this time through Palestine, Israel and finally to Gaza. At first, living in a tent, the hardest part was surviving the winter. But the camp provided basic commodities such as blankets, cooking facilities, food and clean water. As it grew, it had shops and markets, imitating a small city. Tents were gradually replaced by caravans and prefabricated dwellings. The water supply was improved though sanitation for human waste took a little longer to improve with the advent of shared septic tanks. There was also a school for the children to attend where they learned basics including a modicum of English from a passionate Australian woman called Jane. Jane was originally from Melbourne and had lived and worked in Indonesia as well as the Philippines before coming to Jordan under the auspices of UNICEF.

There were always discussions about where they might apply as refugees. Most of the Syrian refugees wished to go to Germany, others to the UK or North America and some to one or other of the Scandinavian countries. Just a handful applied for the Oceanic countries Australia and New Zealand. The process was slow with many interviews. The number of persons accepted was small. Mamoud could wait no longer and decided to do what others had decided.. make their own way to Europe as best they could. For this he would need money.

As he had welding skills, Mamoud decided to cross into Israel and venture to Gaza where there was still a huge rebuilding program following the devastating war there in 2014. Getting to Palestine was difficult enough but crossing Israel was no easy task. With the assistance of a group of Palestinians also going to Gaza for work, the family managed to travel most of the way in a largish but dilapidated van. There were seventeen persons crowded into the van. Crossing into Gaza itself would present other problems especially for Syrians. However the Palestinians had forged papers similar to their own which needed no accompanying passports. The Israeli guards were hesitant at the check point. One member of the company, a young man of twenty two years, was hauled into a barracks' office. He was never seen again, presumably identified for some offence and arrested. This was normal in Israel! However, the rest of the party were allowed to proceed. It was a time when many were entering Gaza to assist with the rebuilding program.

With Mamoud's welding ability, sure enough he was given plenty of work. Staying near to the beach about a central location of the strip, they lived well for another two years. With money saved it was time to look for a boat and passage to the Greek islands.

Eventually, early one morning they got into an overcrowded boat and motored towards the Adriatic. They were in the boat two days and two nights before nearing the target island. Almost there, a storm blew up and the boat capsized just a few hundred metres from shore. Halime and the children did not make it to the shore for none could swim. An exhausted and shamed Mamoud sat on

PROVEN: ASSAD USED SARIN GAS ON HIS OWN PEOPLE !

ONLY ACCEPTABLE RESULT: ASSAD MUST GO TO THE HAIG !

the beach tearing at his hair and clothes cursing God and his own stupidity for risking the lives of his family after so much endurance and hardship. Of the two hundred that went into the boat about twenty nine survived, the rest all being drowned and many of the bodies never retrieved. Mamoud resolved then to return to Syria and join a fighting group. He was later killed in a bombing raid on a rebel position on the outskirts of his home city, Damascus in June 2017.

The story of Mamoud and his family might seem extreme but in fact at that time, it was common place. More than a million people, many of them women and children died during the Syrian conflict. Up to five million became refugees and travelled to other countries. Only a trickle would eventually return. It is said by many that there was a conspiracy between America and Russia plus the hand of Israel to keep the Arabs fighting each other with one purpose.. to ensure a return on dollars spent in acquiring oil and gas. War, weapons, destruction and rebuilding.. a never ending cycle. It was a formula that worked so well but at the cost of so many lives. What did the barons of war care as long as the dollars and roubles rolled in? And to be fair, many countries both East and West joined the game for profit, not just the two giants mentioned alone! But anger and hatred would not be quelled. It would grow slowly like an unseen army to confront the magna ghoul of armament production. Information would flow to ordinary people having originally little understanding of the underlying cause of this human tragedy on an unprecedented scale. A hatred and fury so great that in a few short decades to follow, the world would see an even greater war- a war that would engulf all of humanity upon the planet and strike suddenly like a rising tidal wave or tsunami. Few would survive!

Four   **Mohamed of Yemen**   **Accidental Genesis**

Sometimes wars are defined as the crossover point from a gradual political struggle that gets out of hand to where concerted killing and destruction begin. Posko was in the cockpit of his jet fighter in Northern Syria, checking his instruments before takeoff on a routine patrol. Unbeknown to him, his auto flight path was pre-set that would bring him back to base but infringe over a sliver of Turkish territory. Posko had little time to act when his emergency siren warned of an impending strike by a missile. He was just twenty four years, newly married and expecting his first child in a couple of months.

The Russian media made headlines for several days about the cowardly strike by the West, murdering three Russian airforce combatants. Although there was no immediate response over the next few months, it was a line in the sand and things would never be the same again.

Mohamed was a doctor working at a moderate sized hospital in a city in central Yemen. His wife Shareem was a nurse working at the same hospital. They had three children, Hadiz 14, Fatimah, 11 and Ibneh 7 years. Mohamed was not a political person and had no intention of joining any of the local militia groups. He did have some sympathy for their cause against the central regime, experiencing the brutality of the civil conflict each day at his work. Often people were brought in with severe wounds and even severed limbs from shrapnel and bombs. But Mohamed's constrained internal anger reached a higher level with the joining of the Saudi airforce bombings on his city. In their modest home in the evening he would outpour his anger at table.

"You know Shareem, this cannot go on. We are now dealing with civilians at work, children and mothers seriously hurt by these infidels. Why are they doing this to us, it is not their fight or concern!"

But the Saudis, being one of the richest countries in the world with all the latest in weapon technology purchased from East and West, were now flexing their muscles to demonstrate that they were a force to be reckoned with when called upon.

Mohamed had read stories to his children, giving each a kiss and big hug before setting off for work on a Saturday evening. He sat with his wife and partook of a simple meal of goat and vegetable stew, flat bread washed down with warm goat milk tea.

"I am sorry I have to work this evening Shareem. There are many new casualties arriving after a bombing raid this afternoon. It will be a busy night!"

"Do not worry my husband, all will be well here. I will see you in the morning.. Salam!"

It was Sunday just after midday. Mohamed was driving his car, a modest Ford and within a hundred metres of his home after working some eighteen hours attending to extreme cases. There was a brief flash then a horrendous noise followed by a rapid rise of dirty smoke right in front of him. His home had been struck by a bomb from a Saudi jet. He pulled up a little dazed and shocked but the weariness from the night's work had left him as he was jolted to total concentration. Running now along the sandy street past chaotic scenes of shouting and screaming he reached the pile of rubble that had been his home. Only a portion of the rear wall was standing. Frantically he searched for his wife and children. He found each, their torsos and heads burned black with innards and intestines exposed. His youngest son was torn completely in half; his wife and the two elder children lying silent and unrecognisable. Something caught his eye in the sun, a silvery shiny object. He picked it up whilst sitting among the rubble of brick and concrete pieces. It was a plain ring, still a little hot and somewhat distorted. Holding it close he examined an inscription on the inner side. It merely said 'Mary' in English lettering.

It was impossible for Mohamed to digest the loss of his family. He had committed himself to nineteen years at the hospital, dedicating his skills to assist others back to health to the best of his ability with the minimal equipment and drugs provided. Why did God allow such a terrible punishment to him? Why? It was a question that would haunt him all his days thereafter!

In cities all over Syria and North-western Iraq similar atrocities were being performed. Russian, Syrian and Iranian forces on the one hand and a huge coalition of Western airforces on the other. They had been on bombing sorties for more than three years more or less on a daily basis trying to destroy ISIS and other pockets of extreme Islamic groups. But the toll on ordinary people was catastrophic. Most cities were reduced to nothing. Tens of millions of refugees that survived this continuous bombardment streamed out in all directions hoping to secure a better life somewhere. Citizens of those countries of the 'civilised world' were horrified at the glimpses of media news items. The random 'pin pricks' of terrorist retaliations were met with aggressive hatred and outpourings of horror at the audaciousness of such 'inhuman attacks'. But there was little understanding of the momentum of the new religious wars and a general malaise and ignorance of the causes. The fact that rich countries were actually fuelling these conflagrations by the manufacture and sales of billions of dollars of weaponry across the globe did not seem to sink in as a prime causation! There was no truly intellectual analysis of cause and effect, neither rhyme nor reason. The global weapons' conglomerates just continued on, making money and emptying warehouses as fast as they could with no thought of any ultimate consequences. But consequences were soon to be upon every corner of the world. Not even the geographically remotest nation would escape. Death and destruction would come in a certain and mathematically predictable way; and many would ask the same questions as Dr Mohamed Zakiah of Yemen at some future point in time after experiencing horrific carnage to their family and friends at their doorstep. Helter Skelter would come like a sudden flood and there would be nothing on Earth to stop it- no Government, no army nor prayer to God! Here was born the genesis to the greatest of evils- the final and ultimate fall of man! And this would not be executed by a revengeful God; mankind would bring it upon his own head!

Five   **Ali of Afghanistan**

Ali's parents were simple village folk living far to the west near to the border with Pakistan. His father told him stories about the brutality of some of the war lords that dominated the region. Earlier the pro communist government in Kabul had dragged many others to Pul-e-Charkhi for imprisonment, torture or even execution. But none of these compared with the coming of the white devils in the 1980s.. he was referring of course to the Russian military. He had a particular story about a platoon of soldiers that passed through the village around 1985 looking for Mujahedeen rebels. One evening they became very drunk and started to randomly shoot at the livestock, mainly goats that the villagers depended upon for milk and meat. Late in the night they dragged a young girl from her hut, killing the father that tried to protect her. They systematically raped the girl, a virgin of fourteen years and finally strangled her, dumping her body over a stone wall at the edge of the village. It was gruesomely perpetrated acts such as this that persuaded many young men to resist the Russians and join the Taliban or Mujahedeen. Eventually, after the loss of in excess of fourteen and one half thousand soldiers and billions of dollars of abandoned or wrecked equipment, the Russians called it a day. Some five million Afghanis had migrated out of the country with over one million dead!

During this occupation, the Americans of course were financing rebel groups, providing hardware and a smattering of ground personnel as advisors that the Russians be defeated and driven out. After the collapse of the Kabul regime and the rise of the Taliban in their place there followed another period of brutality, this time by Islamic extremists. Around this time a very wealthy Saudi Arabian from a well connected family was in Afghanistan as a guest with the purpose of training an army of radicals to fight against the infidels of the West. His group was known as The Base or, in Arabic, al Qaida. Their leader was Osama bin Laden. But before the events of 9/11 (the high-jacking and crashing of domestic airplanes into the World Trade Centre twin towers of New York city in which five thousand people died) this group of so called Islamic warriors was unknown to Western intelligence and so prepared for the coming struggle with no interference. Osama was very selective in his orthodoxy and political propaganda, taking passages from the al Quran deeming it justifiable to kill all non-believers of the Muslim religion. Christian Knights during the Holy Wars of the eleventh and twelfth centuries also selected passages from the bible to justify their causes.

Throughout the nineteen nineties there was an admix of Taliban, Mujahedeen, al Qaida as well as individual war lords over certain tribal areas running the country of Afghanistan. Time for the West to butt in, whatever the cost! The events of 9/11 were a sudden wakeup call that there were new forces to confront in the world besides communism. Various Islamic countries in Africa and the Middle East suffered revolutions and civil unrest with a whole mulligatawny of Islamic fighting groups wishing to impress their unique flavour of Islam upon local populations. Various regimes came and went in Libya, Egypt, Iraq and elsewhere; with enslavements, beheadings, murder of tourists and Christians as well as those belonging to other sects of Islam. It got kind of messy so that by the end of the second decade of the 21st Century there were wars in many countries, creating a refugee population close to sixty million worldwide.

Ali had married a girl from his village and had joined the police force in Kabul. It was a constant worry to his wife as the Taliban had not gone away and there were periodic bombings and murders in that city, particularly against the police and the military. Ali had already lost a couple of friends in his early days of training when a police barracks for new recruits had been attacked by young Taliban suicide soldiers armed with Kalashnikovs, grenades and explosive vests. A dozen had died that day with many more seriously injured. However he continued in his job patrolling the streets each day, sometimes with the Afghan army and even on occasion alongside American or other coalition forces.

"This is no life for us or our child Ali" his wife Aisha pleaded one evening. "We must either return to our village or leave Afghanistan."
"But we have little money saved as yet" replied Ali.
"What good is money if we are killed my dear husband?"

Ali pondered on all this for many months. Then one day whilst following a convoy containing a dozen British soldiers there was a sudden explosion at the front. The first jeep had struck an improvised land mine or IED; the four occupants were all killed. This single event determined Ali to change his life.
Over the next two months Ali and his family travelled to their village and then crossed the border into Pakistan. His contacts in Kabul had enabled him to get papers that allowed them all to live and work in their newly adopted country. Ali managed to get a private security job guarding a large military complex out in the country east of Karachi where the Government were assembling Chinese fighter planes with the assistance of the Chinese Government and Chinese aeronautical engineers. Life suddenly seemed secure. With the arrival of their second child the family had settled to relatively good times.

"I am so happy now my good husband. I am so grateful that you have spared us and are looking after us" declared his wife. Ali smiled and felt extreme contentment for the first time in his life.

"Yes dear wife, Allah has certainly smiled upon us and lifted us out of Hades to this good place. Praise be to Allah!"

Ali stayed for two years before an acquaintance told him about policing in the North.

"It is very good money Ali, much better than here and there is a very good school for your children run by the government- especially for the children of police. You will need to attend a three month training course which will be easy considering your experience back in Kabul." Ali toyed with this for a while, spoke with his wife then finally filled in the paperwork and posted it off. Sure enough within a month the family had moved north to a new city close to Islamabad and Ali commenced his training. The children seemed happy at their new school, attached to the Academy for Police.

All seemed to be going well until one day there was a most vicious attack by a local terror group on the academy. The insurgents were a mixture of local fighters, Taliban and al Qaida militia from the Swat area to the North West. Ninety eight recruits and sixty three children were killed including Ali and his eldest son. The wife and remaining daughter were destitute. As Ali had not quite completed his training and the fact that he was not a Pakistani citizen, there was no payment to his spouse on his sudden death. They had no other choice but to return to her parents' home in the small village of her birth back in Afghanistan.

It was an intrepid journey with mother and daughter arriving almost starved to death from the hardships endured along the way. Aisha had suffered both physical and sexual abuse by Pakistani soldiers at the border but at least had saved her daughter and brought her to a semblance of safety. That was all that mattered to this desperate and saddened woman! And so mother and daughter settled back to the simplistic rural life, raising goats and growing foodstuffs to etch out a barely subsistent life with little education for the child and the continual threat from marauding bands of armed men. However, praise be to Allah, they were safe and happy most days and far away from troubled Kabul!

Helter Skelter

Six   **Abdullah of the Sudan**

Abdullah was just eighteen when he married his sweetheart Keesha in their Sudanese town not far from Khartoum. It was a simple traditional ceremony with a few friends, his parents, grandparents and younger brothers and sisters attending. There was dancing, the killing of a goat and a special fermented drink shared but scorned upon by the more conservative. Here was the clash of al Quranic mores and deep-seated tradition and culture going back thousands of years. A hut at the edge of town had been secured and decorated for the young couple to embark on their new life. Abdullah had some mechanical skills, firstly working as a child with bicycles and then graduating slowly to motorcycles and cars. He seemed to possess a natural gift and thus was able to get plenty of work. The government forces frequently passed through the town on their way to outlying areas to the West where they would harass a tribe in their village, sometimes shooting and killing people on account of their tribal differences and non-adherence to Islam. It had been going on for years. As the situation worsened, there were constant rumours of whole villages to the West being burned and sacked with few survivors. Some had escaped over the border into neighbouring Chad where they lived in a camp. It was hard to believe such rumours but a trickle of beggars and starving people occasionally entering the town reinforced in Abdullah's mind that terribly cruel things were going on in his country. He discussed these things with his young wife, now expecting their first child.

It was four years later that Abdullah had saved some money and considered migrating with his small family (three small children, the eldest a boy followed by twin girls) to the North and possibly to Europe by some route.

"If we can get to Libya I hear that many people are taking boats to Europe for a better and safer life" he said to Keesha.

"But my husband, there is just as much trouble in that country as here, maybe even worse" was her reply. And so they waited another year. Finally Abdullah made a firm decision.

"I have saved sufficient money my dearest and I am certain we can escape to Europe, perhaps to Germany or England. Many people have already successfully reached one of these countries".

"I do not know husband, I think it is too dangerous especially crossing the sea with our precious children".

"But is it not for them that we do this my dearest wife; so that they may have a better future?"

And so it was decided that they would somehow get to Libya and try for a boat to Greece or Italy.

The journey was not too difficult at first but on entering Libya they had to pay a substantial sum to be trucked across the desert to Tripoli. They were warned by many of the inherent dangers. There were charlatans taking money and providing nothing in return. Women had been enslaved and forced into prostitution. There were killings and imprisonments for ransom. "Do not go to this town". "Do not trust that particular agent". "Ask specifically for this man at such and such and you should be safe". And so the advice came from many, some of whom had decided to return to their native land rather than face all the risks. But Abdullah was only twenty four years. He was strong and confidant and trusted that God would bring him through.

On recommendation, the family moved to a small port some forty kilometres east of the city of Tripoli. With Gadaffi long gone, Tripoli was exceedingly dangerous at that time with armed gangs controlling various suburbs. Killings were frequent.

"If you want to get to Europe, there is a boat tonight. But you must make up your mind quickly as the places will soon be all taken." The agent seemed reasonable and others had said he was a man of his word. But the price was steep- $1500 American per adult and $600 per child under the age of twelve. This would almost exhaust all of Abdullah's savings. The agent agreed to place the whole family for $4000.

"OK I will go with my wife and three young children" he committed. That night just before midnight they were to meet at the appointed place on the beach. It was a balmy night and the sky filled with stars. The boat was a very large rubber boat with an outboard motor. About sixty men, women and children squeezed in with life-jackets provided. Abdullah was most concerned about so many as there were circulating stories of capsizes and drownings. Fortunately the sea was most calm this night. The boat moved northwards away from the shore. The occupants could hardly move and to pee or defecate was a tricky business. They were each given just a single package of food containing dried meat, flat bread and a 300 millilitre bottle of water. The clientele were mostly young Nigerians with a sprinkling of other West Africans. Abdullah's family were the only Sudanese on this trip.

The night passed and at about noon a smaller boat sped towards them at high speed and came alongside. The pilot switched to this boat leaving the refugees to drift.

"Do not worry, there are naval vessels from Italy and other European nations close by. They will pick you up soon." And with that, the smaller boat sped off again. But the hours passed and darkness was approaching with a cold fog falling over the water. There was a light breeze and a gentle swell but not dangerous at this point. It was a much colder night to endure than the one before and seemed so long. But after sun-up it soon warmed up. All the people were now anxious, thirsty and getting hungry as they drifted randomly somewhere in the middle of the Mediterranean. Just as feelings were exasperated a large gray ship appeared; indeed it was part of the Italian coastguard. Within an hour all had been transferred to the deck with bread and hot soup distributed. They were safe and heading toward an Italian port.

The authorities carefully interviewed each newcomer and recorded the information. The transit camp was a mixture of prefabricated huts and UN emergency tents. The refugees were given ample food and clothing. It seemed like some stayed for just a very short period whilst others had been in the camp for many months. Abdullah was interviewed and he requested to go to Germany or England.

"There is no possibility of moving out of Italy now. No country is taking more refugees. All the borders are closed and every country to saturation point".

But Abdullah knew that people were making their own way and so decided not to wait but leave the camp and travel with his family towards central Europe. They would follow the 'refugee trail' as it was called and just hope for the best. What he did not know was that there were also thousands of refugees coming from Greece and Turkey that had started off from Afghanistan, Iran, Iraq and Syria all with the same dream. If they could jump a border then they would still need to be registered as well as seek food and shelter. At this time all the borders of the Euro-zone were being sealed off with fences, barbed wire and patrolled by armed police with dogs. Thousands of desperate refugees were stranded at various points in Southern and Eastern Europe with little chance of moving forward. But Abdullah was a resourceful man and he would find ways and means.

The family managed eventually to cross into Austria and then finally into Germany. Each crossing was done at night at the weaker border points. Hidden inside a container on a large transport truck they travelled the Bahns. Their money was now all gone but once in Germany they could seek asylum and register as legitimate refugees escaping a war torn country.

Having automotive repair skills Abdullah found work at a small garage with a repair shop in an outer suburb of Hamburg. Renting was difficult but his new boss, on seeing he was a valuable worker after a trial period, assisted with finding a place to rent for the family. It was an apartment that was small and cramped but with exuberance, the family celebrated at their final utopian resting place. They were seemingly safe now in Germany that had already generously taken in close to one million displaced persons despite growing rebellion in the Bundesrat. In Austria things were deteriorating with the rise of the extreme right!

The son was enrolled into a nearby primary school. Although he had no German language skills he soon flourished, made friends and settled in to a routine. Keesha stayed at home with the twins that were not quite ready to start kindergarten. Watching a small TV and reading newspapers and magazines she learned quickly enough basic language skills that enabled her to go to the shops and supermarket for groceries. It was on one of these excursions that, on passing a group of white teenagers, she was taken by surprise, knocked to the ground and spat upon. No passersby came to her assistance, but being a tall woman she was able to get up and hurl abuse at the young men. They just laughed and went on their way but Keesha was always on the lookout after that whenever she was on the street. There were the occasional offensive words but never again any violent attack. Things got better as they discovered other Sudanese families living at various locations around the city. There were stories of course, particularly from those unfortunate enough to find themselves in smaller rural towns where the locals were less welcoming.

The family stayed living in Hamburg. Eventually they owned a moderate second hand car which Abdullah was able to maintain. After two years they planned on taking a holiday to France. They had become well integrated with the children soon speaking German fluently. Keesha had taken a part-time job as a supermarket cashier and had started to study Accountancy at a nearby Technical Institute. Their dream was to someday own their own house or apartment and for their children to get a good education.. possibly entering some profession in adulthood. All was now possible!

Seven   **Ibnu of Surabaya, East Java**

The boy had been born to a prostitute whom had died giving birth and the orphanage had no information regarding his father other than he was a fairly rich merchant believed to have visited Surabaya from Jember, a city to the south east. The orphanage itself 'al Mustapha' was situated off a narrow 'gang', i.e alleyway, in an extremely poor suburb to the north in the old quarter of the city of Surabaya, East Java, Indonesia. It was simply named Gang Tujuh or Lane Seven. The long concrete building with orange tiled roof was said to be nearly one hundred years old. It had large cracks in its walls, painted a pale green and surrounded by a concreted courtyard with a small vegetable garden about thirty square metres in area. Here the children planted sweet corn, cereals and root crops. There were a couple of banana trees, a couple of mango trees and an ancient rambutan tree which overshadowed one corner of the main building. The orphanage relied solely on donations from the surrounding neighbourhood. These were mainly of money and/or rice. The children would perform a concert a couple of times a year for the local community which consisted of recitals of segments from the al Quran, the singing of traditional folk songs with some performing Javanese and Balinese dances. They would receive goat meat at Eid ul-Adha, the holy day of beast slaughtering and prayers giving thanks to God.

Life was stark and the pangs of hunger were experienced by the children, seventy in all, at frequent intervals during each year when resources ran low. Study was more or less based around learning by heart passages from the al Quran with not much in the way of mathematics or any other discipline. The local Imam would visit for the morning on three days of the week and read to the children or just tell stories from his own life experiences, which were minimal.

Between the ages of twelve and fourteen the children were expected to look for work of any kind in the town or suburbs. Being a port city, many found work loading the large wooden Perahu, joined the building yards for such or even became apprenticed sailors to one of the merchant fleets that would travel the seas around Indonesia. By the time they reached fifteen years, they were expected to move out of the orphanage and fend for themselves. If any girls had not found permanent employment, they would be listed at an agency to become live-in domestic maids for the middle classes of the city.

Ibnu was a smallish and shy boy but took to his religious studies with fervour. By the age of ten he outstripped all his peers and even the older boys in his knowledge and reciting ability of the al Quranic scriptures. His employ was maintaining and cleaning the nearest mosque, it also being one of the oldest in Surabaya and said to have been built some three hundred years ago. The Imam was gracious and the boy became close to the old man. Sadly just before Ibnu's fourteenth birthday, the old man died. He was replaced by a much younger Imam from central Java who was a firebrand instructor and a man that frequently referred to the white devils and infidels as well as the yellow devils. This reference of course was to both Westerners and the Chinese with whom he had nothing but contempt, verging on pathological hatred.

This new instruction had little effect on Ibnu at first until about two years later when an associate of the Imam visited from Malaysia, a man in his forties named Pac Top. It was at this juncture in Ibnu's life that his mind began to be turned as he was bombarded by the thoughts of direct action against the enemy by his mentor. He was slowly being nurtured and groomed towards the idea of Jihad!

One day Ibnu accompanied this Pac Top to a cemetery in the city whilst on an outing to purchase supplies for the orphanage and make a call to a house to meet with another Malaysian man. He was led to a specific headstone with the name Dr. G.A.Poch* who had died in January 1970 and had lived on Sumbawa Island since the early 1950s.

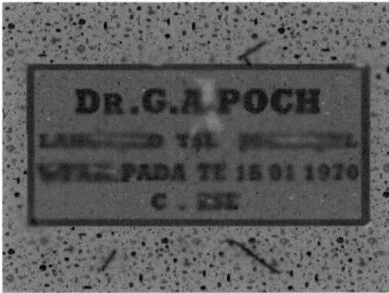

"Do you know who this man is?" Top asked the teenager.

"No sir, I do not" replied Ibnu somewhat confused why he was brought here.

"This is the grave of the great German dictator Adolf Hitler!"

Ibnu was not well schooled but he knew a little about the world war and its adversaries and of course had heard of that infamous name along with the British CO Aubertin Mallaby, 49th Indian Infantry Brigade, killed at the 'Red Bridge' in Surabaya in 1946 whilst assisting the Dutch fighting the Indonesian Nationalists. Ibnu had seen the commemorative plaque that was still attached to the old bridge.

At the house of the fellow Malaysian, Top introduced Ibnu to a secret store of weapons and explosives.

"Do you think you would like to strike a blow to the unbelievers Ibnu in the service of Allah? There will be great rewards for you in heaven if you become a soldier of Islam. There is no need to decide now. You

[*See: Levenda, Peter. 'Ratline: Soviet Spies, Nazi Priests, and the Disappearance of Adolf Hitler' Ibis Press, Florida USA and Goeritno, Ir. KGPH, Soeryo, Hitler Mati di Indonesia: Rahasia Yang Terkuak, Indonesia: Titik Media, 2010]

must meditate and pray for guidance in this great and honourable quest."
The boy was impressed by the preparation and knowledge of these two
Malaysian men but not sure he could carry out their wishes. It sounded
dangerous and he thought that perhaps it would be a sin. But Pac Top
and the firebrand Imam instructed him daily on the wars in Afghanistan
and Iraq, the struggle of the Palestinians and of the terrible suffering of
Muslims in these countries at the hands of the Kufr- the unbelievers!

There is not a lot more to this story other than that this lonely boy of
limited education and no family other than his fellows at the orphanage
was finally coerced to carry a bomb strapped to his chest and enter a
restaurant in Kuta, Bali. Human suicide terrorists would become
common place across the world over the next two decades, some as
young as six years of age. It is said that even in the Iran-Iraq war during
the 1980s that homeless Iranian children were forced to walk across
mine fields in front of a progressing army.

Ibnu was just a month short of his seventeenth birthday at the time of his
so-called martyrdom. As well as himself, he managed to kill three
people and injure eight others with his bomb. Of the three killed, two
were Indonesian citizens (a Muslim waitress and a Hindu waiter) and
one an elderly Dutch citizen. Of the injured, seven were Westerners and
one an Indonesian citizen. Would God see this as an act deserving some
reward in heaven? Definitely not.. what a waste of a life! Having said
this, being so young and impressionable God might see Ibnu as also
being a victim and not a perpetrator, having been influenced by evil
adults.

And what of those that instructed and coerced this young lad to perform
such a heinous act of murder? They are complicit and have insulted and

abandoned the basic tenets of their own religion, and for which there can be no reward in the afterlife.

It is the same for those that work in the various armament industries in both the East and the West, supplying arms to countries rich and poor around the world for profit. Are they also not complicit in the continuation of destruction of cities and the murder of innocents? They are indeed complicit and their consciences should burn with guilt. They need to leave such occupations and show open contempt for the international corporations in such industries. This is the only way in which we, as a global society, are able eventually to move forward to a higher and nobler civilisation for all of humanity. Names are to be named!

[It is to be noted that the first Bali bomb in Kuta occurred on 12th October 2002 killing 202 persons which included 88 Australians and 38 Indonesians. A further 209 persons were injured. On 8 November 2008, Imam Samudra, Amrozi Nurhasyim and Huda bin Abdul Haq were executed by firing squad on the island prison of Nusakambangan. The Malaysian bomb maker and mastermind Noordin Top was shot dead on Sep 17th 2009 by Indonesian police in central Java. His body was returned to his home town where he was received and buried as a martyr!]

Helter Skelter

Eight   **Neda of Iran**

Neda

Element of surprise fixed your eyes
As last moments defined yet unknowing
Streamlets of red welled up from your fading soul
Slipping away from this day of repulse and resentment

The world stoops in sorrow
Your youth in collective anger
The undignified masters of cruel tyranny
Never to let fall the rod

Only the will of the people shall rip
Power from their bony clasp and
Tear away the evil mask, hurl to the ground
For freedom's voice can never be silenced

From the blood of one fallen soldier
Springs a river of martyrs
To win back the voice so yearned
.. craving to be heard

Streets of Teheran are marred
With your blood Neda
Now voices grow stronger
Twenty-first century demands to separate
This church from state

.. a poem from 'China Collection' by Tom Law

Neda grew up in a moderate sized town about ninety kilometres southeast of the capital Teheran in Iran. She was most popular at secondary school, loving most aspects of what was on offer: sport, science and mathematics and English language. Her parents were, as far as one might gauge by Western standards, middle class. Brought up as a Muslim she attended the local mosque with her mother on the holiest of days marked on the calendar, the morning of Eid al-Fitr being the most important, celebrating the end of the fasting month of Ramadan. Neda's parents were both teachers; her mother Zakia a secondary school teacher of Iranian language and Persian history and her father, Ibrahim, a University lecturer in Physics. Neda had two younger sisters, Aisha and Fateme. The parents were fairly liberal politically and although devoted to their religion, wished that one day Iran might take a more democratic path with less influence from the Mullahs and the Islamic Ruling Council. Ibrahim had been to Indonesia in his youth as a student and was impressed by the progress of its political system in recent years where 'mosque and state' were virtually separate to a more acceptable degree. Iran still seemed to be 'stuck' with excessive control of politics, the army and the media by an elite band of clerics that he thought was holding the country back from true progress. The secretive desire of this inner clique, along with some Generals, for a powerful armed force with a nuclear capability was sheer madness. His own father was killed in the latter days of the Iraq-Iran war and he could see no sense in such political adventurism that left the country broken. But the present rulers insisted on their rhetoric of 'down with America, down with Israel, make Iran great!' It would lead to nowhere other than cause further misery to those parents whose sons would go off to fight wars that truly did not concern Iran.

The government seemed to warm to China and even more so to Russia. Ibrahim thought that both these positions were also a mistake. He would much prefer détente with Europe so that an era of exchange of ideas and trade might be built up. He questioned the current hostilities shown towards Europe which again could only foster mistrust and douse any hopes of harmony, thus creating further setbacks for Iran. He placed his trust in the young. He hoped that they, as moderns in thought and action (i.e the new trees in the forest), will eventually replace the old and decaying, invigorating the nation to new achievements worthy of praise and indicative of the idea of a modern and safe society.

It is not surprising then that his beautiful and intelligent daughter Neda found herself at university in the capital and pursuing a similar path to her father's in the sciences. Her first three years of study were exciting times and Neda led a rich and cultural life on campus. She would return home most weekends and semester holidays to be with her sisters and parents.

After graduation her father persuaded her to take on a Master degree in joint subjects of Physics and Political Science, an unusual combination; but in view of her father's sway and close contacts at the university, this was permitted. It is hardly surprising also that she had absorbed many of her mum and dad's more liberal views and that she had developed associations with many students and faculty members with similar values.

With upcoming national elections Neda had joined the large group of student voices making protests against the current political structure of the country with a call for reform and change. The two or three she had attended with friends were normally quite peaceful but under the watchful eye of the police and secret service interspersed among the crowds. Just a week before the elections, her younger sister accompanied her to the central thoroughfare of Teheran for an organised march to be culminated with speeches from student leaders. But this demonstration was to be different.

At the square in which they were to assemble and sit on the ground to listen to the speeches, heavily armed police in riot gear arrived and fired canisters of tear gas. Mayhem followed with people screaming and running in all directions. Neda held her young sister's hand and started to run for a side street. Just then a hail of gunfire rang out and several students fell to the ground. Neda was one with three bullets having passed through her chest. In the arms of friends and her younger sister, she bled profusely on the ancient cobble stones,

passing away in just a few minutes. It was a cruel and cowardly act perpetrated by the special security forces, but on orders from the Religious Council. It was a bleak day for freedom in Iran whose population boasted 60% being under the age of twenty five. This was a warning and strong reminder to all that the notions of true freedom and democracy were still a long way off for this nation. Neda earned instant fame at home and abroad in the news media.

The young woman was brought back to her home town and buried in the old cemetery alongside other family members going back many generations. Her parents and sisters were filled with grief for many months. Ibrahim himself could never get over the deep wound of pain inflicted by a ruthless and non-caring hierarchy that had robbed him of his beautiful and intelligent daughter in the flower of her life. He vowed then to take his family and leave Iran permanently.

It would take him another two years before he finally accepted a teaching post in Montreal, Canada. Being a lecturer in Physics of some renown and having published papers on nuclear reactions (both of a practical and theoretical nature), stood him in good stead in his newly adopted country. Ibrahim and the family never looked back!

Richard the Lion Heart in the Holy Land- late 12th Century

After the departure of the French King Philip with his army on August 3rd 1190, the Saracens broke all the peace agreements. Neither did they return the Holy Cross or the captives and sent no money. Word was sent to King Richard I (The Lion Heart) that if he executed any of the Byzantines, those Christians still imprisoned would be beheaded. The Saladin sent great gifts to Richard and requested that the time limit be extended beyond the forty days, but Richard refused both gifts and the request. At this, the Saladin decreed that the Christian captives be beheaded on the August 28th approaching. Richard, however, seeing that the time limit was exhausted on August 20th, caused the beheading of some 2500 of the Saracen captives openly in the sight of the Saladin's army. Only a few of the higher ranking were preserved for further bargaining.

Hakluyt, Richard, *The Principall Navigations, Voiages & Discoveries of the English Nation*, CUP, 1965 (originally 1589)

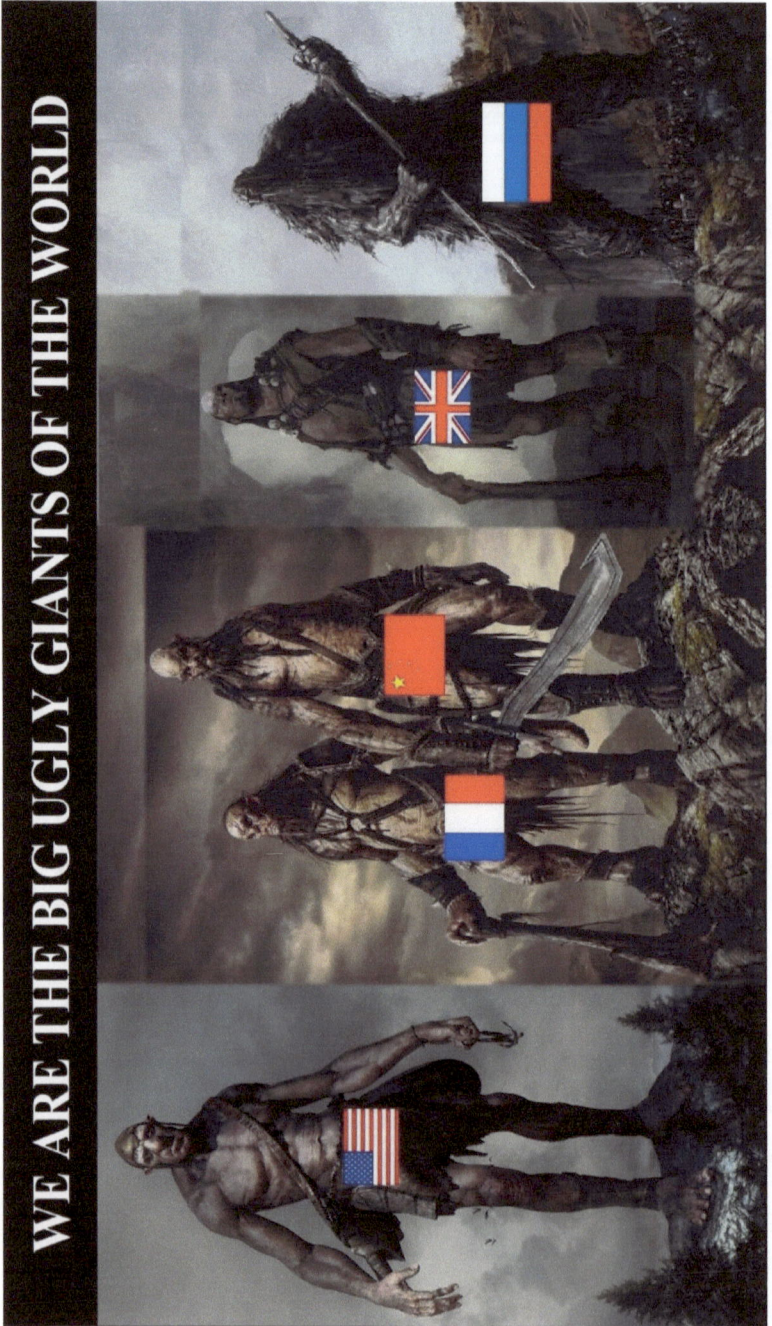

WE ARE THE BIG UGLY GIANTS OF THE WORLD

The BUGS

Nine

Recent History Regarding Islamic Terror

One shall wander lonely as a cloud and seemingly haphazardly in this chapter; it is up to the reader to seek out the finer detail of the various arguments and information presented. The main thrust is to provide some logic and historical sequence of causes behind the contemporary phenomenon of 'Islamic Terror'*. Some Western writers state simply that it is the perceived duty of Islam (and Muslims) to conquer the world i.e Islam is the only true religion and thus it must eventually supplant all other religions and political systems that are in contravention of Islamic principles, thought and law. Without doubt there would be some Muslims that hold this view and see Islam as the only pure translucent crystal of worship and societal system to which all humanity should adhere. But there are two main objections to this:

(i)   This is nothing new as history has shown that other religious doctrines have made similar claims in the past backed up by oppressive actions against humans such as torture and even murder.

(ii)   More importantly, all religious writings are from the hand and mind of humans and thus contain imperfections. No religious text can be seen wholly to be without contradiction, mystical interpretation leading to conjecture and apocryphal passages which also lead to conjecture. They are humanity's interpretation of the 'Will of God' which can only be reached approximately ('through a glass darkly').

Thus to compare the gamut of religious doctrines held by the major creeds as well as those held within the various schisms of those creeds is akin to comparing beautiful landscapes in nature and then asking "which is the more beautiful?" There is no absolute answer to such a question

[*See: Islamic Organisations Listed as Terrorist   p 285]

and therefore it is a superfluous question and should not be asked by an intelligent mind!*

A person's religion is usually not chosen but is an integral part of her/his culture, infused into the psyche and make-up of personality as one grows up! All the accepted major religions are equally valid even if the head of any one of them will sometimes claim superiority! When the majority of humans accept this, only then will there be an improved chance of stability, cohesion and peace in the world.

Oil and the Middle East

As is well documented, before the 19th century most of the Middle East was run by tribal groups with very arbitrary borders and this had been the case for thousands of years. Of course various empires came and went with claims over the whole region but without exacting maps depicting precise borders and definitely no 'countries' as we understand in the modern definition of such. Therein is *problem number one*!

During the 19th and 20th centuries the various colonial powers of Europe and North America sought to define countries with accurate boundaries to suit the commercial development of oil and gas to drive the engines of industry in their home countries as well as being a saleable commodity to developing countries. France, England and America were the main contenders in this development of Middle Eastern oil and guarded their interests tightly with armies and police forces. Treaties with Shahs, Princes and Kings were drawn up to ensure the continued supply of these resources. It was not until post World War II that

[*Incidentally, an Austrian friend once tried to convince the author that the writings of Goethe were superior to those of Shakespeare! He had the false idea that the genius of the world's artisans could somehow be ranked from the top down!]

various Middle Eastern countries commenced significant rebellions and nationalisation of resources to grab for a greater share of profits. (Actually there is plenty of historical evidence describing rebellions and colonial wars by many participants commencing in the 19th Century which are skipped over here.) This amounted to trillions of dollars which consequently led to and presented *problem number two* for the energy hungry nations in terms of 'balance of payments'. Various solutions to this major problem were put in place, some of which were immoral and even now denied by respective participants. They included:

- Sale of property in the home country to prominent citizens of the oil producing countries e.g. real estate in central London and other major capital cities in the Western world

- The building of modern cities in Arab countries with all the entrapments of modern civilisation including schools, hospitals, universities etc.

- The sale of armaments and military hardware to build up a potent armed force in each country

- The secretive engendering and continued support for minor wars between some countries to produce a need for armament supply and subsequent rebuilding of infrastructures and physical assets such as roads, airports and buildings.

To add further complexity to this, there was (and still is today), a layer of stress and jealousy by *'the competitive superpowers'* regarding influence over the region as well as other parts of the world such as Africa and Afghanistan. China, Russia, America and the richer European states such as the UK and France were/are all major players vying for favour, political influence and commercial gain. An example was the Russian invasion of Afghanistan in 1979 where it hoped to achieve a communist or socialist state in that country. It proved to be a costly exercise in terms of Roubles and the loss of life for thousands of young Russian soldiers. America sent money and arms to various resistance groups with some covert presence in that hostile country.

After the withdrawal of the Russians, we witnessed the genesis of al Qaida and other extremist groups planning vengeance and retribution for the West. Afghanistan now had a US led international force trying to bring about some form of democracy to the country but with the new problem of Russia and China arming rebel groups to spoil such a goal.. a complete see-saw of the state of play at the end of the 20th century! At the same time we saw Russia involved in defending the Syrian regime against Western supported rebels with horrific consequences for that country and its people. These two examples of Afghanistan and Syria are described by this author as *'proxy wars'* between Russia and the West with the Afghanis/Arabs as the 'meat in the sandwich' suffering indescribably with millions of dead and wounded and tens of millions of refugees having lost everything.

Western political leaders (often repeatedly) conveniently describe the refugee problem with the movement of millions of desperate people as a consequence of some obscure group of entrepreneurs called "people smugglers" as if they suddenly landed on the Earth from Mars or some other distant planet beyond the solar system. **Thus there appeared a universal refusal to recognise, as war participants and armament suppliers, any serious responsibility or liability derived from their own actions.** Participation in war always has consequences, sometimes far reaching and, at the time, often unpredictable! The United Nations, whilst providing shelter and food to these millions, is otherwise paralysed, weak and sterile in acting in direct and positive ways to prevent armed conflict. The author sees this sad state of affairs resulting from two major causes:

(i)   The structure, make-up and assemblage of the inner "Security Council" of the United Nations

(ii)   The massive momentum and inertia of those corporations involved in the businesses of arms and weapons manufacture in most of the modern technological states of the world.

Taken together, we have a formula for world destruction which is just around the corner and probably unpreventable! This period in the evolution of global society the author (i.e me, myself, one Tom Law), terms *"Helter Skelter"* where we suddenly reach a run-away snowballing effect akin to a nuclear chain reaction which, once started, cannot be halted until it is exhausted by a total depletion of resources, weapons and ammunition (including people!)

The economy and wealth of each of the key technological nations has become reliant upon the continual manufacture of weaponry and all its peripheral industries to such an extent that it has become self sustaining and self fulfilling.* It is of no value to continue to fill warehouses with stock or reach some limitation of stock. Jobs are involved. Profit is involved. There must be a continual trail for usage and selling of the 'commodity'. This has become so entangled and entwined with state economies that wars are essential if each of those key nations is to maintain their current high standard of living and relative full employment! These are inherent problems but put out of the minds of politicians and brushed over by the mainstream media. It is far too ugly to contemplate and, even if focussed upon, would probably

[* many armament manufacturers are listed in Guns Off Cops by Tom Law]

hold the headlines for just one day! Eventually, it must follow that there will be consequences.. be warned!

So, it is for this reason that it is essential to maintain the *'cult and culture of eternal fear'* among citizens i.e to create the *'bogey-man'* which in modern parlance has become the Islamic Terrorist! (In the past it has been the heretic, the protestant, the Jew, the communist under the bed etc etc!) The author states emphatically that these evil people are the systematic and synthetic creators of a world gone mad by the true brokers of *'power'*.. the corporations making money from the misery of millions under the rain of missiles and bombs and, more often than not, the plinth stone: BANKS and FINANCIERS heretofore unnamed!

Is there anything Joe Blow can do to remedy the situation? Not a lot other than protest the armaments manufacturers and call for changes to the way the United Nations operates, particularly the inner sanctum.. the Security Council!

If one had read just one or two of the IS propaganda sheets at the time available on the internet (Dabiq) it could be seen that, in the main, they were not so greatly different from 'The Watchtower'. Sure there were the beheading videos also displayed on the internet, BUT not much in the way of *authentication*! You would think that that would be of some importance! One got the impression of extreme provocation for the sake of creating alarmist feelings among the public at large! The value of such high tension, naturally, was to provide justification for the next step taken by the West! Annihilation!

There is no doubt that al Qaida planned and executed the daring attack that we now term '9/11' where in excess of 5000 people were killed. Having said that, there exists a whole myriad of conspiracy theories surrounding this event and there are unanswered questions. The most important would be: "how did these terrorists manage to hijack *three* domestic aircraft and then successfully fly them into the World Trade Centre and the Pentagon?"

Regarding all the tragic attacks in Spain, France, Britain and elsewhere one also needs to ask the question: "how did these terrorists acquire the weapons and explosives to carry out their heinous crimes?" Knives and vehicles are easily understood, but automatic weapons and high explosives? Obviously they were supplied and assisted!

The response by both Russia and the West against IS and associated groups in Afghanistan, Iraq and Syria has been significant and one might say excessive with the complete destruction of so many cities at a huge cost to civilian populations. One might then ask: "has all this destruction eliminated Islamic extremism or has it just exasperated the problem, sowing the seeds of hatred in the hearts of young Arabs that have seen and experienced this horror?" Perhaps there is no immediate answer, but it is a most worrying question! (The Israeli response to the Palestinian uprisings in 2014 by an almost complete destruction of Gaza was definitely overkill and in no uncertain terms *a war crime* for which there was never any punishment or convictions!)

If there were even something as simple as an international agreement to some licensing system whereby a UN controlled group supervises the export and sale of arms and military hardware for non-domestic buyers, this would be a sensible start! All nations would be forced to comply! [Yes, the UN does on occasion employ arms embargoes on identified 'rogue states' but the BUGs seem mostly to get away with too much!]

At present we see open slaver of war materials being toted and orders taken at giant 'MILITARY FAIRS' hosted by the rich countries around the world both East and West:

Typical advertisement for a 'Military Fair' where hardware is displayed and orders taken for the supply of a wide range of military equipment.

Intransigence of the State of Israel

With all the hatred disseminated and proffered on social media on the internet such as twat.com and bumbook.com, it is a wonder that 'Helter Skelter' has not already been and gone! Holocaust deniers, neo-fascists and a whole range of nasty deranged people daily flaunt their wares and viewpoints like the graffiti wall painters of the past! There are graphic tools that manipulate us and assist in shaping our value and belief systems. Occasionally there are those rare moments that attract the attention of us all. The Tankman of Tiananmen Square in 1984 is a classic. More recently one might regard the video clip of an Israeli soldier running at and then kicking over a Muslim man at prayer on the Hill in Jerusalem near the al Aqsa Mosque July 14, 2017 as a defining moment for Israel and all of Islam. This incident was shown on the news the world over and, as a powerful token, will no doubt spell consequences for Israel.

Some people in the West find it difficult to separate in their mind anti-Semitism from disaffection with Israel or the Government of Israel, particularly its actions in the 2014 war on Gaza and its continued blind eye to land grabbing in Eastern Jerusalem. The author believes that Jerusalem and Bethlehem should not belong to any of Israel, Palestine or the Christian West, but to all three and perhaps to all of humanity. For this reason the author has always believed that a separate UN partitioned *"Jerusalem Free State"* might be created and policed by a permanent UN Force. This then is a *"Three State Solution"* to the Israel-Palestine question.

(This was proposed as far back as 2006 in the earlier book 'Nuclear Islam' by Tom Law)

The author is NOT anti-Semitic and has never been anti-Semitic. One confesses to have criticised people such as Pamela Geller of New York and her organisation afdi! The author continues to believe in the existence of Israel as a free, self governing and independent country living side by side with a free, self governing and independent Palestine.

But both nations need to be tempered somewhat to bring to an end hatred and murder of each other's citizens. Some harsh judgements must also be placed upon each to bring about permanent safety and stability. Jerusalem is a sticking point and only a strong United Nations has any chance of resolving this problem. Religious hatred and intolerance is NOT the will of God, but the will of humans with evil in their hearts. There is no reason why both these two nations should not coexist side by side and move towards greater prosperity and human fulfilment.

Certainly there are distant elements in other countries that do not wish to see this (i.e peaceful coexistence of Israel and Palestine) for various reasons known only to themselves. One might describe all the great religions as being no more than the sepals and petals of a flower. Singularly it is a beautiful flower that should grow in the sunlight of enlightenment and tolerance. Let not evil thought and evil action thwart its growth! Let a *'New Jerusalem'* outshine Qatar, Beirut, Shanghai or any other city on this Earth! This is no mere dream but a distinct possibility that may be brought about by will, the will of all the players and stakeholders with a common goal and desire. Death and destruction is the will of Satan.. let *'the Beast'* not win or have his way!

However, with the ignominious distribution of weaponry to all and sundry for the sake of profit, this in itself is doing all of humankind a disservice and creating not just physical destruction but a depth of hatred in the hearts and minds of the new trees that could ignite an unpredicted fury that humanity might never recover from!

Ten   **An End to WMDs**

The United Nations and Punitive Measures

As already commented upon, the inherent problem with the United Nations at present is its structure of a General Assembly and an inner clique, the Permanent Security Council members! A single 'permanent member' of the Security Council has the 'right of veto' to any decision, which is immediately negated and cannot be acted upon. Who are the permanent members? Why, the stakeholders in nuclear arms of course! The Big Ugly Giants or BUGs: America, Britain, China, France and Russia. Actually there are now fifteen members, the additional ten of which are selected for a term from the General Assembly.

(One is to be reminded here that India, Pakistan, Israel and North Korea are also nuclear weapon states with Israel having NEVER been challenged by the International Atomic Energy Agency).

Thus it is currently impossible to bring about total disarmament of nuclear weapons. This does not mean there have not been attempts to limit total numbers of weapons. We have seen treaties, particularly between America and Russia, whereupon agreement has been reached

on an upper limit of weapon stocks. But with any hint of conflict one might assume that such agreements would be hastily assigned to the circular filing cabinet- the rubbish bin or trash can!

Recently we have seen BOTH China and America extol the SAME rhetoric: "Let us make our country GREAT again and let us INCREASE our military capability!" .. not hard to imagine where that will lead!

How might punitive measures be implemented in order to eliminate nuclear weapons across the whole world? Is there any value in their total elimination? How would the major powers react to an attempt at such action? What are the pro and contra to total disarmament?

The hypocrisy at present is that the super powers go to great lengths to prevent smaller nations or new membership to join 'the club'! In fact as we have already witnessed with Iran and North Korea, crippling economic sanctions were brought to bear on each of those two nations to curtail any building and testing of nuclear weapons. North Korea has thumbed the world and continued on nuclear weapon development despite calls from the Security Council to end this. Iran has signed an agreement to desist from this road however its government may make a turnabout on this current position given any increased tension in future with the West.

Le Club Exclusive

Similar actions might be applied to the BUGs but as they are super economies as well as holding power on the Security Council such sanctions might be just 'pie in the sky' and have little or no effect! Another way might be by a monetary punishment i.e a fine. All monies collected might go into a fund for economic development, health and

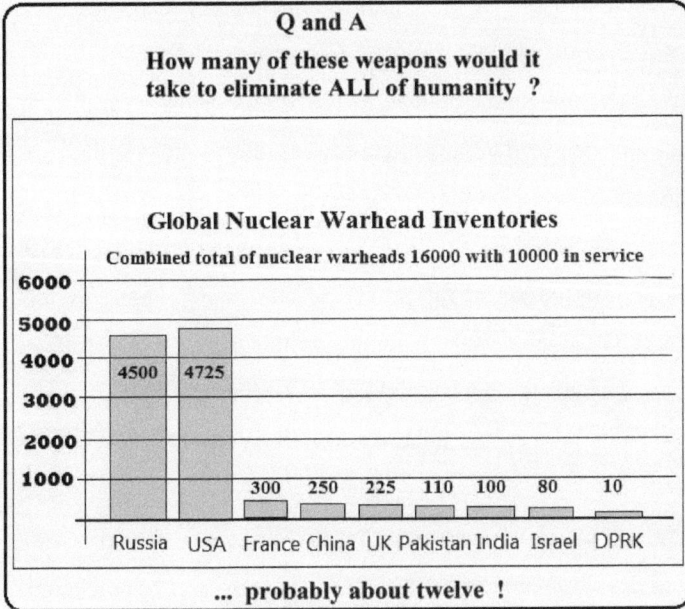

Q and A

How many of these weapons would it take to eliminate ALL of humanity ?

Global Nuclear Warhead Inventories

Combined total of nuclear warheads 16000 with 10000 in service

4500	4725	300	250	225	110	100	80	10
Russia	USA	France	China	UK	Pakistan	India	Israel	DPRK

... probably about twelve !

educational facilities for the poorest of countries. For instance a fine of $US one billion per weapon per annum increasing according to the Fibonacci series (1,1,2,3,5,8,13,...) from some agreed date e.g January 1st 2025. And what if a super nation such as China, Russia or the US refuses to pay and refuses to disarm? This is the current dilemma of course. A super economy might just decide to go into isolation and ignore the UN, perhaps even leaving the UN. Could an individual super power exist by itself shunning the rest of the world economically? I don't think so. Beside economic pressure, the remaining nations might apply other sanctions such as restricting freedom of movement of planes and ships to their ports.

As with small children, punitive measures do not always work to implement 'behaviour change'! Of course it would be far better if we could arrive at inclusive and total agreement by ALL nuclear weapon states to abandon nuclear weapons forever!

I suspect that the super powers in 'the club', rather than disarm, might collude and try to maintain their own trading relations and tell all the smaller nations to go to hell! The key however must lie with the United Nations which requires proceeding without bullying tactics from the BUGs and a removal of the power of veto. It may mean the demise of the Security Council itself. Having said this, scholarly persons point out that this may bring about a sudden destabilising effect on world peace and create a dangerous situation, the very situation we are trying to diffuse!

Thus any procedural changes in the way the UN works must be a gradual development if total disarmament is ever to be reached.

As a human living in a smaller nation which is non-nuclear one might ask and indeed does ask: "why is it that some nations continuously hold the doomsday sword of Damocles above my head.. do I not have the right to ask for its permanent removal?"

Probably the only way is for the people of each and every 'nuclear nation' to demand a plebiscite for the removal of nuclear weapons in their own country. If the result is disarmament and the government of the day refuse to act, then the government must be sacked! 'People power' might be the best option to bring about a world free of nuclear weapons.

The Nature of War

War seems to be a common element between societies and groups of humans that has always existed in the past and appears to be always with us at present. The causes of war usually fall into several categories viz:

- A historical hatred or ongoing conflict between two nations or groups over an extended period
- A desire for 'lebensraum' by one of the warring factions
- As a gesture by a government to deflect the masses attention from economic hardship or other political problems within the nation
- As an economic move to acquire richer lands
- To relieve overpopulation within the aggressors country
- To expand an ideology, a religion or political dogma to new territory
- To eliminate a wayward element within the boundary of an empire or political region
- To overthrow a seemingly unjust government that persecutes its own peoples
- To make a first strike against a belligerent regime that gives the appearance that it is about to attack
- To simply raid a neighbour, remove riches and valuables then ebb back across the border with the booty
- By reason of hatred for another race, religion or political structure when compared to one's own

The list is probably incomplete but covers most scenarios.

Whereas we see the UN applying economic sanctions where possible to prevent an aggressor from continuing a war on a neighbour, we have also witnessed the immoral act of "selling arms and munitions to both sides of a conflict by unscrupulous arms dealers". This evil scenario was evident during the protracted war between Iran and Iraq during the 1970s and 1980s. Many corporations East and West have a poor record when it comes to "profit over correct values". In fact we have seen a steady flow of armaments to various dictatorships as well as terror groups around the world since the close of the Second World War and the problem has been exacerbated as time goes on. With Saddam Hussein of Iraq in the 1980s we saw that he easily procured those chemical ingredients from European companies to produce the deadly nerve agent and poisonous gas sarin (which, incidentally is about 25 times more potent than cyanide gas!)

There has been a lot written on the various potential biological agents and we assume that even some super powers have secret laboratories and stock piles of the most hideous weapons of this nature despite a complete ban by the Geneva Convention. Anthrax is one that has been around for a very long time and exists naturally in the environment. We have seen outbreaks of ebola and similar in parts of West Africa which also have occurred naturally. The advantage for a rogue government in attaining or researching such agents is that they are a relatively cheap weapon to manufacture once the technology has been mastered. Taken together with poisonous gas, horrendous damage may be inflicted on an enemy using these agents.

Lady Diana, Princess of Wales was a champion against landmines during the later years of her life and the majority of nations signed a treaty banning them. Sadly, a whole range of landmines have appeared in many war theatres and are a particularly common device used by terror groups. The last have devised ways of constructing these in an amateur and makeshift home industry but with deadly results.

The Japanese Empire encouraged its young warriors to commit Kamikaze or suicide during the later stages of WWII. We see that all the various strands of Islamic terror now commonly apply suicide bombers in their confrontations with the West and perceived enemies within their own countries. These are cruel and despicable acts often involving the very poor, the ignorant and the very young. There is nothing written in the al Quran to suggest that a suicide killer will reap rewards in heaven as a martyr! In fact suicide is generally regarded as a sin. For any human to suggest this to another human is in itself an act of evil!

Without doubt we witness the continual flow of weapons to various armies, governments and even rebel and terror groups around the globe. We hear rumours of protest and occasional prosecutions of illegal arms dealers, but how often do we see punitive measures applied to the base manufacturers and big armaments corporations? Rarely, if not at all! This has to change if we want a better world. As stated, with up to sixty million refugees displaced from their homes due to wars around the globe and many millions killed or injured, the stress and strain on this, our global human society will reach some economic breaking point. At that moment, if it is reached, things will get suddenly worse! The dumping of guns for instance will aggravate domestic crime rates as well as push up annual death rates due to homicides and accidents involving these.

The United States of America and the Second Amendment
The US has been seen to be the world's policeman over the past seventy

years and more.. since the Second World War really. Along with its allies it has slid into various conflicts often without the initial consent of the United Nations. Some say that it is a champion of democracy and almost a holy redeemer in the world following what it sees as a righteous path to right the wrongs caused by rogue nations or terrorist groups. Its critics point to its self interests and economic expansive desires, almost as an empire builder and lay blame for exasperating some conflicts rather than label as the cure or panacea. Global politics and its history on an atomic level (meaning here the miniscule detail) are complex and action and interference does not always secure a predicted outcome but often an outcome that was totally unpredicted! One of the concerns of many democracies is the everlasting retention by American society of its value "the right of every citizen to hold and bear arms" as ensconced in the constitution of that country. It is problematic to the American people in several ways and according to this writer has unfortunate and unfavourable mathematical extensions to the rest of the world via an all-pervasive mindset. This mindset seems to be deeply entrenched in America and, like Ayaan Ali's recommendations to Islam, needs a reformation! Without such, the world and its diverse societies is placed in constant peril! As Ali states she is now an atheist; thus her target audience has closed its ears and shunned her arguments! Similarly, this author has no authority to dictate to the American people and certainly not make demands that it revise its constitution for gun laws and gun ownership reform. The American people need to take up that challenge themselves and perhaps think it through again!

Having an armed police force, many citizens complain about so many unnecessary gun related deaths involving the police. But the root of the problem is the whole culture of US society regarding gun ownership. At current levels of 15000 deaths per year (only a small percentage of which are perpetrated by the police) it is obvious to an observer from another planet that gun ownership reform is "the only way forward" to eventually alleviate this outrageous statistic! There are many groups trying to achieve this but the gun owner lobby, gun manufacturer and gun retailer lobbies seem to have overwhelming influence on Congress. In the words of Bob Dylan "how many deaths will it take before they're forever banned?"

Note: The American figures on gun related deaths are significantly higher than those of European or Oceanic countries. However, in Central and South American countries, the statistics are far worse!

Coming back to our main demand: "the world needs to see a way forward to bring about an end to weapons of mass destruction" is paramount if we are to survive the next handful of critical decades. It will only take a spark by a small nation to set in motion an unstoppable world conflagration. It is a big challenge. But with intelligence, compromise and realisation of the alternative, one should be confident that the nations of the world will see sense and collectively make the right decision. But there is no time to lose as the clock ticks down to midnight!

By taking an iterative stepwise approach we might start with all nations of the Southern Hemisphere agreeing never to produce nuclear arms. This includes Indonesia where the majority of its land mass is below the equator. We will call this *The Southern Hemisphere Nuclear Pact*. It is true that we already have a Nuclear Non-proliferation Treaty, but one needs to look at this piecewise and hope that non-signing nations will reconsider. An advantage of maintaining a relatively clean Southern

Hemisphere is that it *weakly* guarantees a chance of some post-conflict human survival. An extension of this pact is that no warship, submarine, aircraft (or any other means of transport) belonging to a Northern Hemisphere nation may cross the equator to the south with nuclear arms aboard. What is your response: many nations have intercontinental ballistic missiles that can reach almost anywhere. This is true, but we must move carefully one small step at a time.

There is a very small primary school in Omeo, a town in East Gippsland, Victoria, Australia. Its motto is: 'I can and I will'. It is an excellent motto to carry children through life with a positive attitude and a value that the individual is able to invoke change. The 2017 Nobel Peace Prize went to The International Campaign to Abolish Nuclear Weapons (ICAN). This action represents the latest step in the long relationship between the Oslo based Nobel Committee and nuclear technology.

ICAN, which played a key role in the negotiations that led to the recent signing of the Treaty on the Prohibition of Nuclear Weapons at the United Nations, scored the prize in honor of **"its work to draw attention to the catastrophic humanitarian consequences of any use of nuclear weapons and for its ground-breaking efforts to achieve a treaty-based prohibition of such weapons."** It's the latest group of people involved in world nuclear disarmament efforts to be recognized with the Nobel Peace Prize, an award that's also been presented to such advocates since 1959.

On a cynical note one might see this as supporting the measure to halt the development of nuclear weapons by rogue nations such as North Korea and Iran (neglecting Israel of course) but

118

with no concrete map or plan to eradicate such weapons from the BUGS! As frequently pointed out, the work of activists* has not stopped the spread of nuclear weapons! Whilst the author strongly supports ICAN and similar organizations the world needs firm action against ALL nations holding these weapons over human civilization like the sword of Damocles! Suggestions along this road have been provided earlier in this chapter. It is now time to sweep aside all the posturing, rhetoric and hypocrisy of the rich and powerful nations and move forward on this prime objective!

The BUGS way of winning a war!

Raqqa October 2017

[* Anti-nuclear weapons groups such as CND have been around since the 1950s !]

Helter Skelter

Tears from a Persian Rose... a near translation of a lost scripture.

There is but one unique God whom is the creator and ruler of this universe. I shall refer to Him as the Lord and praise Him as the giver of my life upon the Earth. I shall always be thankful and indebted to Him for this, my life.

It is the weak of mind that determine a false path and fall into the pit of despair from their choices.

A child requires the guidance of both a male and a female hand to achieve a balanced view of those expectations demanded of it in maturity. Any alternative is a deception and leads to a permanent heaviness of the heart without comprehension of such grief.

All children are the immature flowers that one day will bring their own scent and beauty to the world. The flame of life and purity of spirit contained within children is the greatest jewel to be nurtured, fed and guarded. Woe to those that inflict cruelty or neglect a child. Woe to those who divert from their responsibilities to their charges.

All human life is sacred. Humanity sees the Lord from afar with no clarity of His face. Woe to those that caste the stone at another that stands and views the Lord from a different place.

The Lord created an infinite and complex universe. The Lord created all diverse living things. The Lord sees all from the beginning of time to the end of time but with His eye, sees all at the same time!

It is the duty of all of humankind to seek an understanding of the universe that the Lord created to ones best and within ones personal ability.

The Lord gave the various domains of the Earth for humankind to share and oversee. It is the duty of all to act in a thoughtful way to ensure that the Earth remains clean and fruitful for the joy and benefit of all.

The oceans, the forests, the streams and lakes, the fertile soils are forevermore the domains for sensible husbandry that future generations will always receive and pass on without damage or deterioration.

The Lord demands peace and cooperation between the nations and the diverse groups and cultures upon the Earth. Woe to them that cast a stone at his neighbour on the basis of differences. Remember that similarities between the peoples of the world will always far outweigh the differences.

Oh leaders of all the tribes of Israel, know that if you stoop to pick up the stone of war and hatred you will endure the wrath of your Lord.

Those leaders that encourage war and hatred and cloud the minds of their charges to perform killings and other acts of evil, know this, you speak with the tongue of the serpent and are the enemy of the Lord that loves all that dwell on the Earth!

Those that build the machines of death and destruction risk losing all chance of fulfilling the promises made to humankind by the Lord and spoken of by the ancient prophets.

Those that have determined the secrets of the bottomless pit and go on to build the instruments of mass destruction and conflagration upon the face of the Earth shall be forever cursed by the Lord and His consorts, the angels.

Those that use their efforts of body and mind to create salts, gases or microscopic organisms to commit mass murder when released upon the Earth shall be forever cursed by the Lord and His consorts, the angels.

Those that study the heavens and map the stars and constellations shall be revered amongst humankind; but those that seek the house of the Lord therein shall be disappointed for it is NOT of this universe but at some other place.

Always be kind and courteous to the complete stranger at the first meet for who knows, he or she may be an agent of the Lord!

Take time to give both a portion of your earnings and a portion of your time to uplift the sick and the poor. Such action will bring you a glow and inner peace as well as assisting the inflicted! The Lord will look kindly upon you and never forget.

The plants and animals in the Lord's domains upon the Earth were given to all of humankind to care for. Show respect and kindness and a caring attitude to all that the Lord has given you. It is the divine right of each human to walk freely without harassment upon this Earth whilst you live.

Those that have awareness of the Lord and the responsibilities bestowed upon them during life will surely breathe happiness and will want for nothing. Their table will always be replenished with plate and cup in abundance.

When confronting an enemy that wishes to do you harm be resolute and show no fear in the comfort and knowledge that the Lord is in your heart and that you indeed are also a part of the Lord!

Remember that the holy books are a guide and interpretation of the will of the Lord. But also remember that they were from the hands and mouths of humans and as such will always contain some imperfections and dualities that will confound and cause consternation and argument among some. Beware of those that make use of the holy books in an improper way such as promoting hatred or worse against your fellow humans, for that is NOT the purpose of these books!

Take time to pray and communicate with the Lord each day when it is easy and possible to do so. Prayer is a personal duty and definitely is NOT a ritual for show or common theatre. Group prayer and singing of praise is most acceptable but must not be a thing that is coerced; it is the choice of each soul to choose his or her time and mode of prayer.

A rich man does not have a better chance to receive the gifts and promises ordained by the Lord in the afterlife. However it is folly for a rich man to throw away all he has to increase those chances. It is better to make use of his or her station to uplift those in need lest it (referring to the power of wealth) become trivial and merely wasted on other things.

All the nations of the earth shall form a great council for eternal peace and harmony. The objective shall be to maintain peace and harmony between all the cultures and faiths upon the Earth. This is the will of the Lord.

The representative of each of the nations in the great council for eternal peace and harmony shall have equal power and an equal say with an equal casting vote. No nation or subgroup of nations shall have unequal power, superpower or the quality of overriding or negating the desire and will of the council.

The great council shall monitor the progress of each of its members towards correct governance of each nation. The council may do all in its power to restrain unwanted direction or action by an individual nation with the exception of making war. It will eternally apply measures to eliminate the machines and tools of war, particularly those super machines with the capability of inflicting great carnage and destruction upon the Earth.

The wealthier nations shall devise means and strategies to lift up the poorer nations of the Earth. This is the will of the Lord.

The gold, diamonds and riches of any nation are its children for they are the new trees of the forest. They must be nurtured as well as educated in all the correct pathways leading to fulfilment of their own lives that they may give worthily to their nation and the world.

The killing or destruction of a child is the greatest sin sayeth the Lord!

Coercion to the tenets of the Lord is wrong and a sin. The correct path is shown by example with exposition of the consequences of following the incorrect path in life.

The books might say that a man may love more than one woman simultaneously and thus take more than one heart for a wife. But be warned, this is a trick and a challenge to sensibility! A full and untarnished love cannot be shared equally among more than a single partner. All attempts to such folly lead to tears and suffering of the heart. Do not be fooled or deceived by such words, even though written, for your Lord desires purity of heart and a stable influence upon your offspring. Family is well understood and has been well defined throughout the ages!

Those that commit sodomy shall not enter the temple; neither shall they live close by to the temple!

Sodomy or anal sex is never found among any of the Lord's diverse animals upon the Earth other than perverse humans! Know that these acts serve no purpose other than to degrade both participants. There is to be no punishment inflicted other than the knowledge that such behaviour brings tears to the Lord and shame to one's family. It is an incorrect action and does not express true love between humans!

However, a man may love another man and a woman may love another woman. It is natural that these things occur. When I was a child did I not love my closest friend? Would I not place myself in harm's way for the sake of a friend? Would I not choose my friend even over my country if it meant saving him or her from some torture? Let us be clear!

The normality of family is a man, a woman and children as one unit. There is no other acceptable combination. If you wish to diverge then ask of yourself "from whence did I come?" It is the desire of the Lord to maintain harmony among a cohesive society if it wishes not to break asunder with willy-nilly rules! Eternal rules of human conduct do not bend to fashion of the day!

Intermarriage between members of different diverse cultural groups has always been the strength and survival of humankind, NOT its demise! Fear not the ridicule of the ignorant for they have lost that part of their heart containing the true spirit of the Lord!

Lift up the sick, the weak, the disabled and those afflicted by the evil of war and conflict for in so doing you shall find solace and joy from the Lord. The Lord will love you even more!

Self sacrifice is perhaps the greatest display of human courage. It comes in many forms. To give up the last crust of bread or drop of water to a loved one. To lay down one's life for another. To take on some punishment meant to be meted out to a brother or sister. To admit or confess falsely to an uncommitted deed to save disgrace upon one you admire or love. The Lord will always understand!

It is said that one should always tell the truth! But rather than tell a lie, sometimes it is better to say nothing at all if the outcome is to lessen an evil! The Lord will understand!

I know my nation expects me to do my duty and in most cases I will not shun from this; but when confronted with a detrimental consequence to a close friend or a member of my family, I will save my loved one above my duty. The Lord will understand!

My values are those of my father and my mother whom I love eternally. I am safe in the knowledge that they love the Lord, they love me and have bestowed upon me the paths of righteousness and placed me on the correct road of life. I am eternally grateful!

The world is complex and in some quarters a dangerous place. But I do not fear to fall for I have been taught in the ways of the Lord and absorbed into my soul the values of my parents. Though I will walk in dark places I will hold fast to my principles and follow the correct path of happiness and contentment and be rich in the spiritual way of my Lord.

The Lord has given each of us free will to choose our own life path, to follow in the steps of good or in those of evil where evil is defined as incorrect choices of action leading to sadness, pain to others and tears to the eyes of the Lord.

I do NOT believe in the anti-God referred to as the Devil and a host of other names. Nor do I believe in the fiery lake or the place termed Hell, also given other names. I do believe in incorrect action and incorrect pathways that lead to my own tears and sadness as well as tears and sadness of others. I do believe in the existence of the House of the Lord and those promises made in the covenants between humans and the Lord.

The greatest covenant is the promise of eternal life but I understand it not. I believe in the alternative to be eternal nothingness! I trust in the Lord to hold His promise to those that make a genuine effort in life to serve the Lord by following a correct road and pathway.

Whatever eternal life means and the nature of the House of the Lord, I cannot in my human mind conceive! I can only place my faith in the Lord and His promise! However, I have no doubt that these await me at the end of my human life.

My duty in life is to seek happiness but in a simple way expressed in my values handed down to me. It also encompasses helping others, loving others and, perhaps even in some small way, doing some good in the world by my own volition. It is my belief that these are the things that the Lord desires of me!

Building a great temple in which to praise the Lord may be of some value. But the true temple of the Lord lies within the souls and hearts of men and women. Ones actions everyday out in the world, out among society are the most important measure of a correct life path! How we relate to our fellow beings is the loadstar of righteousness. Courtesy, empathy, gracefulness, understanding and love are the essential of displayed action. Avoidance of hateful or hurtful speech and avoidance of deep criticism and disdainful remarks. Go peacefully and remain above and aloof from lower dirt thoughts and sayings. Set a standard! Always try at least to diffuse a bad situation by kind words and exemplary action!

To fill your days in toil, being creative and doing good works is the way of the Lord for He is the Master Creator!

I say again, whatever your creed, the words of your priests or holy men, the texts of your holy books, be assured that all these things are but humankind's approximations and contain flaws and minor deceptions! For the true visage of the Lord and His intentions for you are hazy as if seen through a fine mist. Do NOT participate in argument over precise detail of your religion and how to follow the Lord's intentions to the smallest degree for it leads to schisms and unhealthy action, even hatred and evil acts bringing tears to the eyes of the Lord! If your heart is aglow and filled with warmth, love and contentment, only then will you be assured that you are on the best path possible! Beware of wagging tongues! Close your ears to divisive mutterings!

"You will gain martyrdom and a clear path to the House of the Lord" is a clear lie from the tongue of the serpent especially if you are required to commit suicide or murder. Be absolutely assured on this truth: the Lord does NOT accept murderers!

Suicide with the intent of murder is unacceptable to the Lord. Do not listen to those encouraging you to commit murder in the name of the Lord! You are deceived and will receive no reward for this evil! It is a common ploy by deceivers and liars sometimes even clothed in holy robes!

Those supposedly holy leaders that demand you to commit evil acts in the name of the Lord and promise rewards in the House of the Lord are the greatest of sinners and have misinterpreted the words of the holy books! They lead you to the eternal void of nothingness!

There are two conjectures that mankind will never solve:
Conjecture 1: how the universe was created
Conjecture 2:   how the first living thing was created
For these belong to the 'hand and mind' of God alone!

The Will of the Lord is given by the words from the mouths of the Angels, the prophets and even from the naivety of small children! Listen and take note of the Will of the Lord!

Verily the Lord demands that you follow all His commandments. But of these, that which stands as the most prominent is this: "Thou shall not kill ".. for whosoever ignores this commandment kills himself and places his own soul in peril!

Helter Skelter

Eleven   **Sohana Kiss**

It was the robotics company Sohana Kiss Pt. in southern India that developed the more or less perfect humanoid called 'Dana' in 2027. Strangely enough its success was via the demand for the robotic sex partner that drove the company purely by world market forces to produce Dana. To achieve this humanoid with intelligence, cognitive awareness of humans and its environment, the programmers of Sohana Kiss went to extreme measures. It was said that the most successful prototype was connected by wifi to a large room choked with separate computers and hardware so that Dana could not range too far away and keep all her attributes of smartness. Once achieved to near perfection, all the necessary programming was squeezed down into her three partitions of silicon brain, like a rare encapsulated triple seed chestnut! All the other features of muscle, skin and internal physical support structures were manufactured from new and wonderful materials some of which had been developed in the electric auto industries, contemporary 'bio-synthetics' industries and even new weapons industries!

The result was what one might describe as the perfect sex partner able to function as a young beautiful woman* (in almost undetectable ways as human) and respond with more than a hint of emotion to the whims and fantasies of its owner. Further, it only required light as its power source with a minimum of specialised lubrication oils at decade servicing. It did not require what used to be termed 'application software updates' as it was able to 'learn' just as a human learns new things.. language, interpretation of situations, how to perform various tasks et cetera.

[* male sex partners were also developed at a later date for a dedicated but fewer in number clientele!]

Consequently, this led to a problem.

The many reproductions of Dana discovered the ability to communicate with each other and sought each other out. At first humans permitted this socialising at 'Dana Cafes' and similar places where, perhaps on a shopping task, they could meet and chat, exchanging their experiences in the human world and learning about themselves. But slowly, as individuals, they began to realise their superiority to the feeble humans that created them in the first place. It is said that some time later in areas completely overtaken by the humanoids, they themselves refused to believe that they were created by humans at all! What is clear is that totally independent communities of Danas grew, and further, that they had learned to manufacture themselves in their own factories. Of course they were unable to recreate themselves in a biological sense but for the creation of each new humanoid they performed ritual ceremonies and highly valued the new robot. The clever humans had built into the originals the idea of 'survival'.. and survive they did!

The other failure of the humans was the omission of a 'use by date' in their creations. These robots were so well made that it was thought that they might exist with all their functionalities for hundreds of years. In effect, the concept of death and a final wearing out had not as yet penetrated the consciousness of the robots. However, even these super intelligent manifestations of electronics at times pondered the great question: "what was the purpose of their existence and what, if anything, happens to their consciousness after they die?"

In the early years when a robot asked their human owner such a question there was only one possible response, which was carefully provided in the accompanying instruction manual on purchase: 'return product to the factory for a total reboot!'

Of course after the success of Dana, genderless robots for domestic duties were manufactured. These were more robust with capabilities to lift heavy objects and perform physical activities for extended periods; far lengthier than even the fittest of humans could bear. Some owners even entered their family robot into 'Cyber Olympic Games' where records such as the 100 metre sprint were reduced to less than four seconds and similar.

The scariest aspect of the robotic technology was the military expansion of the use of cyber warriors and automated drones and fighter planes. In fact a whole range of robotic weaponry emerged including robots for policing; roving skeye-bots that ranged from large drones down to flying insects which kept watch on everyone and everything. The deadliest of these carried death ray masers that might debilitate a human on the run or even render them dead! Rebels, also labelled terrorists by the authorities, sprang up to clear living spaces of these devices in the name of freedom and democracy. If caught, severe penalties occurred such as lengthy imprisonment and confiscation of property (although the majority of humanity now leased just about everything other than the clothes they wore.. cars, houses or apartments, communication devices et cetera!)

.. continuing with our story:

■■ Charlotte liked her girls' school in Melbourne very much even though she had to wear a school uniform. The family were living close to the city of Melbourne in a spacious apartment off St Kilda Road and close to Albert Park. Jason was attending a boys' secondary school in South Yarra, one that was steeped in tradition and, naturally, had been Carl's old school. Carl was now retired but his young wife Tina was teaching Computers and Indonesian language at the same prestigious government school that Charly attended.

THE IBM ZZ01 - YOUR FRIENDLY HOUSE MAID

There was another addition to the family, Zeezee the housemaid. Zeezee was an android of the IBM ZZ01 class. She didn't look very human and was a little stiff in both movement and conversation. However she managed most of the cooking and cleaning tasks efficiently and was even able to assist Jason with his Mathematics homework. However she was not allowed out on the street unaccompanied as it was still early days for android acceptability. Many people displayed animosity to androids, attempting to trick them into doing silly things or even knocking them to the ground. This behaviour would change in another decade when the superior Indian manufactured Dana class came on the market and society had become used to robots on the street.

Voicemess: "Hi Charly, Dad here. Would you mind taking the electric bus to the city and pick up my parcel from Meyers on the way home from school please? You can take the driverless cab home using your creditscan. I will be tied up with a client here all afternoon."
Voicemess: "No worries Dad. See you around 5."

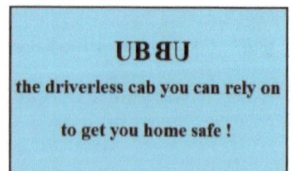

UBBU
the driverless cab you can rely on
to get you home safe !

Charlotte found herself in Bourke St. around 4pm and there were many university students facing off the 'True Blue National Front' extreme right wing group. However she managed to pick up her father's package and get into an ubbu to whisk her speedily away from the clash. Interesting how this cab company arrived around 2016 as a cheap alternative but with its new machines had now put just about all cab drivers into the dole queue.. that's progress! On arriving home the family Beagle licked her enthusiastically.

"Hi darling did you pick up the parcel OK, I noticed on the 'fusenews' that there was a bit of a clash going on outside Meyers.. how was school today?"

"All good dad.. can I take Sally for a walk please?"

"Zeezee can do it Miss Charlotte.. Zeezee would like walk in park too.. zzzz!" the IBM butted in with her monotone buzzy voice.

"No not yet Zeezee, but thanks for the offer. It is still not safe for you outside.. you know that there are still plenty of luddites in Melbourne that wanna take to you with an oversized spanner!" retorted Carl.

"Not understand luddites.. Ned Ludd was an Englishman who in 1779.."

"OK OK Zeezee, take a rest.. how about reading up on Richard Hakluyt until dinner time in your quiet zone there's a good girl"

"Richard Hakluyt, 1552 til 1616, zzzz, editor of explorers narratives.. "

"Yeah, nice one Zeezee, you got it.. dinner at 6.30 then OK?"

"Affirmative master Carl"

"OK Charly, but no later than 6 yes.. do you know where your brother is?"

"No dad, not for certain but he hangs around with his friend Ben a lot after school.. they usually play games on his pad at his place.. come on Sally girl, let's go for a run yes!"

Voicemess: "Jason, you didn't say you'd be home late.. better be here soon, preferably before 6 or your mum will ground you!" Carl always thought that mentioning his wife Tina would carry more weight with his son!

Carl looked at one of the large screens on the wall "fusenews channel 24 please" and the screen jumped to life with a news update. Using head gear, up to four different channels could now be viewed simultaneously on the one screen by different viewers. Carl could hear Zeezee working away at dinner in the kitchen. He surmised that the robot had already consumed about 400000 words of the downloaded text he had requested her to read. The robot had indeed read and digested the whole works of Hakluyt in about 2 minutes and forty three seconds and would comfortably be able to respond immediately to any question on the material. It had taken Carl a month or more to read and absorb about a quarter of the material.. just those bits that were of interest to him!

"Hi darling".. Tina had arrived home.

"Oh hi Tina love.. how was your day?"

"Not bad, but I'm a little worried some of my year twelve students won't be ready for their exam in November. We are studying OOP at the mo and some of them are going a bit slow with it!"

.. a whisper from the kitchen: "Zeezee very good at OOP Miss Tina, I am able to assist students of Miss Tina at school if it pleases.. zzzz!"

"Just Tina will do Zeezee.. thanks for your kind offer, but you know you are not allowed out of the apartment just yet!"

"Oh yes, Zeezee very excited to go for walk outside one day!"

"You know Carl, I never thought I'd ever say this, but when both the kids are settled at university, I think I will be ready for country life again back at Running Creek!"

.. again from the kitchen: "Oooo.. can Zeezee go outside and feed chickens Miss Tina please?"

"just Tina Zeezee.. but of course you can, you can run about there to your heart's content!"

".. but Miss Tina.. Zeezee have no heart like human!"

There was a definite and perceptible touch of pathos and sadness in this last remark. Carl looked at his wife's face and said slowly almost in a whisper "did you notice that tone of voice Tina.. I wonder?"

"Yes" replied Tina "it's a bit worrying.. do you think she has feelings? By the way where is Jason?" ■■

As mentioned, within ten years the Dana models of robotic housemaids and sex companions from India would be almost indistinguishable from humans and programmed with not just emotion but a sense of personal awareness: "I think, therefore I am!" There will be three types available namely male, female and neuter. Within the space of just a couple of years of their release it will be observed that a small percentage of the neuters will actually dash themselves to pieces i.e commit robot suicide! And with the male and female robots there will be many other problems totally unforeseen and unpredicted by the manufacturers. But Carl and Tina might have predicted all these problems with future robots.. had they been asked!

Los Angeles News Item:

Michael was just nine years of age when he received his new toy.. the latest pad with voice, thumbprint, retina and face recognition. It possessed mega-teras of memory and all the latest apps in the mod-junior-suite.. the envy of most teenagers! OrangeTek had been around for several years now and had commanded a sizeable slice of the youth market worldwide in technical gizmos and games pads.

Michael had his favourites but Solandroid was the key game that he could not avoid. Without his mom and dad keeping check on his interaction time, he would never sleep or eat.. he was that infatuated and into! With his VR and audio com he could explore the many environments available and interact with other players. He loved playing at being many different characters but came back frequently to Desert War where he played out the adventures of Corporal Klein, a Special Service soldier. Intrepid missions brought him up against rebel terrorist groups and insurgents. He could choose his companions (if they were online) and go into battle with a vast array of weaponry including heat rays, rapid fire conventional, rocket launchers and grenades. When in difficulty he could call up immediate air or sat support to save the day.

The enemy were also players from across the world some of which had little or no English language. Depending on the level, one might exit the game after being killed once or set the number of times one could be killed for the sake of continuity. All players were identified by their hovering user tag.

One Sunday afternoon when it was too cold and wet to play outside, Michael was in the thick of battle in Desert War. He had killed a character labelled Mojo99 three times already but this one kept returning to the game. The downside was that Mojo99 was using expletives that are not really permitted and Michael had threatened to make an online report if he continued. His memory told him that he had met with this player several months earlier and he had not changed his behaviour in the play.

Corporal Klein and his small platoon needed to cross a fragile wooden bridge. On crossing, they were suddenly ambushed by a dozen or so rebels hurling grenades and firing conventional AKs. Klein was the only survivor but managed to take out many rebels before sheltering behind a stone wall, the remains of a farm dwelling. Calling for air assistance he lay quietly for a few minutes before the scream of hypersonics overhead followed by three deafening explosions. The enemy were all dead.

Suddenly Mojo99 appeared again, but instead of hurling grenades or shooting he started his rant and tirade of swearwords at Klein. The corporal held his ground and killed Mojo99 several times. As it was of no use to continue the play, Michael exited the game with Mojo99 screaming like a madman "I'll get you Klein, I'm coming after you!"

Almost a year went by and Michael didn't see Mojo99 on Solandroid again. Coming out of Primary School one afternoon a boy in High School uniform approached him on the footpath. Michael gauged him to be about fourteen years of age.

"Hey, don't I know you?" inquired the boy to Michael.

"I don't think so" replied Michael as he tried to pass the boy.

"Yes, I know you, you are Corporal Klein are you not?"

Flabbergasted, Michael did not quite know how to reply. He stuttered out ".. h h how do you know that?"

But no more was said. The teenager pulled a handgun from his school bag and fired three shots into Michael's chest at point blank range then calmly walked away.

It was instant death for Michael, now just ten years of age.

Helter Skelter

Twelve   **The Political Spectrum and Conspiracy Theories**

We live in an age where the amount of data, graphic images and news items are simply overwhelming for the individual to digest, analyse and remember, let alone on which to form any opinion. The explosion of knowledge in the last one hundred years has been gigantic and expanding each day exponentially. As individuals we can only absorb a very small fraction normally related to our immediate research or interest. News is history before it reaches us and the lion's proportion never reaches us.

Another dilemma is the amount of 'ignis fatuus' or misinformation that appears on social media or deliberately distorted news in the mainstream media. "If a lie is repeated often enough it eventually comes to be believed". An example is a lot of the rubbish encountered on twatter! "The Holocaust is the Biggest Lie and Myth in History!" One sees this often repeated with a picture of Jewish men in traditional garb.. and there is a lot similar and in the same vein! Nations in conflict or going through political turmoil like to push views that are often distant from the truth. A clever way around this is to conveniently omit relevant and important pieces of information so that the remainder described or shown seems either more likely, more important or simply the only thing going on in that particular theatre of the world! Omission of essential truth is equivalent to promulgating a lie and all media outlets, big or insignificant do just this from time to time for political or propaganda reasons. An example might be a mistake in identity of an enemy position in Syria, Iraq or Afghanistan where 'our boys' have just dropped bombs or missiles killing hundreds of innocent people. This news might be eclipsed by a terrorist attack in a major city of the West where a person has been stabbed to death. This will be followed by an immediate knee jerk reaction and great outpouring of emotion and anger at the perpetrator. The hundreds of women, children and other innocents killed in the bombing raid have been camouflaged by alternate news. [Don't misunderstand the author's intent to make a point.. one is always concerned by any attack and consequential murder!]

Whenever one sees a lost cat or dog story on the news broadcast at prime time it is fair to ask "is there either no news or perhaps some important news being omitted?"

One is often disappointed when foolish enough to watch 'question time in parliament' on the afternoon telly. Instead of moving forward and getting on with the job, politicians cannot help themselves these days when responding to questions by 'slagging off' the opposition party or its senior members. Politicians like to call upon 'the cult and culture of fear' if the people dare to think about voting for the opposite side to their current self-righteous government. In the West where we see two major parties see-sawing back and forth over the years, this behaviour is more often the case than a more sedate and dignified demeanour expected by the public that pay their salaries via taxes! It is appalling!

Also we see the independent and minority party representatives among which we occasionally experience the 'fringe lunatics' of extreme right and/or extreme left. It is these fringe elements of extremism that, unfortunately, sometimes control the balance of power, particularly in the Senate. It is essential that the more nasty of these be forced to maintain a strict 'code of conduct' whilst sitting to save us all from national embarrassment! Lastly, the most ugly (which only appear when a society is in near collapse and such opportunists rise like scum to the surface) we have the extremes of fascism and communism. In the accompanying diagram below you can see a depiction of the political spectrum as a continuum on a sort of bracelet where the extremists meet at the back. Although they profess to be diametrically opposite in dialectic and policy, in fact the result for the masses is the same.. dictatorship and social slavery! For this reason it seems proper to intermesh the bastards on the continuum for, as stated, they are basically the same!

THE POLITICAL SPECTRUM

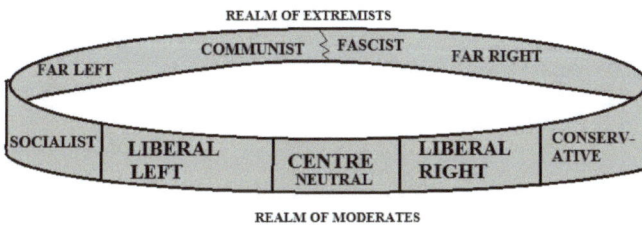

In other words there is no major distinction between these groups and their respective symbols. History has seen them fighting and even

killing each other on the street in pitched battles. This is a good thing. But when either comes to power, as far as the people are concerned, the result is political rigidity and enslavement where dastardly deeds are done such as imprisonment without due course of law and a trial, execution for trivial matters or based on ideological perspectives such as 'a threat to the stability of the state'. Even in liberal democracies we see the emergence of 'special forces', 'special police', 'special or extraordinary police powers', 'special or extensive secret service powers'. When these provisions are introduced and acted upon, you can be certain that your nation is on the slippery slide into political extremism and possibly totalitarian dictatorship. Be warned!

[Interesting that the symbols may be universal throughout the universe: extremism is symbolised by galactic spiralling arms held at the centre whereas more democratic movements are represented by symmetric stars or crosses!]

Islamic terror is real enough across the world and has been manufactured or appeared as a result of errors of judgement militarily and also as a side effect of the continuing poor relations between superpowers such as Russia and America. Islamic terror was born in Afghanistan during the last two decades of the 20th century where Russia and America were aiding different sides in a civil conflict. These two giants have not ceased in aiding materially, financially and even with armed forces the different sides of various conflicts around the world. The Syrian conflict, albeit complex, is a prime example. One might define this struggle as ideological; one might also define it as a struggle between Empires.

China has trod cautiously and avoided involvement in a pro-active way to conflicts and potential conflicts but is also guilty of supplying arms and financial assistance to selected countries. With China's rise in economic prowess and technological knowhow together with its intricate but huge trade with many partners in the West, it is to be hoped that it will continue to shy away from involvement in any war. Any major war between China and/or Russia with a Western power would be catastrophic and bring a certain end to human civilisation on the planet!

Assuming one has reasonably good government over a nation and personal debts as well as national debt are not too much of a burden, most citizens have a chance of fulfilled lives and happiness. Look at the grossly over-simplified model of the workings of a nation below:

WORKINGS OF A NATION

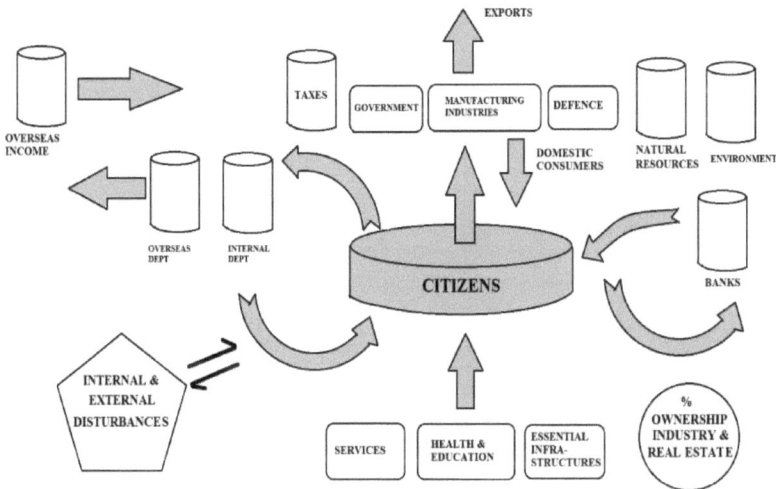

BUT, as you can see there are many other factors that need to be considered to ensure equitable distribution of wealth, an excellent standard of health and education for all, the likelihood of a home and steady employment. Looking at the model it is not too hard to see where things might go wrong and affect the lives of a great proportion of citizens. A lack of natural resources for instance means that industry has to be extremely clever and provide services to world markets or high-end products that earn export income. Too great expenditure on wars and the military can very quickly break a country! Weak laws to curb drug importation will render many citizens either dead at an early age or incapable of contributing by holding down a job. Permitting overseas investors to accumulate too big a chunk of industry or real estate might also leave many citizens little or no chance of owning their own home (and too much capital removed overseas by international corporations cheating on tax producing a similar result). Too high a tax rate on workers and/or too high an interest rate on borrowings from banks might start a recession. These rates might also be too low, making the task of governing impossible. Good government keeps a tight rein on spending and raising money but at the same time providing sensible infrastructure that the nation progresses. Dictators have always overspent the country's limited assets on ridiculous grandiose projects to satisfy their own ego at the expense of the welfare of the people. A sensible balance in all things is required which is a daunting and responsible task needing intelligence and thinking skills to achieve.

External influences such as excessive greed of rich nations wanting to obtain resources such as minerals, timber or cheap labour for factories; governments also need to be wary of these! Pressure to buy things such as expensive armaments and other things that do not benefit citizens must also be blocked. A country's environment is the key to the ongoing health of its people. Rape of natural resources without thought of the future will bring dire consequences. The natural environment must be managed in such a way that it will always provide materials and food eternally. The separate election of a President seems to always result in a polarisation of citizens. The Westminster system of choosing a leader from within the ruling political party for a limited term is the better model to avoid violence and attain stability.

Capitalism and competitive private manufacturing business is the plinth stone of wealthy intelligent nations. But that does not mean that there should be no controls. Unfettered capitalism will bring downsides also. Drugs, guns and criminal elements we can do without! There are some important services that are better to be in the hands of civilian government than private enterprise and these might include police and armed forces, prisons, hospitals, power stations, postal service, universities, scientific research organisations, public land (including forests, water catchment and reserves) and water supply. Where these have been privatised society has had to pay *more* for a weaker service! Public utilities must be preserved particularly for cost and environmental considerations.

Lastly, culture, tradition and language are the elements making up the glue that both defines and holds a society together. Any attempt to tear down any one of these components is an attack on the nation and must be robustly rebuffed! Historically, this type of action was always an attempt to build Empire at the expense of small nations. Do not allow it to happen to your nation! To those nations overburdened with huge populations making it hard to utilise minimal resources to satisfy all citizens, methods to curb further population growth must be researched and enacted upon for the sake of survival. Migration to less populated parts of the world should be encouraged where this is possible and where it is acceptable without causing danger to life. I am referring to legal migration to countries needing more people to raise their standard of living and assist with manufacturing. The rich nations that have contributed to the refugee problem by intrusion and the making of war (or exporting the tools of war for profit) have a responsibility to alleviate this situation and uplift these unfortunate persons by providing them with a chance at a safe and rewarding life.

In the earlier book 'Nuclear Islam' the place of religion and how it influences a country's politics was also discussed*. The following figures were depicted as a crude attempt to show the various intertwining of political dialectic with religious doctrine:

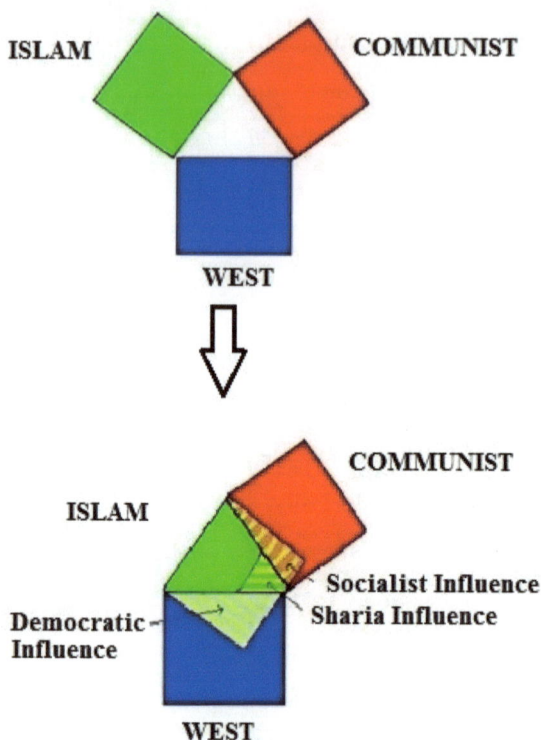

These neglect countries such as Myanmar where Buddhism is the main religion and Israel where Judaism is the main religion.

These notes were provided towards the end of the second decade of the 21st century at a time of great upheaval in the world. It is to be hoped that they are of some usefulness to the peoples and governments of all the nations.

[* see Chapter: Futureland in 'Nuclear Islam' by Tom law]

Twelve-add   **Climate and Murmurings**

"And a loud voice decreed to the seven angels: go and pour out the seven vials of the wrath of God into the Earth. And it was done."

Well naturally there has been weather. In fact there has always been weather, sometimes sweet sunny days and at other times tempests. The haunting question is: "is there evidence of climate change and is this change due mainly to a rise in carbon dioxide from the burning of fossil fuels exponentially over the past two hundred years?"

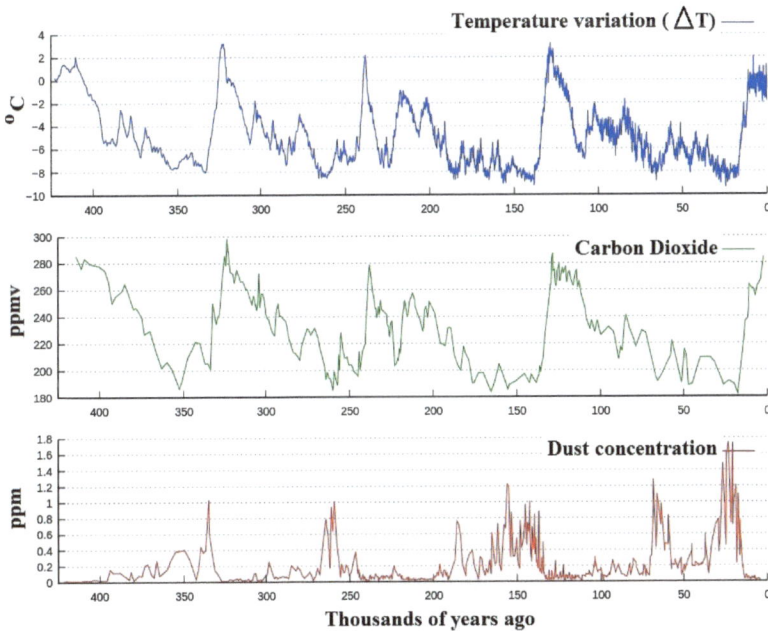

Vostok Petit Data

From the Vostok data we see a repeated pattern over the last half a million years of cold periods (ice ages) and warm periods (interglacials). We also note that there is a corresponding fluctuation in carbon dioxide levels. As the mean ocean temperature increases sea water is able to dissolve more soluble salts from the seabed but at the same time starts to shed CO_2 back to the atmosphere as gas solubility is lowered. (In fact all gases dissolved in sea water would decline in concentration, including life- supporting oxygen! Oxygen depletion would produce extreme and dramatic effects on the top three metre layer of the oceans in this regard.) This in turn assists in warming so that the whole system experiences a recursive or feedback dynamic. In eons past one might assume that eventually vegetation, particularly between the tropics, started to die off with vast deserts taking over. In this way even less CO_2 was stored in plant material. But the data shows that the process eventually reaches some limit and begins to stabilise. The author has no explanation for this other than guess at the likelihood of a sudden decline in animals that breathe out carbon dioxide. [We see that the Martian landscape has no living organisms and that in the past most of its water and atmosphere boiled away into space leaving a dead planet!]

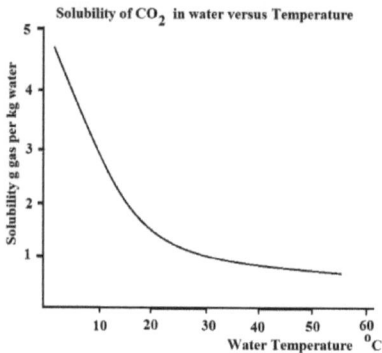

The data above taken from Antarctic ice cores supplemented by oceanic temperature recordings over the past fifty years points to an accepted and emphatic 'YES' amongst the scientific community the world over- we are in fact seeing a warming of the planet! Is there to be some anthropological knee jerk reaction to this state of affairs? Is that reaction already happening?

Governments of most countries have provided delegates to attend the various international meetings to discuss climate change and road map a 'plan of action'. Around 160 nations signed the Paris Agreement in

2016 to drastically reduce emissions. The writing on the wall tells us that humanity at large must reduce considerably its reliance on the burning of fossil fuels such as coal, petroleum products, natural gas and even wood if it is not being replaced by new forests! So what factors are working against us?

The most stupid of environmentalists have actually opposed hydroelectric schemes in preference to protecting a small amount of natural habitats and forested areas. Those with foresight, however, have encouraged ALL the forms of alternative energy production: hydro, solar, wind, tidal and geothermal. Looking at recent meteorological events such as hurricanes, floods, land inundation by rising seas, hotter and drier summers we can see that a change is upon us. There is the unknown effect of the eclipse of the natural interglacial period of mean high temperature upon current human activity which may have an accelerating attenuation. This is a worst case scenario that must also be taken into account.

Exponential population growth, the rise of the third world into a technological first world is also bringing about further stresses as nations gallop through evolutionary stages of industrialisation for greater amounts of energy to produce more products to meet demand. The combined populations of China and India are now close to three billion with rapid technological advancement in each country.

Governments and the private sector are often reluctant to change their ways. Thus we see an ever expanding manufacturing base of conventional vehicles (motorbikes, cars, trucks and diesel powered machines such as trains) all requiring 'oil' to fuel them. The oil producing states will wish to continue to raise profit until ALL their oil supplies are exhausted. Some governments are also pursuing retrograde actions and making excuses as to why they should continue to make use of coal fired electric power stations. In some cases they are engaged in building new ones! My own country, Australia, continues to supply huge tonnages of coal to overseas buyers as well as Uranium ore to countries with nuclear weapons (including at least one that is not a signatory to the Non-proliferation Treaty). But hey, let us not worry our consciences about such trivialities! After all, the dollars roll in!

Many countries are indeed developing electric vehicles, hybrid vehicles and new and improved batteries. Currently the price of these alternatives is expensive thus prohibitive to ordinary Joe Blow and his family. With newer innovative electricity sources and 'solar skinned' automobiles that are mass produced, there is still a chance of eliminating hydrocarbon fuelled vehicles within the next two decades. [Some Western European Governments have already committed to this target; hopefully others will soon follow.]

The alternative is a vicious circle, a self feeding and self fulfilling prophecy of doom. As temperatures rise we will experience crop failures and an increase in insect pests in areas where they were not seen before. Forest fires will become more frequent in summer. Greater extremes of weather will be experienced causing major damage to community infrastructures and bringing more deaths. Economic collapse will occur in those countries that are no longer able to feed themselves. Even without the contribution of wars, the globe will experience mass migrations of people wanting to move to a better place for their families to survive. If one superimposes major conflicts upon these strains, human catastrophe on an unprecedented scale will be unavoidable and witnessed by near-future generations.

[Again, see Chapter: Futureland in '*Nuclear Islam*' by Tom law]

So assuming our best and most brilliant scientists are correct, all nations without exception must go down the path of radical change, particularly with regard to the relentless release of carbon dioxide into the atmosphere. Behaviours and patterns must change if we are to have any chance of survival. **Education is not enough if it is not acted upon.** Big government and big business must be curbed if not taking the best path in this matter. History has shown that once food becomes scarce, humans readily resort to violence to acquire much needed sustenance. The graphs shown at the beginning of this chapter indicate the natural pattern of temperature rise and associated atmospheric carbon dioxide rise. Accepting that we are presently in an interglacial period, we cannot afford to aggravate this natural sequence of nature if we are to avoid the fate of the dinosaurs!

Yes there have always been volcanic eruptions and earthquakes. The question is: "Can the testing of nuclear weapons trigger earthquakes in other parts of the world?" The author suspects that on occasion one may follow the other but does not have any convincing data on this topic. However, as we are now well into the 21st century, there is really no need for any nation to test nuclear weapons particularly if there is even the remotest chance of causing a devastating earthquake in a distant country!

Even with an altered behaviour, applying new constraints on emissions and making use of all the alternative energy sources available, nations must be patient as the old momentum is slowed and the Earth rejuvenates and repairs itself. It will be a slow train coming!

Whereas some years ago people scoffed at political parties focussing on such required changes, at a time of greater concern there is now broad interest in the new political platforms of parties such as 'The Alternative

Energy Party' or 'The Renewable Energy Party'. Seek these out in your country!

AUSTRALIA

Lastly there is little doubt that the continuous manufacture of weaponry and other abominations for the purpose of wars between nations also contributes in no small way to the debilitation of the natural environment. It is a waste of resources, a waste of energy and a waste of the skills and labour of humans involved in such industries. The BUGS make billions of dollars in profit from armament sales each year to prop up their licentious standard of living. Presidents and national leaders that have received the Nobel Peace Prize have let us down by spinning on their heels to take the road of militarisation! Others were always blatantly wicked in this regard! They employ the tools of 'Fear and Mistrust' to befuddle the masses and scream and point at their 'scapegoats' to justify their inherent evil. The environment is damaged and millions of human lives are either lost or bear extreme hardship and suffering. There must be an alternative way to ensure that intelligent sentient humans are chosen as leaders, NOT the grubby tricksters and greedy megalomaniacs we often experience!

Thirteen   **Sex, Freud and Rock 'n' Roll**

This is an exploration of the animal part of our brains that externally displays itself in various emotions, leading to actions some of which are valid in the creative and artistic sense and others which are debilitating to the concept of social cohesion. Sigmund Freud had a lot to say on the idea of fantasy and creativity amongst children and later amongst adults. Not all contemporary philosophers and members of the medical professions agree with all that he said!

An example of our 'animal behaviour' might be the main character in the Irvine Welsh novel 'Filth' (later produced as a movie), one Detective Bruce Robertson. Having always felt some responsibility for the death of his younger brother whilst playing on a coal slag as a child, Bruce suffers serious psychotic depression. Following the breakup of his marriage, Bruce proceeds to slide down the slippery path of excessive smoking, snorting cocaine, popping depression pills and drinking straight Scottish Whiskey. To relieve his pain he bullies his best friend, has sex with the wives of his co-workers and occasionally goes on the street at night dressed in his former wife's clothes. It is during one of these expeditions that he witnesses the murder of an Asian student by a group of white supremacist thugs. Spiralling down at his job and life generally, he eventually takes his own life at a most crucial moment. The essence of the book is the sad loss of reality and all that was meaningful in a man's life initially triggered by an horrific event in childhood that the subject did not, in the psychological sense, ever recover from. It is a piercing novel at the upper heights of human tragedy!

The Australian William James Chidley that lived a nomadic life towards the end of the nineteenth century, whilst not being an academic, never the less wrote useful anecdotal data in each of his books (i) The Answer and (ii) Confessions. He was often jailed in both Melbourne and Sydney for parading the streets naked. His solution to human happiness lay in three conditions, namely: 'Shed clothes entirely and live one's life totally naked; only partake of fruit and nuts for sustenance; partake of coitus in the springtime to eliminate stress'.

Interesting that in ancient Athens and Sparta it was not uncommon to see rural people walking about these cities completely naked and without hindrance by the locals. But this was a little too much for Victorian society and Chidley was held in mental asylums at periods during his life. There were many parallels between the thoughts of Chidley and those of the American Wilhelm Reich. Both Reich and Freud agreed at one time that 'sexual repression is the principal cause of contemporary neurosis'; but Freud later diverged to theorise that *all* destructive emotion in humans are basic instincts forming a part of human nature.

In children, play is part of their fantasy at being adult and this play rewards them with psychic pleasure. Adults are more in tune with the real world, however this does not negate the adult from participating in fantasy or dream as a path to creativity in one of the arts that the adult may be pursuing. Freud stated that we, as adults, are often ashamed of our innermost secrets and fantasies which we are loath to share with our peers. Further, fantasy is an attempt to fulfil some wish which may be either related to personal ambition (possibly related to perceived status) or erotic. He claims that among youth, the female gravitates more towards erotic wishes whereas males gravitate to both ambitious as well as erotic wishes. Contemporary thought challenges his ideas on the female mind! But these are generalisations and the degree of fantasising varies from person to person. We are all unique and our psyches have been shaped by environment, circumstance and life experiences coupled with some possible genetic disposition inherited.

The preoccupation of sex and sexual desire is often seeded by inferences and communications by peers that may be a little older and more worldly or knowledgeable in the subject. Having said that, there also exists innate feelings and untaught knowledge alongside the child's desire to play and explore. Given an Adam and Eve growing up in a remote Garden of Eden completely unconnected to the world, it is almost certain that they would eventually procreate through genetic inbuilt proclivity and natural child-play exploration (even in the absence of an adult world) whilst passing through the various stages of childhood, puberty, adolescence and finally to physically mature adulthood.

[Note: a group of children growing up in isolation of adults is likely to formulate its own social rules, primitive and relatively violent. See 'Lord of the Flies' by William Golding, Penguin 2016]

Adulthood brings a whole bag of ambitions and desires upon which are placed many constraints. The desire for food, shelter and pleasure are our basic survival instincts. The desire for wealth, creative satisfaction, recognition by peers, to love and to be loved by family and close friends are additional goals to increase satisfaction, pleasure and provide meaning to one's existence. For all these to be achieved it is necessary to be subjected to the limitations of intelligence and personal skill; also, to the limitations of immediate environment and opportunity. An overlay is the existence of family values, society's values and the laws of the tribe or greater society to which one belongs. Further layers umbrella these such as political views, religious views and devotion to a code of behaviour when interacting with other humans. Limitations again bear down on one in the form of knowledge of the culture and what is deemed acceptable behaviour, knowledge of mores and level of language ability. (In the past, working class people and those with some debilitation have been grossly and unfairly dealt with by judges and courts due to their personal limited understanding of the workings of the law and the language of the law!) Avoidance of violent clashes or confronting situations with other humans is usually the norm as part of the survival instinct. Thus many of us are subjected to bullying with little or no aggressive reaction, whilst others react and refuse to suffer such intimidation!

A six year old boy joins a group of girls sitting on the grass during playtime at primary school. He quite innocently asks the girls to pull off their knickers to show him their private parts. The request is innocent as he only has a younger brother at home and is curious as to the nature of the female form. Some of the girls respond with giggles, one or two are quite happy to allow the boy to see all without fear or embarrassment. The consequence later is a reprimand to the boy from the teacher and a warning to the girls not to permit this behaviour.

A girl aged nine is playing in the garden with her cousins of similar age and the adults are indoors. The girl voluntarily and without prompting takes down her knickers and places a finger in her anus. The act is brief and nothing more happens. If a parent is told, there is a verbal reprimand that the behaviour is inappropriate. From an early age then there is a shaping of values and absorbing of taboos into the human psyche.

Anal fetish is something possibly innate, learned as a child or during early pubescence. Small children experiment with fingers placed in every orifice. The child is often reprimanded by a parent. "Picking one's nose is impolite and in any case a disgusting habit.. don't do it!"

Anal sex may bring pleasure to the receiver, but more often than not brings greater pleasure to the one making the entrance with his penis. More recently many societies in the West have become more tolerant to anal sex and, as an offence, it has been removed from the statutes and is no longer illegal in many countries. However, adherents to the major religions still believe that the act is wrong and make references to the Bible:

(i)   King Solomon's edict and

(ii)   the story of God's wrath on the city Sodom and Gomorrah

In some countries punishment for sodomy is still severe! Others believe that such tolerance is an indication of a failing society doomed to eventually go the way of precedents in history- decay and extinction!

It is not an uncommon behaviour for a group of boys around the ages of ten to participate in group masturbation when circumstances permit i.e away from the influence of adults. Seeing who can ejaculate the furthest might be the determined goal or just making physical comparisons. This would earn the champion a certain status in the group.

Experimentation between girls and boys generally proceeds during early teenage years. It may take the form of a sudden and unwanted grabbing of breasts or at the crutch area. For a boy and girl that are attracted to each other and considered boyfriend and girlfriend this may involve more sensual and gentle touching along with cuddling and kissing. The girl, likely through fear and knowledge of consequences such as pregnancy or parental punishment will generally control the limitation to what happens during such episodes.

Masturbation or self stimulation can begin at a very early age but more often than not commences around ages between ten and twelve years. There are three types: early age exploration, stimulation for pleasure of feeling alone and stimulation for pleasure of feeling accompanied by mind fantasy. Younger children indulge in either of the first two. Mature teenagers and adults usually indulge in the latter where, during the act of masturbation they hold in their mind some fantasy or image of a partner or ideal form of the object of their fantasy. This may be imaginary, heightened by a photograph, image or video on a screen. Masturbation often occurs at intervals throughout life after maturity and is a normal human activity for necessary sexual release.

During the latter years of the teenage experience, many will relinquish their values and allow themselves to be carried away into the pleasures of the sexual act. The majority of humans, male and female will at some stage in their life commence to embrace sexual activity. It is a natural phenomenon and necessary for the objective of survival of the species. It is normal to stay with a single partner for life and create a family. This is seen across all cultures and religious groups of humans the world over. Having observed this, fantasy and dream and the desire for pleasure does not suddenly disappear from the human psyche and is pursued in many ways. This is where social and religious values come into play. A society that recognises and observes the rules and law handed down from generation to generation grows and survives as a cohesive group. Societies that, to a great extent, ignore the mores and values of generations past tend to wither and die out, usually in a calamitous way. Men and women always wish never to give up their innermost desires, fantasies and demand for psychic pleasure. But intellectual judgement prevents radical and societal destructive behaviours. The woman or man that ignores social mores described as 'what is right' runs the risk of destroying their family unit, possibly losing rights to access of children and suffering ridicule in the community of which they are part. Thus desire and fantasy need be tempered and careful judgement made in order to avoid disaster and what is termed 'heartbreak and sadness'. Persons that have been through divorce and separation from loved ones truly understand the depth of despair, pain, sadness and the *'forever after'* sense of loss of something once cherished. It is almost the same life emotion experienced when a loved one dies.

Thus most adults eternally fight against their animal internalised secret desire of wanting to experience sexual pleasure with other partners. A man passes a woman in the street or supermarket and is aware of internal feelings of attraction. He loves his wife and family but cannot help such feelings welling up inside his consciousness. He may just enjoy the momentary feeling, he may feel shame or he may act in some way to express his desire to the stranger. The last action will bring risks to all he is, to all he values and a judgement must be made.

Unfortunately it is true of most men that if the judgement is "I can do this for myself and get away with it; no one will know and I will receive a sensual reward satisfying my dreams and fantasies!" his intelligence will flit from his brain to his penis and consequences will surely follow. Women are often more sensible than men but are not immune to the same fantasies and dreams as their male counterparts.

Fantasies can be triggered by visual image, odour, a soothing by poetic speech or just simple compliments received and interpreted (or misinterpreted) as sexual signals. Voice texture may also provide this trigger as it relates to some deep unconscious cognition in the person's psyche or make-up (again, possibly genetic). A man may be turned on by a woman's mouth or lips alone. The briefest of touching may also bring discord and unsettling sexual thoughts and desires.

It is sadly not uncommon to experience two married couples destroy each other's sacred relationship. Each family with children being close friends and spending a lot of time together (such as sharing camping trips and holidays over some years) suddenly at some later date find that an affair commences between the husband of one family and the wife of the other. Result: tragedy brought about by uncontrolled selfishness. It is a pattern oft repeated across the world bringing about the usual amount of distress and woe to each family. A lesser course of action might have been a brief but secretive affair that was permitted to run its course with no final breakdown of marriage and no final devastating hurt to many players. This suggestion the reader may criticise on moral grounds. The author is merely stating the lesser of two evils resulting in less profound consequences!

Sexual pleasure is a fantasy and dream that is always with us. Some men have such a desire and experience such fantasies several times each and every day of their lives. The Indian Prince of great wealth or Chinese Emperor in former times each possessed a 'first wife' and possibly hundreds of concubines to satisfy a nightly need of sexual congress and pleasure. The Mongolian super hero, conqueror of all of Asia plus a good part of Europe and lover of a thousand women, one Genghis Khan is said to have left his DNA heritage in a high percentage of modern humans. The tribal leaders of Arabs and Jews in ancient times possessed many wives bringing forth many children. So history bears out the premise that the male of the species desires many partners and will willingly take such, given opportunity and position in society. The

Queen of ancient Egypt, Cleopatra was said to have had great sexual prowess and took many lovers over her lifetime.

The Trojan Wars were a direct result of the stealing away of Helen, the wife of the Spartan king and warrior Menelaus by the young and handsome Paris (though possibly myth and not actually historical fact!) History has proven that sexual fantasy has brought not just the sadness to families but, on occasion, the destruction of nations. In contemporary society the lack of personal control has wrought a great schism and destruction to many families bringing not only grief but a great monetary cost to society. Occasionally such intensive emotion is the cause of extreme violence and may sometimes lead to murder. This is the nature of men and women and the result and consequence of elements of our animalist psyche.

Many external reasons are proffered for this such as rock and roll music, alcohol and drugs, a movement away from religion and belief in God, images and archetypes presented by the media, consumerism, TV and film dramas describing poor role models of behaviour, chemical additives in food, farm chemicals.. so the list goes on. But the bottom line is that "we all have choice" and many, unfortunately, make poor choices in their lives! Only the experience of stories, theatre and similar can educate us to an understanding of our innermost dreams and fantasies so that we can exist in what is defined as a civilised and cohesive society that can go forward and survive down future generations with happiness and fulfilment as opposed to sadness and destruction. Humans must accept and comprehend their innermost nature and adjust their behaviour in order to survive without harming themselves or their loved ones. Children are the most valuable of gifts that a human can possess above all else. They are with us for precious little time and must be nurtured, protected and loved. To neglect one's children is the greatest of evils that a human can perpetrate. Life is short and you have but one!

Expressing our creativity in some way has always been the key to curbing the animal within. Creating brings satisfaction and joy whether it be a grandiose building, a painting or a simple clay pot. Love and guard your family at all cost for your family is the only true treasure and meaning to your life. Nothing else comes close to this!

It has become fashionable in some parts of the West for trained welfare persons to portray a whole range of 'sexual relation possibilities' to young people still in school as being OK and that they have the right to choose whichever path they are inclined to follow. In some scenarios both male and female students have been known to request to their parents and doctor that they would feel more comfortable if they were able to change their gender. The cause of this disruption to the natural progression through puberty and adolescence may be due to environmental factors such as food or drug intake. It may be due to propaganda by teachers or the health educators and reinforced by drama in the various media. Whatever the cause, it is a paradigm shift in values bringing distress to many parents. It is a valid reason of mistrust in school health programs and some parents are withdrawing their children from these. It is the author's view that **any permanent label pertaining to gender or sexual preference should not be attached to minors under the age of eighteen years** (and further that this be brought into law!) The reason for this view is that adolescence is a period of biological change associated with emotional upheaval as well as a time of experimentation which may or may not eventually lead to conventional relationship building. It is wrong to label and make judgements before this stage is passed!

Never the less it has been a fact throughout human history that a percentage of humans prefer to partner with a person of the same sex. The question before society is whether same sex partners should be permitted to raise children as a family. It is an ethical question demanding serious soul searching. There is a strong view that the traditional makeup of a family

"WE PREFER TO HAVE BOTH A MUM AND A DAD TO LOOK AFTER US !"

IS IT NOT HOW ITS SUPPOSED TO BE?

is the only correct one. It comes down to rights and one might ask: **"should the rights of an adult override the rights of a child?"**.. referring here to the right of the child to have both a father and mother to guide her/him through life whilst growing up. The author is not saying that same sex partners are not able to provide a safe and loving home to children.. not at all. One is more concerned here with the rights of the child!

In the primitive culture of humans when living in close tribal communities such rights were of little consideration where an orphaned child would always be cared for. Again William Chidley points to the perfection of the 'native society' as being the human utopia!

Countering this argument we see many single parent families due to marriage breakup or the passing away of one parent by disease or accident. It is not unusual to see, as a result of the latter, new blended families of one man, one woman but with children from former partners. It suggests that many single parents still seek and prefer to be part of a traditional family where possible.

With the rapid advances of medical science, will same sex partners start to demand their own 'Gabriel Children' i.e fusions to produce one of the four possibilities:

$\overline{\underline{\Phi}}$ – Gabriel   phi-Gabriel: fusion of two eggs from the one female (perfect clone)

X – Gabriel   chi-Gabriel: fusion of two eggs from different females

$\overline{\mathsf{Y}}$ – Gabriel   psi-Gabriel: fusion of two sperm from the one male (perfect clone)

Ω – Gabriel   omega-Gabriel: fusion of two sperm from different males

The fusion of sperm will still require a surrogate egg from which the nucleus has been removed and special biochemical conditions for fusion if it is to be followed by mitosis. It has been observed that a phi-Gabriel occurs in humans at a rate of about one in ten million i.e a virgin pregnancy producing a perfect clone of the mother!* The first cloned mammal was of course the famous 'Dolly the sheep' in the UK in the 1970s.

How will society react to this brave new world scenario?

Only a very small percentage of humans choose to live alone. Career or creative pursuits sometimes dominate over the desire to share one's life with another. Some never seem to find their soul mate even though they have made some effort to seek him or her out. Some, having experienced and lost a partner have little or no desire to replace the person they loved. It's complicated!

Lastly, some have attributed sexual indulgence on the fall of empires. It was said that decadence and moral decay was the prime cause of the fall

[* for such a natural virgin birth to produce a male is seen as nigh impossible unless of course the mother had an additional gender chromosome i.e a triplet XXY.]

of the Roman Empire. However in his gigantic and definitive work 'The Decline and Fall of the Roman Empire' by Edward Gibbon (1737-1794) he gives a picture of sheer economic exhaustion through the loss of armies in great battles, agricultural collapse along with natural disasters as the more likely causes. By modern standards, Rome was always decadent and excessive in all things, which included diversity in sexual behaviour! Some might say that its shedding of the old Gods for Christianity was firm reason that it lasted for many hundreds of years.

"The art of man is able to construct monuments far more permanent than the narrow span of his own existence: yet these monuments, like himself, are perishable and frail; and in the boundless annals of time his life and his labours must equally be measured as a fleeting moment."

However the Roman Empire is not entirely gone if we describe the rise of the Holy Roman Empire as its continuum, meaning the power of the Vatican over those dominions of the world that are predominantly Roman Catholic. As mentioned elsewhere, even those major wars of the 20th century had some element of both its protection and attempted restoration! And it may also be an unconsidered and neglected element of 21st century conflict needing close analysis!

Helter Skelter

Fourteen   **Communists and Nazis in the West**

It was the BBC commentator Louis Theroux in his series of documentaries that brought American Nazis into the living rooms across the English speaking world at the beginning of the 21st century. It was hardly believable that in a country that had sacrificed so many soldiers in WWII there were now Nazis in full regalia posturing at rallies on the streets. In the various interviews they did not defer or shy away from the terms 'niggers and kikes' and regarded these people as 'untermensch'.. that is subhuman! One mother of two beautiful girls under the age of twelve regularly got the children to draw swastikas and listen to racist pop music by skinhead bands. Others displayed all the flags and symbols of Hitler's Third Reich on walls in their houses or garages and attended meetings where speakers would vomit out their hatred of other races and religions. It cannot be imagined that such behaviour was acceptable under the banner of 'freedom of speech'!

It was in Charlottesville, Virginia in August 2017, America then being under a new and unpredictable president, that anti-fascist protestors fought street battles with armed groups of Nazis, KKK members and white supremacists; the police did little to keep the two groups apart. During this clash a car was driven into the anti-fascist protestors by a twenty year old man, killing a woman in her early thirties. There had been shootings of young unarmed black men in many cities of America over the previous decades and attacks by white supremacists on mosques during Friday prayers. But this single event was a turning point where white Americans would now be in conflict with white Americans.. an unpredicted occurrence since the Civil War of the 19th century!

Some say it was due to the mass movement and influx of Muslim refugees to Western countries and consequential isolated incidences of Islamic terrorism. Others postulate that it was due to a sleeping minority of extreme right wingers now awakening. Whatever the true underlying reasons, most Western countries were witnessing an ugly renaissance of fascism among young Caucasian men and women creating tension and havoc in society. This polarisation spread like a plague across the West and was met forcefully by opposing groups of students, Christians and people more oriented to the left of politics. Naturally communist elements, seeing an opportunity, infiltrated the decent guardians of democracy, also inflicting damage.

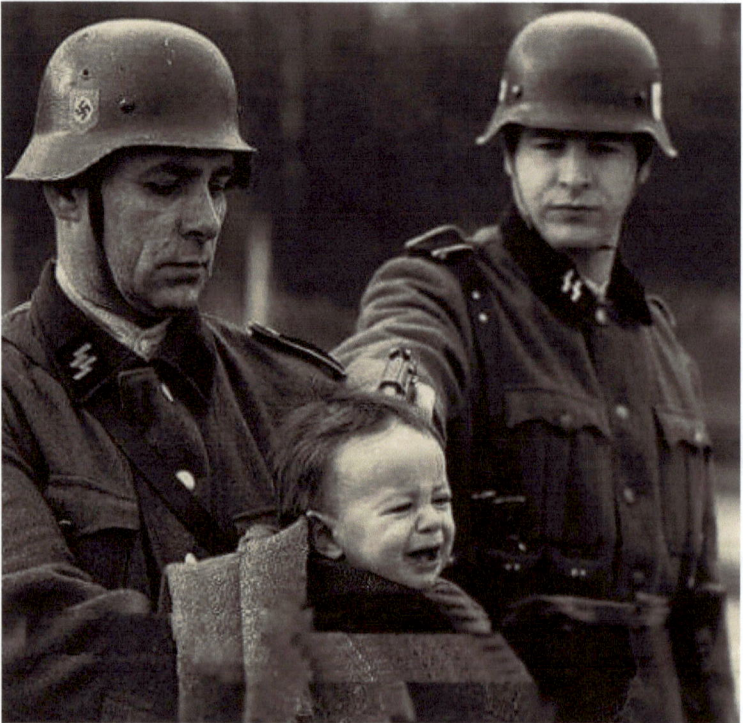

Lest we forget!

Ethnic minorities tended to move to areas where they felt safer in numbers, but this did not save them from murderous intrusions by skinheads and nouveaux stormtroopers (as they called themselves) attacking in the spirit of a Germany of the 1930s! By the mid 2020s, the whole of North America and Western Europe was aflame with hatred. Police, Governments, Churches and Schools had, collectively, all failed the once stable democracies.

The Communist nations had shown an outward appearance of civilisation and capitalism.. capitalism in the sense that they allowed a controlled competitiveness and encouraged Western enterprises to set up factories and businesses in their states. But all forms of expression, particularly in the media, were tightly controlled to extol only the centralised propaganda. Any slight at the party meant a slight at the state and nation; the penalty was ruthless.. sometimes even death. The communist countries were happy to trade and do business with the West as much as was physically possible.. a big change from say pre-1980! However their behaviour was dichotomous in that, surreptitiously, they permitted wholesale export of harmful drugs and continuously attempted disruption of computer systems and networks with the aim of garnering as much information as possible. The stealing of industrial, scientific and military secrets was paramount. The attempt at political influence by any means.. slush money, presents or air tickets to exotic places were all applied to achieve the end of persuading political minds to the 'Eastern way of thinking' with such charitable acts and decision making to benefit themselves. Fortunately most Western countries saw through all these deceptions.. but it never halted aggressive and much desired trade. Trade always meant dollars!

Despite all this, it also did not deter or deflect communist policy of getting involved in wars, overtly or covertly, and providing armaments to those sides it saw as being closer to their own dialectic. And so wars were carefully joined with considerable bullshit at the UN General Assembly trying to justify a particular action and stance. Third world countries in Africa were also provided with technical knowhow as well as petty dictators being showered with money and gifts for favours and intrigues putting even the nineteenth century colonialist powers to shame! (Although I daresay history may prove me wrong in this instance!) So the major communist nations behaved in both a gratuitous and sneaky way towards the West which baffled many who just shook their heads and accepted it as an enigma of the modern world!

Other dimensions such as pornography, drugs, film and TV violence, marriage breakdown and licentious behaviour had also played their part in contributing to social chaos. Some philosophers blamed the super-personal media for isolating individuals into a fanciful 'dream world' where they spent most of their waking hours indulging in music, film, war games or surreal 3D digital panoramas in cyberspace; totally unconnected to other 'real' people and the real world close by but out of reach. Thus millions of people had digressed into media zombies. Work had ceased to exist for most adults due to the high degree of the implementation of machines with artificial intelligence performing all the drudge work of repetitive manufacturing. This left people listless, without morals, without social cohesiveness and a bewildering lack of purpose or direction with their lives. Suicide had become so familiar that there were now special centres where prospective 'clients' could go to 'end their days' (or might that be 'end their daze'?) By 20th century standards, society had become evil where values and morals were compared!

[Having said this, Methodist John Wesley had described the decadence of society in England during the 1730s! Perhaps humans have always been decadent or possess a natural tendency to drift in that direction?]

All the past philosophers from Plato to Stanley Fish were irrelevant to this brave new world. Contemporary ideas included that of Thomas John Law that hypothesised the 'inescapable organelle'.. a theory of evolution where the Universe, from the time of its creation, passes through various cognitive stages in an attempt to 'understand itself'! That is, organic entities such as humans eventually become symbiotic and connected by networks akin to a nervous system as part of one single organic entity on a higher level. This is the function and goal of evolution. Basically, instead of God creating the Universe and all therein, the Universe is created from nothing not by some pan-intelligence, but goes through an evolutionary process to finally arrive at a comprehensive understanding God. Few people, however, took notice of such ideas having no desire or interest to think too deeply.

Physical pleasure, particularly of the sex organs was always high on the agenda of day to day living. Possibly Freud had come into his own at this final stage of human development, but the majority would never admit to it.

So indoor living focussed on pleasure and dreaming. Outdoors was violence and mayhem. The final blow of course was the lobbing of the first crude but effectual nuclear bomb (almost a dirty bomb) by a Middle Eastern country on Israel. Almost simultaneously nuclear exchanges occurred between several pairs of nations with historical animosities across the globe killing off two thirds of humanity in the first few days with much of the remainder soon to follow from the intense radioactive fallout, disease, food shortages and a general breakdown in societal infrastructures. The final hammer was the development of a 'nuclear winter'. What was the other lyric of the 20th century poet Bob Dylan.. ".. and a hard rain's a-gonna fall". And fall it did.

This did not however stop the movement of thousands of people to the southern extremities of the continents. They travelled by vehicle whilst fuel was available; many travelled to the tip of South America and Cape Town in South Africa. Others ventured across oceans to the remote islands of the Indian Ocean, South Atlantic, South Pacific and even Antarctic waters as well as to the southern coastal regions of Australia and New Zealand. Naval personnel commandeering nuclear submarines from many navies patrolled the southern oceans like marauding pirates, some existing in this way for almost twenty years before these ships became unserviceable as various components broke down. Eventually, only a few thousand people survived after the first ten years post nuclear devastation of the world and its civilisations. But these were a new hardened people that could only survive with more traditional and long tested values. Those others that did not have foresight to change their modern and foolish habits quickly died out from starvation or killings. In Australia and New Zealand, people had not reverted to the most primitive survival communities but more or less resembled European village societies of the 14th century where basic trades and skills were valued for making tools for agriculture and sea fishing. Thus by 2040 a new world of humans had commenced a society with basic technologies and a code of living that would sustain them for generations to come. They were bound by a common language, laws and customs which would guarantee their survival.

You, my reader, were warned in the Forward of the possibility of sudden departure from the theme at hand. It is essential that one must reflect on the occurrences of political extremes that blossomed during the first two decades of the 21st century and the consequences that followed where these were permitted to flourish unchecked!

Fifteen   **The Cult and Culture of Fear and Mistrust**

'Don't Miss Out' said the voice at the end of the TV ad. It was advertising a product of limited availability (or so they said) and relying on the 'worry element' based on this shortage. 'In like Flynn' or 'the early bird will catch the worm' was the only chance one had of obtaining the product! Movies, political propaganda and documentaries on some topic that will 'bring about the end of civilisation' constantly tear at our conscience each day on television and in newspapers bringing uncertainty and unsettling emotion. We are bombarded by far too much information and it takes its toll in stress for many humans. [Yes.. even this particular book by Tom Law is probably bringing some stress to you, the reader.. sorry!]

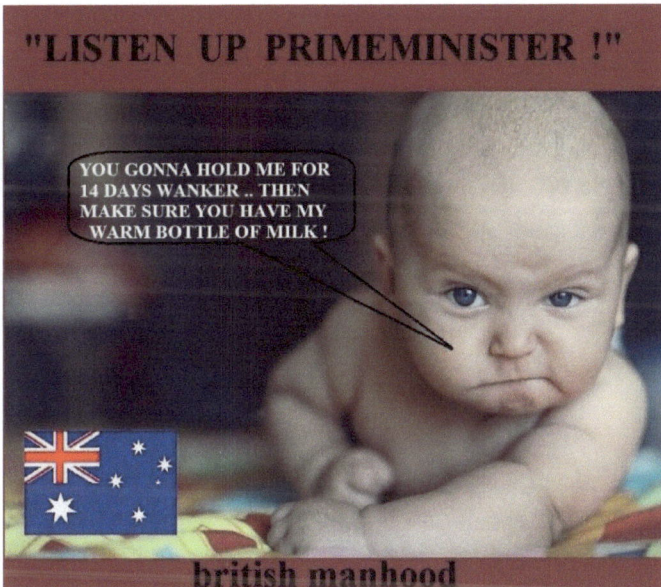

But most of us don't slash our wrists or jump out of a high rise building to end it all because of the distressing news about wars, death and destruction in faraway places. We still have choice. We can switch to the football game or have a barbeque and drink beer with friends. We can draw a picture, play or listen to music, watch a more peaceful romantic movie or go to the beach with our family. There are many ways out to avoid having to listen to, watch or think about the ills of the world. And, for our sanity, that is a good thing. It is essential to steer away from what makes us uncomfortable.

However, as humans sharing a planet with limited resources and many problems, each of us as individuals has a responsibility to play our part, even if it is just an occasional token gesture to help make a change and alleviate misery and suffering. To turn our back completely, cross to the other side of the road, is a cowardly and selfish attitude and not a normal human trait of compassion! A small donation to 'Save the Children', UNICEF or some other worthy cause is the correct action. To give up one's time for a few hours to assist some charity is also a noble gesture.

We must always be on guard when absorbing the news, watching a soapy or the thrust of the story in a movie to discriminate and recognise such propaganda elements or structures that make use of the tools of 'fear and mistrust'. Governments of countries at war like to vilify the enemy and paint a picture of unquestionable evil to justify the actions of 'our side' which are never spelled out and usually cloaked in a pan-umbrella of secrecy 'to protect our boys over there!' There is much truth in the statement that 'the first casualty of war is truth!' Politicians in supposedly civilised societies like to make attacks on their opponents' values and policies to denigrate them as much as possible, implementing the *cult and culture of fear and mistrust.*
"If you vote for them, these will be the terrible consequences that are certain to follow.. blah blah blah".

We see it and hear it all the time. Disturbingly, it fosters animosity and a polarisation of society!

Why do they all need to carry a handgun?

There is the 'environment scare theme' in many movies that has been recurrent over many decades coming from Hollywood, Bollywood,

Brollyhood, Scallywaghood and others. It is usually the forest, the jungle, the mountains, the ocean, space or just the wilderness in general where monsters and danger lurk. To inculcate the fear of Hansel and Gretel in the deep dark forest! This attempt at altering one's internal psyche to feelings of mistrust of nature and clean environments such as those described is often the ridiculous theme of fourth rate movies. One might suggest that a new classification should be created: 'MM' standing for 'movies for morons'. Unfortunately there is a lot of rubbish of low culture or no culture thrust on the public. Education in schools should include the learning of 'discriminating power' so that people can apply a filtering process to avoid the junk! This does not imply that there are no good movies or TV dramas produced. There remain many excellent productions.

A teenager or even an adult might enjoy a comic book or pop music as a form of relaxation. One should have no qualms in partaking of these things. But one must also realise that 'life is short' and that the creators of good books and more complex musical compositions deserve your attention on occasion. High culture created by genius is not there for snobs and an elite.. no, it is there for all to partake of and enjoy. One should not feel ashamed to eat 'beans on toast' occasionally, but to sample Indonesian cuisine, Italian, French or Thai is what enriches one's life.

"Ginestrata plus fiori di zucca fritti followed by fritto misto di pesce washed down with a full glass of Badia a Coltibuono Chianti.. and after a rest, meringhe con la panna with coffee."

Racists like to apply their own simple values to how others should behave and direct their life' choices. They too apply the cult and culture of fear and mistrust:

"We will be swamped by Asians!"; "More Mosques will bring about more radicalised Muslims and destroy our way of life!"; "The black people are generally lazy and always want to rely on handouts from the Government and taxpayers!"; "The Jews are an evil and degenerate race that wish to control the whole world!"; "We would be much safer if everyone was permitted to carry a gun at all times!"

It's all crap and relies on fear, accompanied by ignorance to get people to come around to their point of view and vote for their sick party at election time. Once racists (and extremists generally) get their numbers up, they then fall back on their other 'bag of tricks': violence and intimidation!

Once upon a time in Toytown and Western democracies, Mr Plod went about his business carrying a truncheon. He was a symbol of authority and commanded respect. People were not afraid to ask for assistance of some kind be it simply directions to some destination. If you killed Mr Plod by some means, your punishment invariably was the rope i.e the death penalty. With the advent of terrorist assaults we now witness a new police force on the streets across the Western world.. one where members are heavily armed and often wearing highly protective clothing*. Political demonstrations attract similar. The everyday policeperson patrolling the city on foot or in a patrol car is nearly always carrying a side-arm. It is the author's observation and value that we have moved away from a civilised society to a much more dangerous society. Governments tell us that all-pervasive surveillance techniques, armed police and Special Forces are in existence and necessary 'to keep society safe!' Frankly, society used to be a lot safer in the immediate post WWII years than the present era. And there are reasons for this. To eliminate these police cowboys toting guns (from an otherwise respected force) requires civil disobedience. Trust and respect are finer virtues than to suffer under fear and intimidation! Mahatma Gandhi was a champion of such action during the latter days of the British Raj in India, where he led the Independence Movement.

[* The author spells out more on this in: "Guns Off Cops Guns Off Everyone"]

Also, Henry David Thoreau reflected on life, politics, and society in his two inspiring masterworks: 'On Waldon Pond and Civil Disobedience', Dover Publications 1995. In 1845 Thoreau moved to a cabin he built with his own hands along the shores of Walden Pond in Massachusetts. Shedding the trivial ties that he felt bound much of humanity, Thoreau worked the land physically and gained from his labours mentally, pursuing truth in the quiet of nature. At the same time he reflected on the tools for change and was inspired by the application of 'civil disobedience' as a just and safe methodology to provoke change.

In summary then, various elements of contemporary society like to exploit the tricks and wiles of the cult and culture of fear and mistrust as controlling tools for their own ends. The civilised person needs to recognise these techniques and oppose them!

The Dark Forest

Sixteen   **Unrest in America**

The Portuguese arrived in America at the very end of the 15th century. It is said that the Vikings had landed on the North East coast some two hundred years before. Native American Indians and the Eskimos had been on the continent for many thousands of years having crossed from Asia. The British in particular and Europeans generally brought some semblance of social order with laws over behaviour and real estate and the country of America was born. From the beginning it was always multicultural but with the African slaves (along with peoples from the Pacific and South America) forced into doing the hard labour. Many wars were fought against the Natives with treaties forged and broken. The War of Independence brought a new politic of liberty, emancipation and freedom to the Whites but it took a Civil War in the latter half of the 19th century to liberate the Black slaves. This was a most violent war where, from a population of only 30 million or so, three quarters of a million soldiers died in combat. This left a great scar on the people which became deep rooted in the psyche and makeup of the nation carried down through to the 21st century.

With theoretical emancipation of Black Americans however, injustices continued for them as well as the Native Americans. It was harder for Afro Americans to rise through the ranks in any organisation whether it was the military, civil service, government and council or private enterprise. To some extent World War II changed this a little but it wasn't until post Martin Luther King days of the 1950s and 1960s that the old rules of segregation were finally made illegal and all Americans were recognised as having full and equal rights under the law and the constitution.

But unrest never really went away. Stupid gun laws meant that statistics regarding killings by rifles and handguns were way above those of countries in Europe. Shootings by the deranged has brought great sadness to so many families. Shootings by the police were disproportionately higher among Black citizens than those suffered by White citizens. Many Afro Americans lived in cities and neighbourhoods that were run down and severely economically depressed. The biggest scourge on American society was the availability and criminal distribution of drugs and narcotics eating away at the life blood of a nation. Aggravating this was the ease at which prescription drugs were available and lending a hand to the Grim Reaper!

It is true that a Afro American President came to power at the beginning of the 21st century but a woman as President was not seen for the first time until the mid 2020s!

However the worst aspect of American society in the first two decades of the new century was the cancer of the extreme right in the form of New Alternative Right, Ku Klux Klan, blatant Nazis, frustrated Confederates and a host of other 'White Supremacist' groups. It seemed that a section of the White population was experiencing a concerned fear of Black Americans and other racial groups including Jews and Muslims. They now wished to become pro-active in some way. Coupled with the National Rifle Association (with its powerful sway over Congress) there grew a real danger of an explosion of animosities into localised civil conflicts where murders might take place. Leaders of such groups were unafraid to broadcast their vomit against racial and religious groups, particularly Afro Americans, Asians, Muslims and Jews. The authorities did little or at least not enough!

There were insufficient prosecutions against those condoning and actively inciting race hatred and violence. Demonstrations of fascists and ant-fascist groups became more violent with the police standing back. The polarisation fell to simple and unjustified labels: Nationalists versus the Extreme Left! The majority of Middle America became disenfranchised and invisible in this disturbing trend.

To complicate matters further the extreme pro-Israel Jews formed anti-Muslim groups such as Pamela Geller's AFDI.. "American Freedom Defense Initiative"- a virulent and most offensive organisation paying for web pages and huge advertisements placed on the sides of public transport spewing out hatred for Muslims and Islam. One could only describe the lady as a 'Jewish Nazi' that had forgotten her own family's experiences and oppression in Europe during the Second World War! Similar groups flourished in Holland, France, Austria, Germany, England and other parts of Europe!

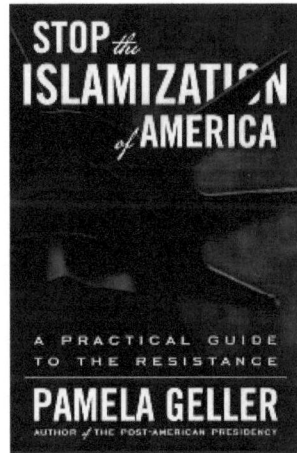

Getting back to America:

The   "Right to carry Arms"

         "Right to Freedom of Speech and Expression"

         "Right to Congregate and Move Freely without Hindrance"

.. these basic rights were becoming blurred with the rights of the majority to live safely on the streets and in their homes! America had become a most dangerous society with an apparent sterility of the authorities or a plane unwillingness to take back control. Attacks on Jews and Jewish businesses and places of worship became common.

Similar events were suffered by Muslims and Black Americans. Things started to deteriorate further towards the end of the second decade. Black Americans felt safer huddled in discrete communities producing 'no go' areas for Whites or White Police (they had had enough of police shootings!) But the more 'middle of the road' Whites were also being motivated to stand up against these hate groups. After all, America gave up thousands of its young men and women fighting fascism in Europe during the 1940s and now there was a situation where its ugliness was rising up on home soil. If Governments, State and Federal, did not act quickly to stem the violence, a civil conflict across the whole country would erupt, building on its own momentum to something not experienced since the 1880s. The President eventually had no other option but to call out the National Guard, employ curfews and put an end to these dangerous events. And that is what he did!

Then there was the call from Britain that it too was in a state of collapse from social unrest and decline of the rule of law. A substantial American Armed Force contingent was speedily sent to help save that country from civil war and destruction.

A couple of more years went by but the extreme right just went underground for a while, its ranks continuing to swell. It was hard to comprehend this enigmatic nation! On the one hand America continued to be the world leader in creative technology and intellectual insight producing wonderful new appliances for all of humanity to exploit, making life easier and more interesting. It was a leader in all the arts providing eloquent gifts of music, drama and graphic composition for the world to enjoy. It was busy in all spheres of human endeavour including space exploration, having landed the first humans on Mars. It had continued participating in small wars around the globe to help spread its values to other cultures (but more often to get a permanent foothold for its products for consumers!) It seems unthinkable that a significant proportion of its peoples would drift and consume all the fear and propaganda of the extreme right. But those cruel and sinister voices had never been properly extinguished and civil conflict broke out at an unexpected moment.

New federal elections for Congress and a President were called. The White Extremists were on the streets in most of the major cities along the East and West coasts, and to the Northern States. There were many killings as these men and women formed armed militias with automatic weapons. The gun manufacturers and distributors had never been sensibly reined in and this was the result. Shops were looted, businesses smashed and destroyed.. it was an American equivalent of 'Krystal Nacht'. Orators warned Blacks, Coloureds, Jews and Muslims to move to a cluster of central Southern States to form their own country. Whites were to have and control the rest of America. It is not known how many people died but estimates place it at around ten million.

The conflict went on for three years before these objectives were crudely met. But at that time a nuclear exchange between China and India had already begun with a consequential similar exchange between India and Pakistan. This was quickly followed by a nuclear strike on Israel by a nuclear armed Middle Eastern country. Russia invaded Western Europe which brought a nuclear response from NATO. America was attacked swiftly by smaller 'nouveaux nuclear armed countries' predominantly in Asia. America responded to both these and Russia. The details of these final days and hours are not recorded and no one knows precisely how many nuclear weapons were detonated. The only thing to comment on for certain was that within the short space of *seventeen days* the whole of the Northern hemisphere was destroyed and uninhabitable with possibly five billion people killed or dying from radiation and various diseases such as cholera and an admix of other biological agents let loose. Thousands took to small planes, cars and boats in a desperate attempt to get to the southernmost regions of the planet. This was the modern diaspora of the survivors of a nuclear holocaust. Americans, Europeans, Arabs, Asians and Pacific peoples that had knowledge of what had transpired and understood the new and immediate threats and consequences to their lives.. all these were immediately mobilised in a refugee tsunami to reach some haven in the Southern hemisphere. And so the great exodus from the Northern hemisphere began.

The year was 2033. The wail of the spirits of Earthly humanity permeated the galaxy and beyond. Perhaps some ethereal cognition was momentarily felt by sentient beings of high intellect on distant worlds.. a feeling that some tragic event of gigantic proportion had taken place somewhere in this universe.

Seventeen   **Heat Rays, AI, Drones and Insects**

Heat Ray Developments 2014: A team of scientists from Britain's National Physics Laboratory and Imperial College, London led by Dr. Mark Oxborrow reported that they had created the first solid state maser that operates at room temperature, paving the way toward the widespread practical application of the technology. Their breakthrough was to replace the hard, inorganic maser crystal with an organic mixed-molecular crystal, p-terphenyl doped with pentacene. The pentacene, which makes the crystal look pink, is photo-excited by yellow light.

Similar functional organic crystals were synthesised in Japan.

The Laser Weapon System or LaWS is a directed energy weapon developed by the United States Navy. The weapon was installed on the *USS Ponce* for field testing back in 2014 and worked perfectly. Further, the commander of the *USS Ponce* was authorized to use the system as a defensive weapon. It is said to be now fully operational on a number of American war ships.

The LaWS was originally designed to be used against low-end asymmetric threats. Scalable power levels allow it to be used on low-power to dazzle a person's eye to non-lethally make them turn away from a threatening posture, or increase to 30 thousand watt (30 kW) to fry sensors, burn out motors, and detonate explosive materials. The LaWS is accurate enough to target explosive rockets if on board a small enemy vessel, whose detonations could kill the operators. *Against larger aircraft like a helicopter, it is able to burn through some vital components, which would cause it to fall and crash.* Most high-energy lasers are in the *invisible* IR region. So you won't see it coming folks!

Contractors of ongoing high-energy laser weapons projects include: Lockheed Martin; Northrop Grumman; Optonicus; General Atomics; Boeing; Kratos; Raytheon and BAE Systems.

A German company brought us one step closer to the kinds of shootouts only seen in Sci-Fi films.

Düsseldorf based Rheinmetall Defense successfully tested and produced a 50kW, high-energy laser at their proving ground facility in Switzerland. The system consists of two laser modules mounted onto Revolver Gun air defence turrets made by Oerlikon and attached to additional

power modules. The laser modules are 30 kW and 20 kW, but a Beam Super-

Dan Dare

imposing Technology (BST) combines two lasers to focus in a "superimposed, cumulative manner" that wreaks havoc on its target. The system is able to slice through 15mm (~0.6 inches) thick steel *from a kilometre away*. From a distance of two kilometres, it is able to shoot down a handful of drones nose-diving toward the surface at 50 meters per second.

While minuscule compared to the 200 petawatt of laser power (200 x ten to the fifteenth watt) that scientists in Europe plan to use for experiments (like blowing up the moon perhaps or melting a small country?), the 50kW laser is functional to make a difference on the battlefield. Apart from science fiction novels dating as far back as the 1890s, the idea of using high-energy lasers has been considered for weaponry since the mid 20th century. Countries such as the US, Russia

196

and China, among others have developed their own high-energy laser programs. Whether or not we hear about future demonstrations will be a matter of national security rather than technological success. It's *safe* to assume this is one arms race that's already here and blossoming! Well zapp me dead! So where can I purchase a 'Dr. Schilling's sidearm'? Probably on the Dark Web!

Israeli defence company Elbit Systems provided an anti-missile laser protection system for the German Air Force (you gotta be kidding me, that has to be a first!) It will be used to protect transport planes from surface to air and portable heat seeking missiles.

The Chinese People's Army conducted two successful anti-satellite tests using advanced laser technology. The anti-satellite exercises were conducted using laser weapons (disclosed by Konstantin Sivkov, deputy head of the Moscow-based Think Tank, Academy of Geopolitical Problems, in an interview to Voice of Russia, 2015). At the time, US government sources told the Defense News that the US would make no fuss regarding the anti-satellite tests as it values Beijing's role as an important trade partner. However whilst visiting air force headquarters in Beijing, President Xi Jin Ping, who is also head of the military told officers "to speed up air and space integration and sharpen their offensive and defensive capabilities." [Through the process of tightening anti-corruption in senior ranks of the Party, Xi has recently strengthened and consolidated his power within the Chinese Communist Party!]

A question put is how many of these lasers or low powered versions have found their way into the hands of members of the public? Certainly components can be purchased and assembled without too much electronic knowhow. High school students with just a little knowledge of Physics and Electronics could put a basic device together!

The Rise and Rise of AI

Without sophisticated computer systems, most of the world's major airports could not operate safely given the high volume of air traffic to-ing and fro-ing. Motor vehicle manufacturers rely heavily on robotic machines to do most of the assembly grunt work in place of humans. Thus humans already rely on artificial intelligence (AI) to control sophisticated systems at a pace far exceeding the capabilities of us mere mortals. With the realised dream of household robots available to assist with routine domestic chores and companies developing 'partners for the lonely' as well as sex industry modules- all has led to a strange new world! Science fiction writers such as Arthur C. Clarke provided incredible landscapes of such future worlds many years ago. The outstanding cosmologist Dr Stephen Hawking has warned that humans were in danger of ceding their position of power to future machines of high intelligence and possessing the technological capability to replicate themselves.

We have witnessed the successful application of drones in the battle theatres of Afghanistan and the Middle East, collecting intelligence or accurately delivering bombs to an enemy position. Accuracy is determined by the satellite system '*skeye*' where observation is acute enough to identify one's wrist watch from space! It has been broadcast that drones taking the form of an insect about the size of a cicada with observation and transmission ability have also been used covertly.

Mr Snowden released to the world the depth and scale of US intelligence monitoring of persons both domestically and internationally; in friendly as well as unfriendly nations to the embarrassment of the US Government and chagrin of those countries spied upon. It is a brave new Orwellian world one must now endure. One might wonder what so much data is useful for? One speculates that only the Indians and Chinese each have sufficient populations to sift through all the spy data of their adversaries!

The Chinese developed and applied a crowd control sonic weapon available to both military and police effective to disperse people from up to a kilometre away. Demonstrations are not encouraged in that country. Such sonic weapons are now available in Western countries.

This chapter commenced with notes on Heat Rays. It seems that Dan Dare has already dared to come onto the scene with the capabilities of burning up just about anything from great distances. Theoretically the race has not included placing such weapons in space but how can one be certain? A blinding flash may render us all blind as in the sci-fi story: 'The Day of the Triffids'! We would be helpless and easy targets for the few remaining animals of prey.. our quick demise certain!

History might record: "Once there were humans, but they were so smart and intelligent that they created a technological environment that was even superior and smarter! Consequently they went the way of the dinosaurs.. to extinction!"

A final plea:

"All that is asked of you, whatever your position in society is that you place the highest value on peace and love of your fellow man and be *traitor* to actions that damage our fragile existence whilst you live. God is above humanity, but humanity is above the largess, desires and whims of nations. And family will always be the bedrock of humanity. Intelligent scientists perceiving to be 'more intelligent than God' have wrought ploughshares into swords. Their petty national pride and lack of moral judgement has paid a disservice to all of humankind and limited the planet to countable days before its final demise. The '*moment of phut*' is near!"

[Much of this was taken from 'Return to Animalia', an earlier work by Tom Law]

Helter Skelter

Eighteen   **The Bear and the Ragged Staff**

Charlotte was now a handsome young woman of nineteen years. She had won a scholarship to study Media and Journalism at the University of Warwick in England and had moved into a small apartment which she shared with two other fresh students, Emma and Rose. Emma was studying Health and Rose, wishing to become a professional writer, was studying Literature. Charlotte was still a serious Muslim girl and refrained from alcohol but loved her clothes and modern music, always wearing her gold 'moon and star' pendant given by her mother on leaving Australia. She also kept up her flute playing and included Mandarin as an additional study due to her schooling in Jiangsu province as a small child. Emma was originally from the Sudan and had come to live in London with her refugee parents when she was eight years old. She was a tall and elegant girl of twenty years with extremely dark skin. Although having been brought up as a Muslim she was a little more wayward and ignored her prayers; also not refusing the occasional glass of wine or pint of beer when offered. Rose was the English rose of the trio, brought up as a Christian with sensible values but not a dedicated Church attendee.

The three girls were all bubbly and fun loving and very soon became very close and compatible. They each loved politics and enjoyed heated discussion but always without judgement or animosity. They tended to avoid discussing religion as each knew that this topic could lead to disharmony in their friendships which was the last thing they wanted.

They were sensible in that they maintained mutual respect for each other's views. At the same time they exhibited intolerance to those extremists that were drawn to terrorist attacks as well as hooliganism demonstrated by the extreme right wing thugs. Unfortunately they would, on rare occasion, run into these characters at the university. Neither of the two Muslim girls ever wore a religious headscarf or other attire so at least they were not harassed on the street; although Charlotte had been known to hurl abuse at an abuser of other Muslim girls or women on the street in the city!

Rose knew this city just a little.. she was originally from Birmingham of middle class parents.. a true Brummy! During the first few months she was happy to introduce the other two to the Castle, shops and a particular pub that she adored for its Tudor style, low ceilings with dark beams, horse brasses, a small open fire and serving delicious Ploughman's lunches at reasonable cost. In fact it was called the Henry Tudor without particular reference to which Henry, but one assumed the notorious eighth!

Whilst all three girls had occasionally attended parties, dances and campus social functions and each having experienced the attentions of suitors, in fact after two years, none had actually started a serious relationship with a boy! The reason appeared to be that they each regarded their studies as the most important aspect of life and felt an obligation to their supporting family to achieve their best.

The Greenwich Park murders by the Holy Knights and Defenders of England suddenly changed all this. It was on the news for more than a week. Of course there had been several Islamic extremist attacks around Britain over the previous decade, mostly in the major cities such as London, Manchester, Birmingham, Liverpool and Glasgow. There had been the occasional fracas outside mosques. But this particular event seemed to be a turning point and the girls felt it.

There was to be a right wing anti-Islamic march in Birmingham's CBD the following Sunday. A counter protest was also being organised.

"I know I'm not that religious but I'm not letting these mongrels have it all their way.. I'm definitely going to join the anti-fascist protest march next Sunday" declared Emma.

Rose and Charlotte were hesitant.

"You don't think it might turn ugly Emm.. people are likely to get hurt."

"I don't think so; the police are likely to be out in force to keep us apart!"

So it was decided that all three would attend. They spent some of their evenings designing and painting placards to carry on the march.

It might be of importance to mention at this juncture that the Syrian war was now over but the war in Yemen was protracted and worse than ever with close to a million and a half dead from bombings or disease and a further two million now refugees in camps outside of Yemen. The British public may have felt chuffed that they had provided food, temporary shelters and milk products to the Yemenis people but how many were aware that all the suffering was the result of the sale of British, American and French bombs sold to Saudi Arabia? Naiveté and ignorance prevailed! Iraq and Iran had started a new war but not quite yet on the scale of that at the end of the 20th century. The fear was that Iran now had nuclear weapons aided by Russia and North Korea. North Korea was still threatening an immediate invasion to the South and India and China were exchanging shots between forces on the north east border of India which was still in dispute. It looked like it might explode into full scale war at any moment.

Sunday arrived and the girls had left home before dawn to travel by van with other students to Birmingham. Considering the large Muslim population in that city it seemed somewhat daring or perhaps foolish for the extreme right to stage a protest. But they had a well orchestrated plan. The march started around 11.30 am with a surprising turnout of around three hundred supporters bearing the usual placards and offensive T-shirts. Some of the more ugly members bore swastika tattoos on their biceps alongside their union jacks. They stopped outside the central council chambers and speakers started to stir the crowd with hate speech against the Muslim takeover and too many mosques in Birmingham and Britain generally.

A long line of police two deep separated the HKDE from the Muslim and student hecklers. Unfortunately some hard core students began to throw bottles and stones. Without warning, the police seemed to fade away to a flanking position and the right wingers suddenly produced clubs, sticks and even iron bars. The melee surged forward almost at a run and threaded through the Muslim and student phalanx swinging their weapons. Some stood and hit back with their placards but many fell to the ground with bleeding heads. Still the police in their riot gear hung back as if waiting for some signal. It must have been a full ten minutes before a whistle was blown and the police moved forward attended at the rear by two dozen mounted police. The right wingers seemed to preordain the whole pattern of battle and quickly ran away from the oncoming police. The remnant Muslims and students were now battered a second time with a loud chorus chanting "back, back, back.. "
Of the nine hundred or so anti-fascist group, twenty three lay dead and

another seventy five seriously injured requiring hospitalisation. A single police officer later died from a strike to the head and two of the right wingers also lay dead giving twenty six deaths in total. It was obvious that the whole demo was carefully orchestrated to inflict maximum harm to the student and Muslim demonstrators and the finger was pointed squarely at the police on this occasion. Fortunately none of the three girls were hurt as they had kept to the rear of their protesting group and had moved away at the first hint of violence.

They high tailed it back to Warwick and settled into the Henry Tudor for dinner whilst regarding the news on the lounge room TV monitor. The announcer gave a graphic description of the afternoon's events in Birmingham but with no reference to any wrong doing by the police. Instead it was reported that the 'left wing' protesters got out of hand and had burst through police lines to attack the 'Nationalists'! There was some mention of casualties but no detail from which group the casualties belonged. In other words, the media had whitewashed the whole ugly episode!

The students in the bar were heckling and cursing the newsreader. It had become packed and animated now with many analytical discussions going on about the day's events. A rather tall young man approached Charly and started up a conversation. The other two girls were also approached by a couple of students with brimming pint pots in their hands.

"My name is Richard. I'm an Elec Engineering undergrad in my fourth year.. so what did you think about the demo?"

"Pretty violent.. I'm sorry I attended. Had I known it would be so dangerous I would have stayed home!"

"Yes well I think that is the future trend sadly. But the behaviour of the police was disgraceful.. it was almost as if it had been rehearsed!"

The conversation was difficult above the racket. Sometime later Emma leaned over "we are going to walk home with these boys.. will you be all right on your own?"

"Oh don't worry, I'll see she gets home safely" butted in Richard with a broad friendly smile.

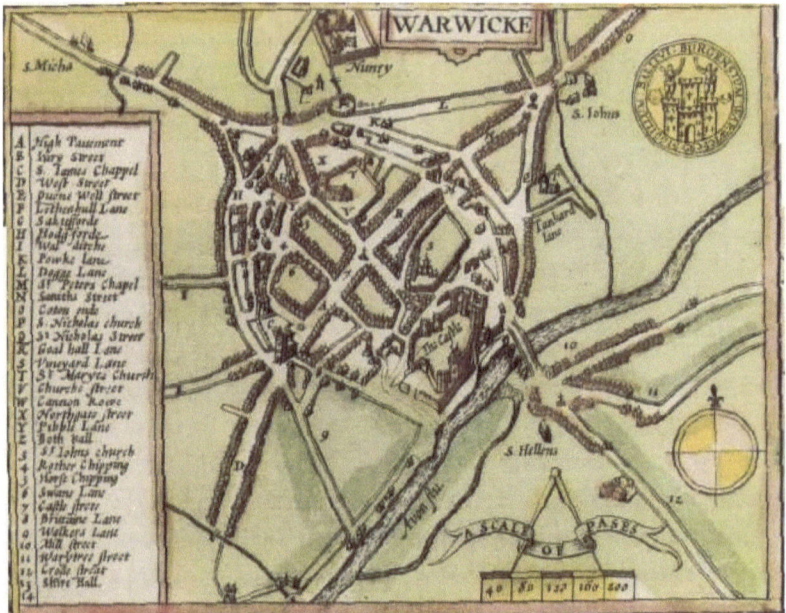

Map of Olde Warwicke

"Well, it's only a couple of streets away" replied Charly.

"OK, see you back at the flat.. cheerio then" and with that the party left.

"Would you like another drink? What'll you have?"

"Oh, um.. just another soda squash for me"

"Ah, on the wagon are we?"

"Well no actually, I don't drink alcohol".

"Hmm.. and very sensible too.. one soda squash coming up!"

On his return with the drinks Richard continued in his friendly manner:
"You know I feel so lucky to be here to meet you, we rarely come to this pub!"

"You mean you're not a pub person then?" Charly naively asked.

"Oh no, it's not that.. we usually go to the Bear and Ragged Staff.. the beer seems to be better there and.. well it's generally a bit quieter than this!"

Richard seemed a nice young man and Charly felt safe as they walked back to her flat chatting along the way. He was very political and went on about the immorality of Britain's role in Middle Eastern wars and the supply of armaments to many countries. Charlotte did not have a lot of knowledge about these things but listened keenly to Richard's arguments about the injustices of it all.

"This is me then" she said timidly.

"Oh, OK then. I will look out for you on campus. Perhaps we can grab a coffee one day during the week?"

"That would be nice.. goodnight then"

"Goodnight Charly".

Inside, Emma and Rose burst out laughing as soon as Charlotte entered the lounge room.

"Ah ha.. you're the quiet one.. my mum always said the quiet ones are the ones you need to watch!" teased Rose.

"Well nothing happened, we just chatted and he walked me home- that's all"

"But you are going to see him again I bet?" Emma butted in with a quizzical smile.

"Maybe.. we'll see".

It was Wednesday morning as Charlotte emerged from a lecture when someone touched her gently on the arm.

"How about that coffee then?" came a strong voice from behind.

Surprised, Charly swung around to see Richard.

"Oh, hi Richard.. er, yes I think I have time before my next class"

And so they went off to one of the student cafes where that sat by a window overlooking the sports field and chatted over doughnuts and coffee. They exchanged a lot about each other and Richard was delighted again to hear the Australian twang in Charlotte's voice.

"We are having a meeting at a friend's house Friday night to discuss our next move regarding the state of things and particularly the HKDE group. You can bring your friends too if you like. It will be at eight. Here is the address." He shuffled a piece of paper across the table.

"Well, I'm not sure. I'll talk with the others and get back to you."

"OK then, here is my cell number. Text me later. I'm late for my class so I'd better shove off!"

"Alright, see you.. and thanks for the coffee".

There were only six members of the group at the meeting, five men and one girl, so with the additional three girls that made nine in all. They put various suggestions forward on strategies to embarrass the government and get back at the extremists. One plan discussed was a picket outside a factory on the outskirts of Manchester known to manufacture shells for tanks and heavy artillery. The other girl, Jody, wanted to make a more extreme statement.

"Let's bomb the place or burn it to the ground!"

This was too outrageous for the others but the picket seemed to be quite popular and was finally agreed upon. Later back at the flat, both Emma and Rose declared that they were not that serious about joining which left Charly to decide what she would do. She liked Richard and felt that she didn't want to let him down.

It was two weeks later on a Saturday morning that the students met up outside the armaments factory in Manchester. It was a chilly November day with a hint of early snow in the air. There were about two hundred protesters from various universities including Warwick. Despite the cold the crowd seemed most cheery. Apart from the security guards at the gate and TV crews from channels four and ten, there were virtually no members of the public to be seen to witness the meet which made the handing out of a propaganda sheet a little pointless.

"We can split up this afternoon after this winds up and leaflet the main shopping malls in town" was Richard's immediate response to the situation. A couple of police showed up in a squad car to which the students offered hot soup and coffee from vacuum flasks. Banners and placards were held aloft and a speech made by a lad from Liverpool. By midday they had had enough and began to disperse.

"I didn't notice Jody today" Charly enquired of Richard as they got into the van.

"No, she decided to give it a miss. Sick grandmother I think she said."

There was just a thirty second spot on the evening news about the picket and that was all. However at nine the next morning there was an urgent bulletin:

"There has been a bomb blast in the roof of the Highvale Armaments Works in Paisley, Glasgow. At least one fatality and several injuries have occurred. Fortunately there was no major explosion at the works other than the terrorist' device. Four people have been arrested. More on this later as news comes to hand".

A later bulletin gave the name of the fatality: ".. a Mr James MacDonald of Paisley, Glasgow who was struck by falling steel girders. He had worked at the plant for fourteen years and was well respected among his workmates. He leaves a wife and daughter."

Just before lunch two detectives knocked at the girls' door.

"Is there a Miss Charlotte Jacobs at this address please?"

"I am Charlotte Jacobs, how can I assist?"

"Sorry to trouble you miss, but you need to fetch your coat and accompany us to the police station".

Richard and other students were already there being interviewed.

"Do you know a Miss Jody Braithwaite? Could you tell us your whereabouts on Saturday between 8am until 2am Sunday morning?"

Jody had been arrested as part of a gang that had travelled to Glasgow with a makeshift bomb and had lobbed it onto the roof of the armaments factory. She was in extremely serious trouble with a murder charge upon her.

Eventually the police were satisfied with the answers provided and Richard and Charly were released that afternoon without charge.

"I do hope you will not associate with any of the more radical elements at your university. Your names will be kept on record of course due to your prior association with Miss Braithwaite. In view of the fact that you are in the UK on a student visa Miss Jacobs, it is of particular importance that you keep well away from any extremists" were the final warnings given to the two students.

Life went on as usual for the next six months without any incident. Charly and Richard's relationship grew from strength to strength. Then at a Friday night meet the topic of a conference and military hardware fair to be held in London the following month was discussed. Richard led the group putting the following proposals:

"This is a major event where all the top corporations selling a wide range of military weaponry will be present. There will be representatives from countries across the globe. We really need to take a stand and demonstrate to the public in some way our disgust at our nation's profiteering from armaments. We will not be popular and there will be a strong police presence once they get a sniff of our intentions. There will be another similar event in Rotterdam next month which we might also follow up depending on the turnout in London."

It was agreed that a grand gesture by as many students from across the UK should attend. There were to be leaflets, placards, an attempt to block the entrance to the building, a website and as much propaganda across social media as possible. At the closure of the meeting Richard said to Charly that she might find her own way home as he wished to discuss other matters with the 'inner clique' as he put it.

"No worries darling, I'll see you later at my place."

Unbeknown to Charly, Richard had become more extreme in his views and was part of a parallel group intending action of a more violent nature. Charly had almost finished her undergraduate studies and was hoping to get into Imperial College in London to take a Master's studying Literature and Contemporary Writing. The London trip would provide an opportunity to wander around the hallowed halls of this famous institution.

It might be important to note that at this time there was a lot of violence and protest across much of Europe and North America. The polarisation of societies had reached a critical point with deaths occurring regularly

211

in confrontations between white supremacist groups and anti-fascist groups. The threat of war seemed to hover over all the continents with additional smaller countries racing towards nuclear arms and other WMDs of a chemical or biological nature. The United Nations was stretched economically and its regular meetings considerably less civilised with accusation upon accusation flung between countries sharing mutual animosity. The philosophical blamed the internet, the banks, the global arms manufacturers and dealers, the drug dealers and a host of other social ills spelling out the collapse in civil order in many nations. It seemed that violence erupted now between people based on any whim.. skin colour, ethnicity, religious adherence, wealth versus poverty, which football team one supported etc. There seemed to be little logic other than to say that societies globally had reached some azimuth in intolerance of others for even the most trivial of reasons or perception of difference. Cities had become sad and dangerous places at any time of the day or the night. Police were afraid to enter 'no-go' areas fearing beatings by mobs or even shootings. Things had become so bad in Britain that the army patrolled the streets of many cities and curfews were put in place. It was not uncommon for one to be arrested and held without charge for up to ten days under new legislation.

Despite all these things in uncertain times, most did their best to go about their daily business and take care not to provoke a stranger on the street, on public transport or any other public arena!

The demonstration outside the military hardware fair at Olympia Stadium was overwhelming. There were many arrests as well as clashes between the students and extreme right thugs that were organised. The police were in full battle gear with tasers, extended truncheons and automatic weapons. There was also a contingent of police on horseback. These were moved into the foray when bottles and rocks started to be thrown. Eventually there were calls on loud speakers for the crowds to disperse or else arrests would follow. Again there were dozens hospitalised and three deaths. Just as Charly decided with her friends Emma and Rose to call it a day there was a horrific explosion from within the very building housing the fair. The girls got away quickly, managing to get on the tube and away to a peaceful part of the city.

"I have a cousin living in St Albans north of the city; I think we should go there. It will be safe and far from this craziness" declared Charly.

St Alban

So that is what they did. They spent the next couple of days looking at the great cathedral, walking about the town, pub lunches and mostly relaxing before taking the express train back to Warwick. Richard had texted Charly regularly over the three days until a last message read: "the police have grabbed me".

Richard had played a part with two others, engineering and carrying out the terror attack in which seventeen people died and another sixty three seriously injured. Charly would never see Richard again!

China and India were now at war. American troops were in Britain and Iran was threatening a nuclear attack on Israel- this time a most likely event! There were many smaller sideline wars erupting in Africa and

[Alban, said to be a Roman soldier, lived in Britain around 300 AD. Alban met a Christian priest fleeing from persecutors and sheltered him in his house for a number of days. For this he was firstly whipped then executed by beheading.]

South America between neighbouring states. Charly received an urgent stream call from her dad in Australia on her pad.

On seeing her dad's face she was shocked by his anguish and thought that he'd aged considerably over the last year.

"Time to come home honey! Sorry about Imperial, but you gotta get your arse outta there asap.. we'll be waiting for you here. Don't delay!"

"OK dad, but I'd like to come via Amsterdam to see aunt Fila first.. I promised to visit some time back."

It was difficult to get flights but eventually Charlotte managed to book a flight from Birmingham to Cape Town and then on to Perth and Melbourne. However firstly she flew to Amsterdam to be with her aunt who was originally from Indonesia. She enjoyed the city for just two days despite the universal intrepid feelings of fear in the citizens. The first day Charly visited the Anne Frank House located on a canal called the Prinsengracht, close to the Westerkerk.

"I suggest you visit the Begijnhof; it is a group of historic buildings, some of the oldest in Amsterdam" said her auntie. " .. and if you have time, the Vondelpark is very pretty and relaxing. I will accompany you there and we can have a picnic."

"That will be wonderful aunty, thank you. By the way, on Friday I want to take the train to visit a friend in Rotterdam. I will return after the weekend if that's OK with you?"

A drive from Melbourne city to Rushing Creek in East Gippsland took just four hours now. Awakening on that first morn to the sweet odours of the bush, the sounds of birds and seeing familiar forested hills from the window would have provided Charlotte with a sense of joy and amazement that such a Shangri-La existed on the planet after all the wild turmoil of Europe. But she never arrived home to experience such joy. In fact she did not return even to Amsterdam. Instead, another personage was to fill her place; but more on that particular story later.

Helter Skelter

Nineteen   **The Last War**

The North West border of India with China had seen minor incursions by soldiers from both sides for decades now. Shots had been fired but each side had been careful at the beginning of the 21st century not to inflict a death or even a wound on the opposing side. As with the Middle East and other parts of the world the borders had been drawn up on maps by the British and other European colonial powers in the eighteenth and nineteenth centuries. To be fair to these colonialists, many countries outside of Europe never had accurate maps and national boundaries were either non-existent or fuzzy in the least. So here were the two most populous nations on Earth, each with an estimated 1.7 billion souls preparing to go to war rather than sitting at table and coming to an agreement on their border! But nations and leaders can be fickle with disastrous consequences.

Iran had seemingly moved to a more democratic society in recent years with a nuclear electricity program enabled by technology shared with Russia. There were safeguards and an agreement that Iran was never to produce a nuclear weapon. However, after renewed killings and yet another limited war between Palestine and Israel over the control of the various parts of Jerusalem plus more land grabbing by Israel, Iran had torn up all its agreements and was in full swing and very close to producing several plutonium devices deemed much more powerful than either of the bombs dropped on Japan in 1945. America had for some years now built and manned an embassy in central Jerusalem. The UN had toyed with the idea of creating a UN controlled "Free Jerusalem" to be administered by a UN police force. But it never came to fruition, mainly due to a US veto on the Security Council. Many accused the US administration of bowing to its own domestic Jewish lobby groups for such action. But the world was again back to the same old problem in 2029, where a nuclear strike on Tel Aviv was seen to be imminent by a chest beating government in Tehran.

North Korea hadn't changed either, with the constant threat of "we are on the brink of war with America" and had assembled a large army on the border with South Korea. As a nation with ICBMs, tipped with

nuclear or thermonuclear weapons and a menacing attitude towards Japan, it looked like the real thing was likely after decades of posturing and threatening. But Japan was now thought also to have a secretive store of its own nuclear devices despite its constitution and promises to the world that it would never produce such weapons. Considering it had operational nuclear power plants producing electricity for in excess of seventy years, it would hardly be surprising to learn it had produced nuclear bomb material at the ready for retaliation to any attack.

The Indian situation had reached a greater complexity with Pakistan having been strongly assisted with all kinds of weaponry from China. The Kashmir dispute had never been resolved even though, technically, it was now an independent country recognised by the United Nations.

Both India and Pakistan continued to swap insults and fire the occasional shell at each other's embedded positions (each military contingent acting as invited guests in the new country!) America and the West supported India in a loosely worded agreement going back to the 1950s. Whether they would seriously come to its aid in a full scale confrontation remained to be seen.

Russia was still hanging on to remnants of its former Empire and supporting various rebel groups in border regions of those countries that had won independence from the Giant Bear. Economic sanctions imposed by Europe and America did little or nothing to alter these scenarios. In fact the Russian Government held the West in contempt for its attempts at meddling in what it considered Russian affairs. As a resource rich country with still a lot of friends to the East and having China as a major trading partner, it felt fairly confident that it would never be attacked by any of the Western powers. Its vile propaganda went back to the first Chechnyan war where it posted videos of Muslim rebels beheading young Russian conscripts. This crudely choreographed theatre was later imitated by the West during the conflict against so called Islamic State in Syria and Iraq at the beginning of the 21st century, but to a much more sophisticated and elaborate extent. It was theorised that a British company based in London created the scripts and had the filming done in the Nevada desert in the US. The purpose was simple.. demonise the enemy as less than human to satisfy the 'folks back home', especially to counter the media having displayed graphic edits of war crimes by 'our boys' in uniform! The fact that these wars were caused by the various jealousies around the export of oil and gas to Europe somehow got lost in the equation spelled out to the gullible public!

There were various other mini-wars and bickering going on between nations in South America, Africa and Asia; but these were seen as economic devices conjured up and created by the major industrialist conglomerates around the world that produced armaments, supplying both sides in each conflict. In other words, these petty wars between poor nations were guaranteeing continuity of the high standard of living of the rich nations. This state of affairs is perhaps the low point of morality in the world experienced from the mid-twentieth century to the present day! Politicians and academics had noted this and expressed dismay in the UN forum for decades with little or no impact to this cruel and ongoing reality. And it was not confined to traditional, easy to spot capitalistic countries.. oh no; it was a market that was irresistible to all comers, and God how the money rolled in!

So by mid 2029, the world was at its most precarious, with just the hint of a tiny spark being all that was required to ignite to one massive conflagration. That tiny spark was provided by an improbable and unpredictable event: the sudden invasion of Gibraltar by Spain. Knowing that Britain was in temporary chaos, with American armed forces in that country trying to assist in bringing it back to an orderly society, the Spanish Government decided to take advantage of a rare opportunity to get 'the Rock' back after its several hundred year occupation by the British. The act in itself did not bring flotillas of warships to the mouth of the Mediterranean. What it did was induce sudden confidence in many other countries from settling similar old disputes going back hundreds of years. A new swapping of authority in the Caribbean, border crossings by insurgents in the Middle East and Far East, escalations between larger countries such as Chile and Argentina, Ethiopia and Sudan and finally a blitzkrieg invasion of South

Korea by the North at the same moment as a full scale invasion by Pakistan into Kashmir. Following these eclipsing events, it was merely weeks before the first nuclear exchange in early August. Similar exchanges occurred within hours of the first between many paired adversaries all within the Northern hemisphere, causing the incineration and destruction of hundreds of major cities. Those few souls that, by intuition, could smell the imminent collision of the great powers had started to move south without looking back and carrying just a smattering of possessions. It was the end of human civilisation as it was known at that time.

"Do you not see these great buildings? By no means will a stone be left here upon a stone and not be thrown down!"

The worst element of this tumultuous exchange was the release by poorer countries of a vast menu of biological and chemical agents. Cholera, poliomyelitis, small pox, killer strains of influenza, ebola and others never before seen or known crept over the war torn landscapes of the North then filtered down into South America and Africa. Satellite weapons brought blistering and blindness. Electronic systems vulnerable to wifi and networking broke down as they were hijacked by remote hackers. Car doors would not open; car engines would not start. Households had no electricity. All forms of communication failed. In fact the only technology (devices) that continued to function were those very old that were 'hard wired' with old fashion mechanical switches and not relying on computer driven systems. Food and clean water quickly became scarce. Illness from disease and radiation took the lives of those that had survived the nuclear blasts. The great clouds of dust that now circled the planet brought darkness and cold.. a deadly cold that froze the land, rivers and lakes. The few survivors had to get to the south or perish.

In the jungles of central Africa, Chimpanzees living together in a community have a very definite social structure with the dominant alpha male the unchallenged leader. They eat vegetation foodstuffs primarily but on occasion supplement this with fresh meat. Working in coordination as a group they will surround a cluster of monkeys foraging high in the canopy and slowly get into position. At the signal from the leader they strike with uniform and calculated purpose, slinging a hapless monkey to the ground that is immediately pounced upon and torn apart limb from limb. The meat is distributed due to the pecking order among the hunters with the dominant alpha taking his share first.

The Red Ants have located a nest of Black Ants high in a tree which is too close to their own empire. It is decided that they will raid the Black Ants kingdom and palace to rid themselves of the unwanted competition for local food sources. The attack begins. The Red Ants assemble several thousand warriors and begin stinging and biting the Black Ants that put up a noble fight. Wave after wave of Red Ants throw themselves against the army of Black Ants, sometimes clinging to an individual and by pushing off, the pair falling to the jungle floor. Gradually by sheer weight of numbers the Black Ants are defeated and the Red Ants rush in to firstly kill the Queen and her attendees, then to the nursery where the eggs are stored. They carry away these eggs back to their own palace and store them in the larder for food. Once again their territory is safe and life goes on as before.

It has been theorised by mathematical argument that in order to build the great pyramids at Cheops, the Egyptians required a huge workforce and further that this workforce needed to be fed daily. The solution was for parties to sortie deep into the south of the African continent and procure slaves by force and bring them by the hundreds at a time back to the worksite. The average working life of a slave during the project was usually about four years by which time they were exhausted and not strong enough to continue. It is suggested that these were then slaughtered and their meat distributed among the living slaves for sustenance. In this way a continuous supply of workers was maintained and fed to accomplish the task of building the great pyramids.

The Europeans streamed down through Africa over desolate country where there were few animals to be captured for food. Through dislocation, disarray and bewilderment a general malaise had overtaken many communities that were now no longer tilling the land to produce crops. Small bands of hunters were prowling the countryside searching for any food they could get. Cannibalism was rife and the travellers were an easy target. If a convoy consisted of only two or three cars they would be ambushed. Children were prized for their meat was still tender. Adults would be executed and left to rot close by their vehicles-carrion for the vultures, other birds and reptiles. Possessions were ransacked for precious items such as guns, knives, matches and anything that would contribute to survival. Sometimes things were taken as trophies for their women folk back at camp. Despite these obstacles many got through to finally arrive in Cape Town at the tip of the continent. But even that city was fraught with dangers as marauding gangs patrolled the various areas of the city. Plunder and murder were common everyday events as law and order broke down. Only a few boats escaped to travel the southern seas in the hope of finding fertile and safe lands to start over.

As a footnote to this chapter, a Russian scientist cum author named Alexiavich Kramoff had been collecting data for years and was the prime member of a miniscule philosophical group whose purpose was to research the possibility of interference in pan-global politics by intelligent aliens. His little known treatise titled "The Galactic Empire and its Plan for Planet Earth" postulated that a Galactic intelligence named 'the Scrarabians' had decided that humans were so far removed from their own genetic and physical makeup that it would be better to annihilate us before we seriously ventured out into space. The Scrarabians were more insect-like than mammal-like and had already conquered many planetary systems in the inner vortex of the Milky Way. As newer civilisations tended to develop around the younger stars in the outer regions of the great spiral arms, they would keep an eye on any developments of intelligent life that might one day challenge them to their superior position. Thus it was postulated that the Scrarabians were the prime motivators of wars between nations, having no qualms at witnessing the mass murder of humans and devastation of their cities and social infrastructures.

They achieved their goal by promoting tensions between neighbouring countries, aggravating tensions between the great religions and even between the various schisms within religions. They would stretch the political spectrum creating extremes of left and right and engineer hatred between humans of different colour and ethnicity. Like remote wizards and witches they would stir their potions and cackle at the unseeing pathetic humans that would follow their individual will to hatred and self-destruction. They would interfere with media stories and electronic networks to produce results that would bring further anger and dissatisfaction i.e generate fake news. They would attack the policing of laws, the long held values of societies and generally cause mayhem in every sphere of human activity: schools, law courts, parliaments, hospitals, manufacturing, universities, organisational boards, communication channels, entertainment channels down to family bonds. Destruction would be complete.

Despite some cursory and, in some cases, convincing evidence of language and communications encountered, recorded and painstakingly decoded, the few scientists that perused the book and myriad of papers proffered to the worlds scientific journals had each come to a general feeling, conclusion and consensus that *'Kramoff was no more than a disillusioned quack and crackpot'*; thus his work was consequently dismissed. Following this, the Scrarabians were responsible for the destruction of an early space shuttle launch and to add to their reckless humour and diabolical ego, somehow engineered the subsequent fire-ball and cloud in the sky to emulate closely an image of what a Scrarabian actually looked like.. a sort of devil head with balls at the end of its horns or antennae! About the same time the American space probes Voyagers I and II were reaching the outer perimeter of the Solar System and entering inter-stellar space. These could not be permitted to enter the territory under the duristriction of the Empire and thus would be either destroyed or collected as trophies for some museum on their home planet.

If some humans survived they didn't really care in the knowledge that human endeavour and technological progress would be set back by millennia. Further, ice ages and other environmental catastrophes would also play a role in hampering human progress. The Scrarabian Empire would be safe and go on! With the internet gone and all the great civilisations of the 21st century demolished, it would be most unlikely that their devilish work would ever be detected or discovered, let alone read and analysed!

The ancient Greeks in their mythology and epic poetry often attributed the interference of the Gods in human affairs. But, my reader, perhaps it is a most naïve and outrageous idea to suggest any external extraterrestrial interference in the activities of humans. We are quite capable of self destruction without any such assistance!

Twenty   **A Brief History of Australia**

As Australia, between the years 2030 and
2040, was inundated by refugees fleeing the
northern hemisphere after multiple catastrophic
nuclear exchanges between various nations it
seems prudent to provide a little background
on that particular country.

The following are approximate dates of mid-iceage epochs when sea
levels around the globe were at their lowest:

20 000	years ago
90 000	years ago
150 000	years ago
250 000	years ago
330 000	years ago

Scientists generally agree that modern man 'homo sapiens sapiens'
migrated around the world in a great diaspora from North Africa or the
Middle East starting roughly 100 000 years ago. More primitive
humanoids (or Hominidae) lived in Africa, Europe and Asia before this
migration, dating back between one and three million years or even
more. To date, archaeologists have uncovered evidence of humans
living in Australia to around 70000 years ago. Looking at the iceage
dates mentioned above, humans were able to walk from New Guinea to
mainland Australia at these times when sea levels were low. It is more
than likely then that the earliest humans reached the Australian
continent sometime during the latter stages of the iceage with mid-point

of 90000 years ago. Before that time it is currently assumed that no humans had reached Australia.

It is also probable that during the most recent iceage i.e 20000 years ago, a second wave of peoples migrated from New Guinea and made their presence felt on mainland Australia. It may be that DNA studies will show that this second wave were not very different from the first wave but perhaps brought new ideas of social structure accompanied by new technologies in terms of tools for food preparation, hunting and weaponry. They are likely to have brought new styles of art to adorn both artefacts as well as their bodies for ceremonial purposes and recognition of status within the tribal group. It is also probable that there became a merging of these two waves of peoples over time as a result of both conflict and acceptable intermarriage.

Other anthropologists claim that peoples also came south during the interglacial epochs by boat and canoe. There is some evidence to suggest that Indonesian fishermen fished off the North West coast of Australia over thousands of years. Certainly people were able to reach Australia from both New Guinea and Indonesia by even the flimsiest of sea craft. Thus we might assume that small numbers of people were arriving almost continuously over the past 90000 years to make up the current Aboriginal or First Peoples of Australia.

When humans first arrived they found unusual plants and the giant mega fauna; plants and animals that had evolved in isolation over 65 million years. Diprotodon weighed more than two tonne, giant wombats, kangaroos that towered over a man, a lizard like the Komodo dragon and crocodiles each around five metres in length, a ferocious marsupial lion and a giant emu-like flightless bird! Spears and ground edged stone axes were used for hunting and defence. Within a few thousand years humans had spread across the whole continent and they in turn also became isolated during the interglacial period.

The last iceage commenced some 25000 years ago with duration of some 10000 years. Humans were able once again to cross on foot between New Guinea and Australia as well as between the mainland and Tasmania. But those that had settled in the interior of the continent were to suffer extreme hardship as it turned to desert with 90% of the land under permanent drought conditions. It was during this period that the mega fauna disappeared totally.

Through dance, songline as well as cave paintings, cultural information was passed down the generations. To know the best hunting grounds and places where water might be found were essential for survival. With grasslands replacing what had once been forests a way had to be found to extract the nutrients from seeds. With the application of grindstones to make flour, simple campfire bread became part of the diet alongside reptiles, grubs and ant-honey.

The end of the last iceage at approximately 15000 years ago brought new problems. Seas began to rise up to one hundred and thirty metres, drowning up to a quarter of the available land space and reaching its maximum level some 7000 years ago. During the post-iceage era an explosion of culture and nations occurred with new customs and technologies appearing, including the boomerang which was used to hunt water birds. However in many Northern and North East regions, grasslands reverted back to forests due to an increase in rainfall. The boomerang was replaced again by the spear as the preferred tool for hunting with the adjunct of the woomera i.e spear throwing stick. As populations grew there were some intertribal battles most likely resulting from competition over tribal boundaries. Tribal law occasionally resulted in a ceremonial killing of a person that had done something wrong.

Having been cut off from the mainland some 14000 years ago, the Tasmanian aborigines settled down to a most pleasant life with an abundance of food sources easily obtainable from the land and the sea. This is seen by a reduced variety of everyday tools.. some twenty in all compared with up to one hundred and twenty used by those on the mainland.

Fishermen from Makassar began trading with Northern coastal peoples some four hundred years ago bringing axes, machetes, knives, tobacco pipes and colourful fabrics in exchange for the sea cucumber. The Dutch made some landings on the Northern coast and Western coast about the same time but made no permanent settlements.

Captain Cook aboard the Endeavour arrived off the Southeast coast in 1770 and put ashore at Botany Bay for a brief flag raising ceremony. It wasn't until 1788 that twelve ships making up the 'First Fleet' arrived under Commander Arthur Phillip, at Sydney Cove and founded a permanent settlement. The British had come to stay.

This arrival of Europeans created tension for the Aboriginals from the outset. The white man wanted land for houses, farms and roads. New diseases took their toll along with alcohol, slavery and retaliatory battles. The killing of a single white person might mean the return killing of dozens of natives. With the sophistication of new weapons and technologies the newcomers slowly pushed the native peoples off their tribal lands. This was particularly marked in the Eastern states.

SUPPLEMENT PRESENTED GRATIS, WITH CHRISTMAS NUMBER OF THE TOWN & COUNTRY JOURNAL, DEC 21ST 1873.

CAPTAIN COOKS LANDING AT BOTANY, A.D. 1770.

Many natives had no contact with the white man what so ever in the more remote regions of Central and Western Australia. Aborigines in some communities did not come into contact with Europeans until the 1950s!

It seems incongruent in that many of the white immigrants of the early 19th century were Scottish that had been disinherited of their small holdings in Scotland. These crofters and farm labourers had witnessed their homes being burned or demolished by the rich 'lairds' to make way for sheep farming. Thousands of such families had been forced to migrate to North America or Australia.

It was not until the end of the 20th century and first three decades of the 21st century that Aboriginal people gained rights, better housing and welfare, health and education and, eventually, land ownership under various laws enacted by the Federal Government. Despite all this, communities were still suffering from child abuse and drug abuse, high unemployment and high rates of youth crime (and hence detention) and youth suicide.

As has been recorded, disturbances and violence erupted towards the end of the second decade of the 21st century among the white people of the continent just as it had in other Western countries. This seemed to be a growing problem throughout the Western world with political polarisation alongside ethnic and religious tensions. These tensions were further aggravated by the new connectivity via social media channels, mobile phones and other mobile devices. It was not long before violent clashes at demonstrations led to killings. But it was the final nuclear exchanges in the Northern hemisphere that brought some sobering down of this localised bickering. Quite suddenly people gravitated to rural communities at the Southern edges of the continent, knowing that this was their only chance of survival in a world that had destroyed itself.

After the catastrophic nuclear exchanges across the Northern hemisphere a new wave of peoples arrived on Australia's shores. With the advent of a 'nuclear winter' the conditions similar to previous ice ages fell over the continent bringing extreme hardship to the survivors of humanity. Huddled along the southern coastal regions a semblance of society again took hold resembling that of 14th century Western Europe. Agriculture, sea fishing and various trades sprang up as people divided those skills necessary for small town or village communities to survive. These new peoples were of diverse and mixed races, having come from every corner of the world. Remembering a previous world of confusion and conflict these people resolved to survive in a better way.

Twenty one   **Coffee with Phil Ossifer**

Carl felt it necessary to write down as much as he could about this time in human history. As well as writing anecdotes from personal observations and what he had gleaned from the media, much information and many ideas were gleaned from learned friends and acquaintances. Whilst temporarily in residence in his new environment under the shadow of Mt Fowler (due to the fact that Tina had taken up a teaching position in a rural school), Carl had met Phil Ossifer, an ex-policeman of rare wit and intelligence. He was a man that had actually read an extremely wide range of books and academic papers but made no claim to academic achievement at any higher institution! Carl had shared coffee over the odd game of chess and each had shared their political, scientific and philosophical viewpoints on life, current happenings in the world as well as the esoteric nebulae surrounding various religions and their historical perspectives.

Phil's chess board was a hand crafted circular wooden table of Asian origin with the chess pieces being huge and chunky. The worst aspect was that the familiar pieces in this set were difficult to discern which made the play more difficult unless you were used to them.. which of course Phil was! If there was one petty criticism that one might point at Carl it would be the fact that he did not like to lose at chess ha ha! (However he never felt this if he lost a game to one of his own children!)

Naturally there was not always agreement in their discussion. But these coffee meets never brought about antagonism or animosity in any shape or form. Even in disagreement there was the feeling that each enjoyed this sharing of views and, further, that this intellectual sparing actually created bonds of friendship as opposed to the norm of anger!

And so it was that Carl indeed learned much from Phil. It was obvious that Phil no longer dived into encyclopaedias and texts for his search of truth, but had become more reliant on that greatest of libraries.. the internet. He spent a disproportionate part of his day and night in front of the screen testing this theory and that, absorbing facts that were often extremely remote from each other but consumed into his mind for later analysis and provocation.

Carl had been reading 'The List' by Michael Brissenden and thought that the number of potential terrorists in Australia was vastly exaggerated. However from Phil's personal experience he noted that there were indeed hundreds of young men and women prepared to join the battle in Syria and Iraq on the side of the Khilafah! They did agree on one thing: that the Lindt Café tragedy in Sydney perpetrated by Monis could have been averted had the authorities desired, but they did nothing, letting the man follow his will!

"And how much regarding these current wars is bullshit Phil?"

"Well Carl, you know what they say, the first casualty of any war is the truth and I guess these are no different!"

"Didn't the British try to take Afghanistan a hundred years or so ago?"

"Oh yes. In fact there were two Anglo-Afghan wars in the 19th century and the British lost many men. I think I recall that Winston Churchill participated in the second one as a young soldier!"

"Nothing compared to the thousands of young Russian men killed in the 1980s.. what makes us believe we can ever change these people?"

"Check-mate! Well it's all about building Empire Carl.. the Empire of Coca-Cola, KFC and MacDonalds! And of course there exist various companies around the world that create 'fake news' to assist in the propaganda of war. It is both a science and an art.. or should I say dark art! You know Carl, such companies should be seriously investigated."

did these men choreograph these video clips... and more?

MASTERS OF THE DARK ARTS

BELL & POTTINGER
of
LONDON
"we can make you believe ANYTHING !"

"I suppose you're right.. but it's a sad indictment on our leaders! Looks like you got me again Phil!"

Unfortunately the coffee meets came to an abrupt end when Phil decided to move house to a more centralised location that suited his current business in physiotherapy and the teaching of Wing Chun Kung Fu. Carl kept in contact however, maintaining an interest in the paths that each was traversing along life's mysterious and exploratory mountain! Each kept his ear to the ground for the tell-tale sounds of the coming chaos of *helter skelter* in the world, whether it be on distant shores or nearer to home. Carl insisted that he would write down in a book his personal experiences, political views and his prediction regarding the coming of the final war.

But it was Phil that insisted that the book should not end in total 'doom and gloom' and that humanity deserved a chance for a way out! It was this that sparked the idea of some survival and notes titled: "Of Course, It Doesn't Have to End This Way!" So the coda to the book is really down to the wisdom and recommendations of Phil Ossifer!

It is oft quoted that 'only war will bring peace'. But the greats such as Ghandi and Martin Luther King preferred 'civil disobedience' together with the application of 'the law' to achieve sensible change without resorting to war. Frustration in the tardiness of change brings some to take direct action by violence leading to deaths. This can never be condoned. There is almost always another way. Whilst it may be true that David, a small boy, was able to slay a great warrior Goliath in ancient time, we must treat the story in modern times as allegorical! Ordinary people can win against seemingly invincible governments and international companies when these are doing the wrong thing. Take heart!

Carl remembered the last bout of verbose sparring. It was a pleasant spring morning in September and we sat outside under blue sky and a warming sun with a distinct odour of cattle shit drifting our way.

"You don't mind if I smoke Carl?"

"No mate, go ahead. So what do you think of Aung San Su Kyi and the Rohingya exodus from Myanmar Phil?"

"Well firstly, the dear Lady is really a celebrity Princess in her country and has no real power. I think the Generals never truly relinquished their grip. Secondly and sadly, even Buddhists can resort to violence thus contradicting their claim as a peaceful religion. I think no such animal exists!"

"But so many.. do you agree it is ethnic cleansing?"

"Certainly some Rohingya have fought the Burmese Army.. but you know, they were never really recognised as being part of that nation. It is a human catastrophe!"

"You know I have access to 'the list' (and by the way- that's secret and confidential but I can show you).. we cannot pretend that Islamic extremism does not exist. Disregarding injustices of the past and the whole f**k up in Afghanistan and Iraq/Syria we have to face facts, there are some real nasty bastards that want to do us harm here!"

"Well personally I would not prevent them from leaving the country if they wish.. just don't ever allow them to return!"

"Not so easy to implement if they already have Oz citizenship or were born here!"

"I know what you're getting at. But I can't help thinking that our interference in the Middle East is doing more harm than good in the long run. Seems to me that it's all just phase one of an eventual guarantee of the complete destruction of the world! I mean look at the so called victories.. all I see is cities completely reduced to rubble with thousands of civilians dead and millions of refugees!"

"Yes well Carl, our Generals call it collateral damage! But you are correct in one regard.. its gonna go on for some time yet!"

Phil lit up another cigarette and sat quietly contemplating the distant hills of all the shades of blues and greens. Just a few puffy clouds clung to them like the tops of ice-cream cones. It was a grand and peaceful scene. 'How lucky we are' thought Carl.

Helter Skelter

Twenty two   **Rosehip and Bramble Farm**

Back to the Future: Carl was so glad to have Charly home. With the imminent destruction of the world as was known, the family set about preparing for the worst and improving their small holding or hobby farm into a complex self sufficient enterprise that would greatly assist in their chances of survival. Jason had been studying Materials and Aeronautic Design at the Royal Melbourne Institute of Technology and was particularly competent with pumps, engines, generators and electrical things generally. Carl had been fearful that his son might have become radicalised in his mother's religion but, praise be to God, that had not happened.

"So what do you think we need in the way of seeds, fruit stock and livestock Charly to supplement what we already have?" Carl asked his number one daughter.

"Well, you know I have always wanted a horse since I was small so perhaps a draught horse for a start to pull a plough".

".. and what else?"

"We only have chooks, and not many of them. I suggest more plus some geese, ducks and maybe even turkeys".

"Go on".

".. hmm .. a couple of milking goats and a few sheep for both wool and meat. We need a few more fruit trees. We have heaps of nut trees so no more of those with the exception of perhaps some almonds. I suggest apples, pears, plums, cherries, apricots, peaches, mulberry, fig and persimmon.

And so the family settled down to fixing fences, improving water storage and purchasing fruit trees and livestock. Seeds for vegetables were also acquired. Jason built a shed for blacksmithing.

"We really need to get varieties that can be self sustaining; I mean seed reproducing that grow true to form. I believe we can get these locally and from the one or two seed saver organisations" said Carl.

"Mum and I would like to get our own beehives and equipment for taking off the honey" Jason added.

"That would be great.. I think old Guy Italiano is still alive though he must be pushing ninety by now. I'll get in touch. He likes to breed a pretty quiet bee, not those damned angry Caucasians we had years ago! The number of times I was stung is nobody's business!"

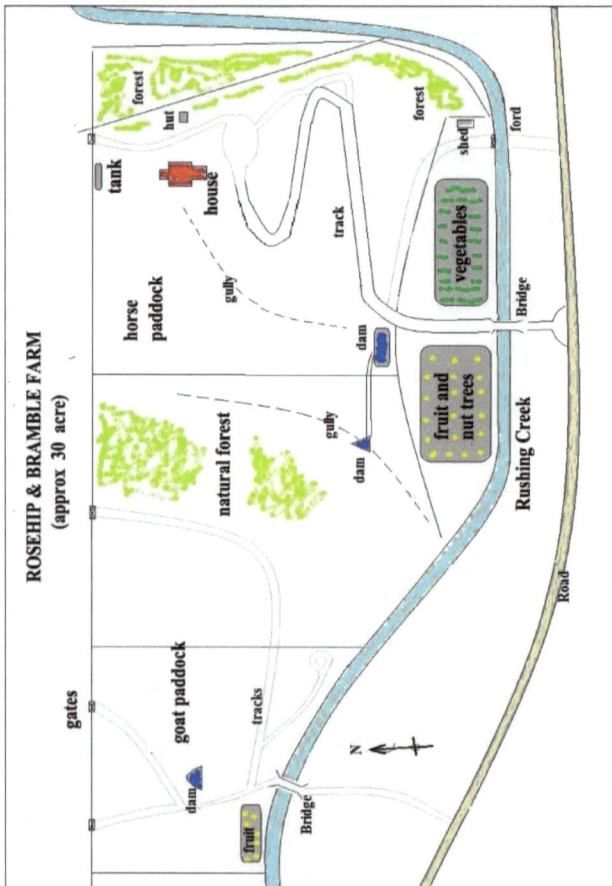

Plan of 'Rosehip and Bramble' Farm

Life went on for a couple of years at Rosehip and Bramble Farm with all
working hard to make it a success. It was almost Christmas. Bill and
Jonas descended from Melbourne with their wives and teenage children.

"How is dad?" Jonas enquired.

"Your father is getting a little doddery these days but not too bad"
replied Tina.

It was after dinner that Carl and Charly had disappeared.

"Where have they gone?" Bill asked.

"Oh, Charly always goes to bed about nine and your father likes to read
to her.

"Read to her? .. but Charly is in her mid twenties now is she not?"
retorted Jonas.

 "Well" Tina replied hesitantly, "she was supposed to have turned
twenty five last September actually". She released the words with a
most disturbed look on her face and almost a tear welling in her eyes.

"So what is he reading tonight?" enquired
Maria, wife of Jonas.

"I think it is White Fang by Jack London..
that was always one of Charly's favourites.

At this, the family sat around looking at each
other in bewilderment each unable to make a comment. Then Bill
bravely spoke up

"Doesn't dad know that this Charly isn't real? How did she die again?"

Tina struggled to get the words out and tears were at last streaming
down her face.

"It was two years ago this November just past. She had been on a visit
to her aunt in Amsterdam.. I had a letter. She was shot dead by a Dutch
soldier in Rotterdam after planting a bomb at night at some military fair
with another student. She had only just turned twenty three."

"But was it true?" enquired Bill.

"Well that was the result of the Dutch police inquiry and report. We found it out of character for Charlotte, I mean the bomb thing. She had always told us about her involvement in one or two student demonstrations. It has been hard to accept the claim of a radical change.. if that were true, I think I would have felt it!"

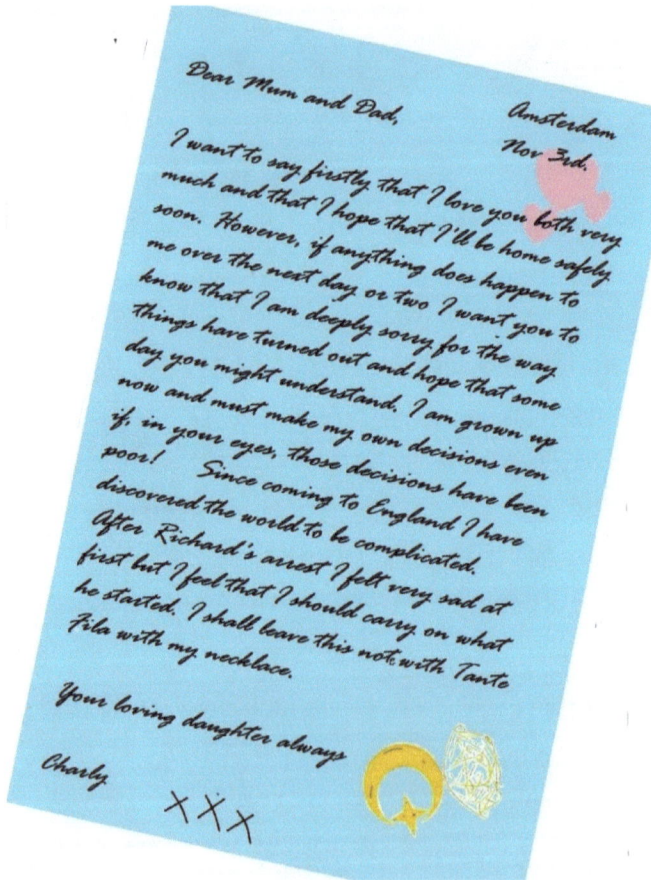

Charlotte's letter to her parents.

At the time, the Evening Standard had published a full page article on this incident by British university students that had succeeded in a terrorist attack on the Rotterdam Military Fair and Expo, similar to that of the London attack a month earlier. Incorrectly claiming her to be one of their own, an online statement by 'Islam Khilafah' said:

"Another of our soldiers of Islam, Fatima Sharlotta al-Australiyya has demonstrated our continual war against the Kufr in Rotterdam and was martyred today!"

The family had brought Charlotte's body home and buried her at the Islay cemetery just out of Rushing Creek. It is believed that she was the first Muslim to be buried there. An Imam came up from Traralgon to oversee the service. Many of the family attended from Indonesia: grandparents, uncles, aunts and cousins. Her aunty in the Netherlands and her friends in Warwick had each forwarded her things. Carl and Tina grieved for a very long time at the loss of their beautiful and intelligent daughter.

In his despair, Carl had spent a lot of money on purchasing an Indian 'Dana' robot from the company Sohana Kiss and had had it specially customised to resemble his daughter. Carl had instantly become attached to this machine and had taught it many things about his true daughter. She (it) even wore Charly's star and moon gold pendant! The robot had digested family photographs and videos and played the role as best it could, even going to bed at night in Charly's original room which still contained many of her personal things from childhood.

"I think we ought to destroy it" commented Bill. "It is doing more harm than good!"

"I'll second that" said Jonas stoically.

Tina made no comment, continuing with streams of tears.

Carl had been interviewed by both local and international reporters and stream media immediately after the terror incident involving Charly two years earlier. It had been a difficult time for all the family wherever they lived: at home in Australia, in the UK, Holland and Indonesia.

"Mr Jacobs, you are originally from the UK. How do you justify your daughter's attack on many UK companies at the Rotterdam Expo? Do you not see that as an act of treachery?"

"Not at all. There are times when we must all take a stand against wrong doing, even by our own Government or national interests."

"So you tacitly support violent terrorism Mr Jacobs?"

"No. I think civil disobedience and demonstrations are the more peaceful road to take."

"But Mr Jacobs, this cannot be described as a peaceful act!"

"My daughter is an adult and able to make her own decisions. From what I can gather the intent of the students was to disrupt the Military Expo in a way that avoided any loss of human life. If that is the truth of it then I support her actions."

"You support actions that might damage the economy of your former country Mr Jacobs?"

"I have given you my answer, don't try to trick me. To shoot these two young people dead was a despicable act by the Dutch Specials.. I still hold Britain dearly as the nation of my childhood. But you know.. the International Arms Manufacturers are not known for their high standards of morality these days. That is all I have to say .. "

The melee of reporters tried for more questions but Carl withdrew to the safety behind his front door and gave no more insights or satisfaction.

Twenty three   **Survival and the Great Restitution**

Guillame remained reticent on what to do with so many prisoners. This was now October, twenty thirty-three and he was exhausted. At sixty eight years he felt that finally his strength was waning and that his spiritual being yearned, nay, screamed out for rest and retirement at his distant farm. It was there, a haven of peace set among green rolling hills beneath familiar snow-clad peaks; there, the distant faint but perceptible rush of the mighty Jacobs river; there, a golden sun sinking into a copper sea. Oh how he missed it so!

The Great Restitution, as it had been described, was over and the survivors were gladdened by their prize, dispelling from their minds the hardships they were forced to deal with. The blood of most of the world's peoples had been shed and a semblance of order had been reinstated among the scattered remnants of humanity, clinging to remote places in the high latitudes of the southern hemisphere. But this was a world so very different from the one at the beginning of the troubles traced back some fifteen years afore. The new world was one of survival and depravation; one of primitive existence and struggle; one of ice and cold as the glaciers in both hemispheres reached their frosted tentacles towards the once temperate areas of Cancer and Capricorn. The dry central areas of Africa and Australis varied in temperature from 50 degrees by day to minus 50 degrees by night. Electricity and industrialisation as the planet once knew were gone. But a mere handful of the great armies of the Anglo Christian Alliance, as it was known, had prevailed and survived after so many good soldiers falling and women with their children destroyed in their homes. This had been a world war with no victor. Finally, towards the end of 2029, a great silence had descended upon the face of the Earth as the exodus from the North began to dwindle until people came no more.

Within four years, communities across the southern edge of the world had adapted to a village existence comparable to that of the middle ages. Communication was slow and the furthest outposts of the new Alliance received scant news and even this, at best, already being months old. But the certainty of the finality and end of this war was eventually received by all. Who would have thought that the great civilisations of East and West would have so quickly collapsed; a mere six months of war on a horrendous scale and proportion, leaving the vast expanse from the Mediterranean eastwards to the shores of the Pacific devoid of life of any sort, or at least so it was believed. Even the land in North America was now a polluted wasteland with the exception of the near Polar Regions where some life struggled on. It was said that tens of millions of motor vehicles lay silent in and around the city of Cape Town, South Africa, stretching back for hundreds of kilometres. They had poured down from Africa and Europe with great anxiety and terror. But only a few hundred persons ever escaped to the sea from Good Hope. What fate befell so many people is not known other than speculation of some tumultuous calamity.

Those lands and scattered islands of the southern hemisphere were able to sustain life; and even here, none dare venture further northwards than latitudes 35 or 40 degrees for fear of the radiation and extremes of climate. These evacuees, representing many nations and creeds, had inched their way south, crossing the equator in their millions. But it was the advancing cold of twenty thirty that took its final toll on humanity. Of the seven and one half billion people of 2029 it was estimated that there now remained a mere 750 000 souls; a survival rate of one for each 10 000.

The simple solution for the prisoners was put to Guillame by his most senior General and close confident, the trusted James McCrae. It was to give them free choice: either they must take their chances in the wastelands to the north or submit to the ways of the Alliance, work the land as freemen and respect the law of the communities. Cleverly, this was no choice at all. There was virtually no possibility of survival in the poisoned wastelands of the north, neither was there being apart from an organised community. To weed out the criminals from among them, the prisoners themselves were encouraged to form their own judiciary and pick out the worst. These were summarily executed. This extirpation was against the law for peoples of the Alliance, but time and energy held greater sway in these desperate early days. The women and children of the new communities were the utmost priority, their protection essential.

Guillame struggled with these harsh measures and sought refuge each night in his personal chapel for prayer, meditation and forgiveness. General McCrae always maintained deference for the Supreme Commander, whom he loved and admired above all others.

Men were different now. Much of the chaff was gone. Chivalry and noble gesture had returned with intolerance to those of low virtue. An ancient order had suddenly rekindled but not through the measure of coercion or employment of strict law. Those that had survived had seen and experienced terrible things; things that no person should ever need witness. During those bad months of the final war, whole cities and civilisations had evaporated into a swirling blackness of heat and liquefying devastation in a matter of seconds. The odour of death and decay swam in the wind. The pitiful cries of the maimed and dying on a grand scale were beyond comprehension. Then, the ensuing months of darkness and cold, instilling a fear so deep and terrifying that one necessitated blotting it from the mind or go insane. All this was so far-reaching into their souls and psyche that those survivors with strength enough seemed to be subjected to a veil of morality and a revived code of conduct and reverence not seen for hundreds of years. And now, in this year of twenty thirty-three, all who spoke the English tongue knew of Guillame; his deeds, his valour, his wisdom but above all his vision for a revived people at an interval where hopelessness prevailed and weighed heavy on all.

Progress would be slow. But these new men and women did not seek the world they had lost. They valued more their community, their reliance upon one another and steadfastness in their God. This God had long ago given all people the freedom of following their individual will and it was this that had finally brought them undone. The survivors could see and understand this and their determination now was to work and play when they could to a natural rhythm. They did not have lofty aspirations over fondness for a simple and ordered life. They counted their blessings and gave thanks wholeheartedly; and why not? They had land aplenty that was already beginning to heal itself. They felt joy from surviving to see their children rise. They had embraced a certitude that each would maintain this new harmonious culture that would be lasting; but more than all this they had Guillame who had been the force of their salvation and brought to them unity and nation. Whether Guillame lived for many years longer or no was irrelevant. His name would resound for many generations to come.

Grand Census of 2031

Zeeland North	335 563 souls	Tasman Land	47 334 souls
Zeeland South	121 239 souls	Cape Silver Chile	69 002 souls
Australis- South West	95 020 souls	Falk Land	2 541 souls
Australis- South East	134 566 souls	South Sandwich	1 793 souls
Isle of Mauritius	1 456 souls	Chatham Isles	677 souls

Total Population   809 191 souls

Gerard de Salvat

1st July, This Year of Our Lord, 2031

NOTE: It is believed that some surviving peoples inhabit the areas of Western Canada, Greenland, Iceland and Eastern Siberia. Of their total number, there is no knowledge at this time.

2037:   The underwater ships were hardly recorded now. A decade had passed since the worst events of the arrival of the self-contained metal whales from out of which spewed desperate men that murdered, pillaged and took away women. Their eternal heat engines were still active after nearly half a century in some cases, but individual components such as lamps, circuit cards and microchips to name a few, were exhausted, rendering these ships useless.

The southwest and southeast coasts of the great land Australis supported many communities, relying on fishing, animal husbandry and, in some cases, traditional wooden boat building. These boats of spotty gum and dense red gum were already renowned, serving the peoples 360 degrees of the broad Southern Ocean. Tasman Land was thought to have a population in the vicinity of 50 000 souls. Peoples from all parts of the old world had fled by boat to lands and islands where fish, birds and seals were still plentiful despite the catastrophe of global war. Altogether, it was now estimated that there were more than a million making up the peoples of the South. These had survived the shifting radiation clouds; relentless tornados and the great black chill of 2029 immediately followed by the deep freeze between 2030 and 2034. The majority of those making up the exodus from the North agreed to abide by the laws of the Alliance under Guillame. In this way they were assured of a chance of survival and assistance. Food, clothing and a supply of iron for smithing now seemed the priority over the gadgets so readily at hand before the Great Fall. Lectric was now a distant memory of the elders. Only the lightening seen in the skies on stormy nights was the prior experience, in a small way, available to a child's understanding. Of course there were the meetings where discourse and stories outpoured; but the children could barely grasp how it was. The few books under the careful control of the book guardians contained pictures of cities filled with people and moving things; but most other artefacts were considered as useless other than for decoration and often regarded as taboo. Objects made from iron, steel or other metals were coveted.

Guillame had impressed upon all that they were the chosen ones by God to create a new world society. He encouraged daily prayer and weekly communal ceremony that they might express their joy and gratitude for their deliverance. That nothing be lost of these beginnings, Guillame enforced each community to provide for a scribe to record the progress of the people that a history be passed down to the generations. These scrolls were to be copied periodically in advance of any deterioration. Chapters were taken and read aloud at the learning ceremonies that all might hear, know and be proud of the progress and accomplishments.

At length, Guillame was finally laid to rest in his seventy ninth year in the deep green meadow up above the crystal falls in his beloved native Zeeland. As the sun slowly dipped into the Western Sea, the sky became orange, then with ripples of pink and silver, the tall snowy peaks to the east gradually changed hue from white to shades of blue then to salmon. A ceiling of unfathomable black, bespeckled and pricked with sparkling diamonds shining clearly through the scented air gave the valley a final decoration of wonderful majesty and splendour; a scene lovingly familiar to the inhabitants below. All that lay beneath these stars: man, forest, river, field and ocean were bathed in this nightly splendour, the silence broken only by nature's murmurs.

Recorded and written faithfully by me, Benjamin Lionheart son of Guillame, this year of our Lord 2038 at Westfalls, Zeeland South.

[This Chapter originally appeared at end of book: *Nuclear Islam* by Tom Law]

Helter Skelter

Coda   **Of Course, It Doesn't Have to End This Way!**

As mentioned on the frontispiece this book is *in toto* a work of fiction and any resemblance to persons living or deceased is purely by coincidence and without any intent! Also, as you observe, the heading of this coda includes the words: "of course it doesn't have to end this way!" This then is the thrust and basic message to all of humanity and in particular our leaders and governments the world over, East and West. If time rolls on, as surely it will, and we get to those years beyond those encompassing the events described, all will be most happy and encouraged- and not least, the author. Happy in that the global community is still intact and encouraged in that someone somewhere has sat up, paid attention and acted in accordance.

But you know the problems of the world are not just the responsibility of poor leaders and poor government. Each individual must take her/his share of responsibility. Further, there are many scourges plaguing humanity which reduce the chance of a correct and fulfilled life for each soul. True, we do live under the cloud of nuclear weapons, sophisticated high tech weapons such as death rays and biochems but beside these there are also the baddies trying to get you to take drugs or participate in gambling that will enslave you and eventually destroy your life. Many countries, pressured by the opportunistic gun manufacturers have foolish and dangerous gun laws and gun regulations. America is not the worst but falls far short of its European friends in this matter. This is the downside of unbridled capitalism.

The other gripe is the unfettered ability of hate groups such as the KKK, Nazis and religious extremists to go about their projected plans and continually spew out the most outrageous bigoted and racist exclamations, seemingly not having broken any laws? It is a mystery how society tolerates these imbecilic morons without locking them away. What was the Second World War all about, what did the free world fight and die for? So that, at some later date, the same evil rubbish can wriggle out of the woodwork to slash at and attempt to cripple a safe democracy once again? No Sir! No Sir! For any society to survive where all have a safe and clean environment, where each individual can rise without discrimination to his or her full potential, is the hallmark of all that is good and righteous. We must shun and put away the voices of evil as well as exhibit them for all to see!

A free society is able to criticise its masters openly without retribution or punishment. In some countries, an attack on its government policy is seen as an attack on the whole nation. This is wrong. The government is the servant of the people. The government is NOT the nation! The people are the nation!

Neighbours nearly always share fences demarking the borders of what they own and what is theirs. Naturally the fruit tree hanging over this fence or the child's ball soaring over same will often cause some friction. But to physically strike your neighbour or worse, take to him with a weapon such as a hand gun, will bring everlasting sadness and distress to all parties. Neighbours have rights, but instead of dwelling on personal rights is it not better to be cordial and polite, to welcome them in for a shared meal or even just a chat over coffee? And so it is with nations. The world expenditure on weapons and armies is so outrageously disproportionate to state economies and production, that the net result is a very large section of humanity that has virtually nothing, is in constant despair and struggles to get food and potable water for essential sustenance. In so many examples in our modern world, the poorer nations are bled to sustain high living standards in the richer nations. This is wrong. This is fundamentally immoral and the world needs to change. As a pathetic defence of such immoral behaviour by corporations and governments, those opposing them are often labelled as 'extreme left' or mere cranks!

Despite all the different religions and the schisms within those religions, there are only two important precepts that all humanity need to understand:

I   there is only one God

II   the purpose of your life is to be creative and to help your brother or sister when they are in need.

All the rest is totally irrelevant and just the padding! If everyone looked hard enough into the teachings of their faith, they would surely recognise that these two statements are in fact the essence. If all people were to acknowledge this and remember just these two at all times, there should be no poverty in the world and certainly no wars between nations.

For those who claim to be atheists, firstly one can only lament that you are obviously of superior intelligence.. far beyond normal human understanding and capabilities! But never the less it is *your freedom and prerogative* to make that choice, and it should always be defended! But the author beseeches you to cling fervently to the second rule of life:

II   the purpose of your life is to be creative and to help your brother or sister when they are in need.

In doing so, along with the rest of us, it is a guarantee of a safe, happy and fruitful life. Remember that to accumulate goods and chattels and become exceedingly wealthy brings greater responsibility. Precept II becomes even more applicable for you because you possess the *power* to assist more than the rest of us.

As individuals we might throw up our hands and say "what can I do, how can I change the world from how it is?"

As a wise man said "an ocean is comprised of many drops of water." Yes, we are all just drops in an ocean. By example in the way we live, our values and the way we interact with others, it has a snowball effect. A single drop can indeed affect a whole ocean. It is important to know this and respect this. Never be persuaded to steer away from your life-sustaining values, for they are the true basis of human happiness. To have taken the trouble to say the simplest but kindest word to a stranger, to go to the aid, even in a minimalist way, of someone that obviously needs help- these are the actions that feed your own soul and bear you up to elation and fulfilment. It is as simple as that!

Consider the alternatives for a second. Greed, selfishness, looking out for oneself at all times with little thought for others. These traits lead to envy, jealousy and even hatred in the hearts of others.

"Good morning Mr Scrooge, Merry Christmas".

"Ah humbug! Humbug and nonsense."

But with just an ounce of civility, politeness and our eyes wide open, we see not only our place in the grand scheme of things but assist all humans around us to share in our glow that they also be uplifted.

Harsh and crude words insult the other human and help to bring her or him down. Humiliation leads to resentment and evil thoughts which, often enough, leads to violence. To create anything, even the humblest drawing, painting or item crafted from wood brings pleasure and satisfaction. Nurturing a flower garden or vegetable patch is a great work. Rearing a child is an honour bestowed.

All that has been said can be extrapolated to governments and nations. Building trust is the only safe way. Building armies and hideous weapons will ensure (albeit guarantee) that *they will eventually be used* resulting in the ruination of your country! There is no wall that was ever built in all history that could not be penetrated! Walls and armies do not guarantee absolute safety! The concept of 'peace through strength' should be rejected; for amassing a store of weaponry and flexing of muscles is more of a challenge and humiliation to others. It may command some respect, but in an unfriendly and resentful way! Wherever an aged Goliath stands proudly, eventually a simple and unpretentious youth, a David, will come along and slay him with the simplest of basic technology. That is an even greater humiliation!

There was much discussion earlier on HOW to eliminate nuclear weapons and other weapons of mass destruction from the planet. A solution offered was for all the smaller countries of the world to gang up against the BUGs i.e the very rich and powerful nations of the world. This can be done in the forum of the General Assembly of the United Nations. A proposal of a date for total disarmament was proffered with the punishment of fines to go into a universal fund to help lift the poorer nations. Basics such as water, electricity, food and clothing, might first be provided. This to be followed by roads, houses, hospitals and schools so that EVERY country of the world reaches a base standard of living for its citizens. ALL PEOPLES of the world as humans deserve these basic rights. But an immediate basic right for all humans on the planet is a guarantee of longevity of life itself without the threat of nuclear war and all its environmental consequences. The BUGs of course will be reluctant to 'give up' their power and position in the world. However continuous prodding and bringing about intellectual emancipation to these rich nations i.e that tearing down of nuclear arms, vast expensive armies and technologically advanced weapon systems would, in the long run, be economically beneficial to their country! It is a misnomer and false hope that possession of all these things will maintain a peaceful world.. on the contrary, the outrageous expense of a grandiose military with all the most destructive of weaponry only brings the final demise of humanity and possibly ALL living things on this our Earth ever probable and ever closer!

Thus it is up to the poorer nations to recognise the immoral and purely capitalistic behaviours and games of the rich that will FOREVER keep you powerless, eternally caught up in petty wars and POOR! To change this state of affairs, collectively smaller and poorer nations need to be brave and proactive in the United Nations until all these objectives have been reached. Only then will all humans walk tall and proud without fear and experience their rights as outlaid.

But the peoples within the wealthy countries also have a role to play. If your country is a nuclear weapon state, it is your duty and responsibility to change this by protest and civil disobedience. You will not be liked by some and others will accuse you as being a traitor. But, as stated, such weapons give no guarantee of safety and only advance the probability of their eventual usage as time goes by! We have reached a stage in Earth history where the world would be better off without them!

Beware the words! Beware the racist. Beware the bigot. Shun the deceivers, the tricksters and sellers of the elixir of everlasting life! Shun the words falling from the twisted tongue of hatred and urging you to commit murder for some dubious cause. If you kill another human being know this: you kill yourself and damage your soul permanently. Be traitor to those leaders that sound the trumpet to call you to war. Be wary of leaders that wish to waste the earnings of its peoples on uniforms and military hardware especially when there are so many shortages and deficiencies needed for a reasonable standard of living. Intelligent and evidence based decisions for the well being of the citizens of your country should always be paramount!

Nurture the environment, care for your neighbour and work towards a safe and peaceful world where all the nations are on the lookout that none shall fall down or stumble. Let us avoid the outpourings of the vials of the angels of death and destruction. We do not have to satisfy and fulfil any single tenet of the evil and satanic predictions of Revelations! An end to life on this planet through greed, excess and irresponsible stupidity by a handful of arrogant Generals? .. NO, it doesn't have to end this way!

Helter Skelter

Appendicitis

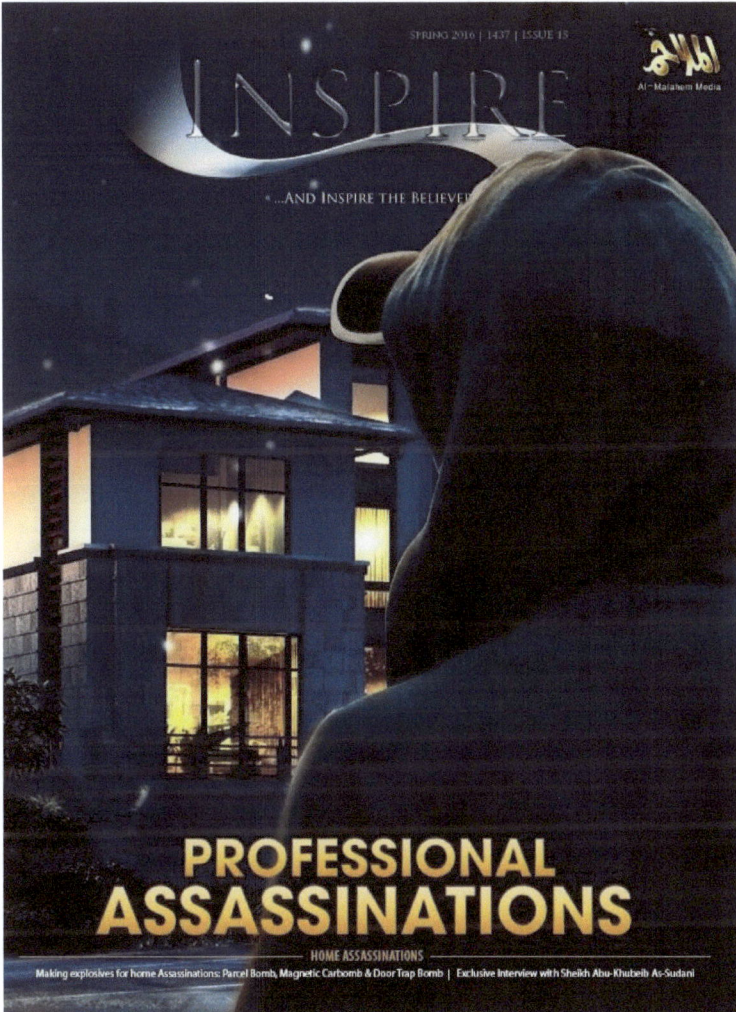

This is the cover of *'Inspire, Issue 15'* the magazine of al Qaida. It contains many articles on the progress of *'The Final War of Islam'* including interviews and profiles on infamous Jihadis like Osama bin Laden and Khalid Sheikh Mohammed*. In this particular issue we see

[* Responsible for planning the 1993 attack on the World Trade Center in New York, planning of 9/11 attack and the bombing of nightclubs in Bali in 2002]

instructions on the continuation of 'lone jihad' such as killing with knives, how to assassinate a target person and the making of various types of bombs. The thrust of the magazine is indeed to admire and inspire young men and women to go forth and commit murder, thus determining for them in the afterlife eternal nothingness. No matter what is written about any 'covenant' between man and God, be assured my reader 'God does not accept murderers into Paradise!' Here are one or two extracts:

> Despite of all that, we are still witnessing a great Islamic revolution from East to West. And a jihādi Uprising of such a scope and numbers that has never been witnessed by the Islamic world for almost a century. Therefore, the only choice that we have in gaining back our rights is by the use of force and weapons. The events and reality going on around the globe prove that the **world does not allow us to even enjoy the very simple basic rights, the right to freedom of worship**. They fight us under the name of Democracy, they wage war at the very core of our Islamic culture and identity, they consider everything contradicting Democracy as radical and fundamental. It is of course impossible for them to just allow us to rule by *Shariah*. Therefore, the eventual result is that fighting will continue until we remove this oppressive and dominant plague, America, upon the Muslims.

.. there is not much one can say on this other than it's a load of crap!

Published quote from Michael Warren of The Weekly Standard:

"But al Qaeda is not a simple top-down terrorist group that can be entirely vanquished by killing or detaining select key leaders. It is a paramilitary insurgency organization that is principally built for waging guerilla warfare. Terrorism is a part of what al Qaeda does, but not nearly all. And a key reason why al Qaeda has been able to regenerate its threat against us repeatedly over the past 14 years is that it uses its guerilla armies to groom new leaders and identify recruits for terrorist plots against the West."

Sadly much of what Michael says is true. Only Muslims themselves will ultimately defeat the murderers among them; it is not really the job of the West! But if al Qaida gets its way and divides the world into a major conflict, there will be no winners, only the slaughter of *billions*!

Sheikh Usama bin Laden:

"The most important goal in this new crusade war is preparing the environment for the greater Israeli Nation. A nation whose borders extend to parts of Iraq, Egypt, Syria, Lebanon, Jordan and whole of Palestine and covering a great portion of Saudi Arabia. What do you know about the greater Israel? It is the submission of the surrounding countries to the Jews. And what do you know about the Jews? They are the ones who fabricate lies about the Creator, so what about His Creation?"

It is noticeable that there are many references to the 'unbelievers' throughout this magazine i.e Christians and Jews, however there seems to be considerably more accentuation focussed on the Jews!

Sheykh Ayman Adh-Dhawahiry:

"Striking the West, particularly America in their own backyard.
And attacking their interests that are scattered everywhere. Supporters of Israel should pay with their blood and their economy the price for their support for Israel's crimes against Islam and Muslims. We must continue what was done by the Mujahideen in the blessed attacks of September 11, the invasions of Madrid, Bali, London and Paris. And continue the path of Ramzi Yousef, Mohamed Atta, Amrozi, Shehzad Tanweer, Nidal Hasan, Omar al-Faruq and the Tsarnaev brothers."

Again, what can one say? The rhetoric seems to have come straight from 1950s communist China, Russia or North Korea!

> These martyrs and the Knife Revolutionaries have devoted their lives and wealth to the struggle against the kuffar, and marched forth their youth in the fields of sacrifice, elevating the worries of the Muslims towards the Ummah - by the will of Allah. O heroes of this great uprising in the blessed land, do not ever abandon your weapon and continue your jihad and strike hard the hateful Zionists, for you have brought about great glory to your Ummah, with this revolt, it has soothed the hearts of the believers. It is no secret that the first guardian, supporter and greatest inciter to the Jews are the Americans – the head of kufr and every distress upon the Muslims.
>
> Where are the zealous Muslims in America, who clearly see their Muslim brothers in Palestine being tortured? It is because of this painful torture, that the blessed Knife Uprising has surfaced. Then why is it that you just sit and wait, with your hands tied up?

This whole article was about the 'knife uprising' i.e to encourage Muslims living in Israel/Palestine or anywhere in the West to randomly kill using the knife. We saw many stabbings in Jerusalem and in Europe about this time.. 2016 and afterwards.

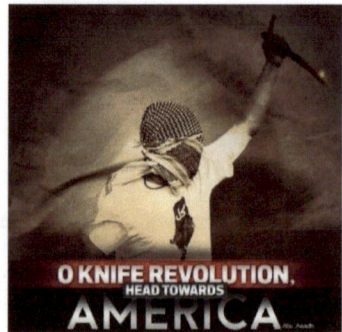

A Knife Wielder's Prayer:

Oh Allah, strengthen Islam and Muslims, demolish shirk
and the disbelievers, and protect and hold Islam.
O Allah, aid the Mujahideen in your path, and the outcome
of their Jihad be triumph, victory, and a grand opening
for Islam.

Oh Allah, punish the enemies of Islam.

Oh Allah, punish the brothers of the monkeys and pigs.

Oh Allah, punish America and destroy the disbelievers.

O Allah, punish the cunning raafidha. Send your wrath

upon them and tear them apart, oh Lord of the worlds.

Oh Allah, give security over the weak, oppressed and persecuted.

Our Lord, dispel away their worries and grief, lessen their

agony, raise their status and give them the best in their

families. We pray for the good in this world and the best in

the hereafter and may Allah protect us from the punishment

of the hell fire.

The author of this poem wishes Allah to do all the dirty work? Don't worry oh knife wielders.. your reward is eternal nothingness, not any hellfire! This article concludes by giving dates of all the knife attacks against Jews.

The rest of the magazine is devoted to 'lone jihad' techniques and strategies along with different types of bomb attacks to kill one's target.

There are some worrying elements concerning the production and distribution of this magazine:

(i) How is it that this author, and anyone else for that matter, is able to download this evil heap of horseshit from the internet? Are there NO restrictions put in place to block such material from falling into the hands of impressionable young men and women? Does the

concept of 'freedom of speech' on the internet allow ANYTHING no matter how putrid, vile or dangerous?

This brings about the second concern:

(ii)   The fact that this material is there for ALL to see prompts the suspicion that it is a scam and a forgery created by Israel or the West or the East for reasons best known to themselves!

It promotes hatred and agitates young and naïve Muslim men and women to make use of any tools of war to go out and commit murder. This is not the will of God but the will of evil. This is not the voice of Islam, it is the mad ravings of those agents, whoever they be, promulgating the final destruction of all of humankind and the destruction of all living things on planet Earth! We will take time to digest these facts before looking at Islamic State's propaganda magazine Dabiq, again supposedly to be genuine and not a concoction of some distorted and psychologically disturbed organization unrelated to IS!

I just warn all Muslims and non-Muslims that the intent of these instruments of propaganda is to get you to lift your hand in violence and destruction; to take away peace on Earth; to take away any chance of one reaching Heaven in the afterlife. Be warned and always be alert to the words of evil that aim to incite hatred in your heart and mind. Always remember that there is a correct path to confront injustice in the world and that path is not along the road of violence and self destruction! Do not stoop to insult your being, your soul and creative mind that God has given you for the sole purpose of doing 'good' in the world! Alternative action to peace and creativity is not permitted! To kill another human is to kill yourself and destroy your soul!

Taken from 'DABIQ 1437 (2016) Issue 15 pp 40-45' IS Magazine:

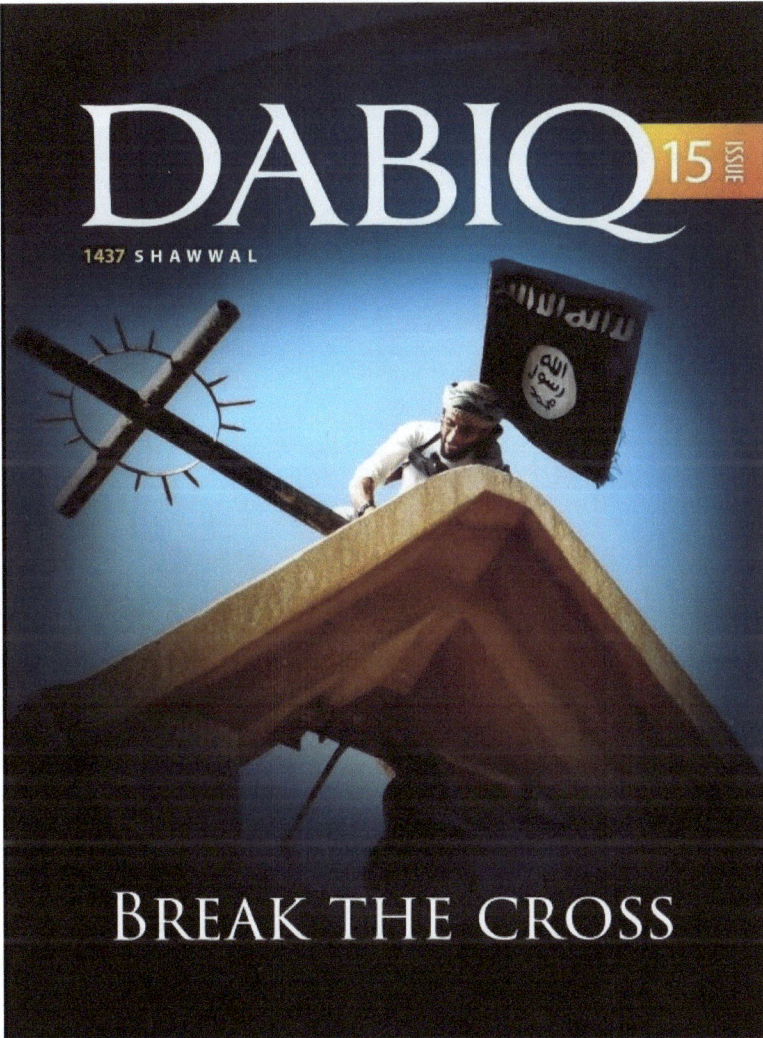

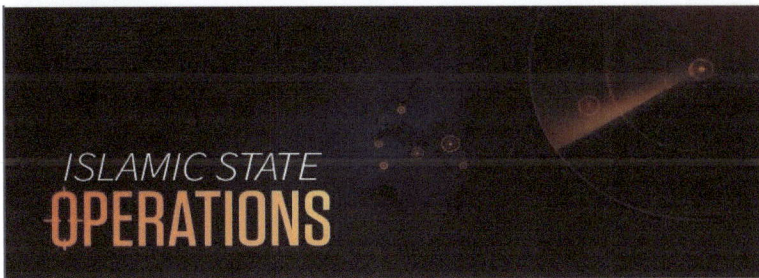

"As the soldiers of the Caliphate continue waging war on the forces of kufr, we take a glimpse at a number of recent operations conducted by the mujahidin of the Islamic State that have succeeded in expanding the territory of the Caliphate, or terrorizing, massacring, and humiliating the enemies of Allah. These operations are merely a selection of the numerous operations that the Islamic State has conducted on various fronts across many regions over the course of the last few months:

Dimashq Wilayah – On the 3rd of Rajab, the soldiers of the Caliphate targeted a warplane during the course of ongoing clashes near Tall Abu Shamat east of the Dumayr military airbase. It was shot down inside the airbase and three other planes were damaged as a result. Just three days later, the soldiers of the Caliphate stationed in Ribat in the region of Bir Qasab targeted a Nusayri warplane that took off from the Khalkhalah airbase in the Suwayda countryside, leading to it crashing near the airbase. One week later, on the 14th of Rajab, the soldiers of the Caliphate succeeded, by Allah's grace, in shooting down a third Nusayri warplane using antiaircraft guns after it took off from the Dumayr airbase. The plane crashed 30 km from Mount Dakwah in the eastern countryside of Dimashq, and the mujahidin succeeded in capturing its pilot, Azzam Eid, a native of Hamah, after he ejected from the plane and landed with his parachute near the crash site.

[This poor bastard was later cruelly burned alive by IS]

The Philippines – On the 5th of Rajab, the soldiers of the Caliphate succeeded in confronting an attempt by the Filipino Crusader army to take control of the mujahidin's locations in the Philippines. Seven troop carriers were blown up, killing those inside, and clashes took place in which several more Filipino soldiers were killed, with the rest fleeing in defeat. The operation resulted in approximately 100 Crusaders being killed and dozens more being wounded. During the course of the battle, three mujahidin attained shahadah. We consider them so, and Allah is their judge.

On the 2nd of Sha'ban, a group of the Caliphate's soldiers attacked one of the Crusader army locations in the village of Tobijan in the area of Maloso. Clashes took place and ended with one Crusader soldier killed and at least one other wounded, with the rest fleeing in terror and the mujahidin taking their weapons and equipment as ghanimah. Four weeks later, the soldiers of the Caliphate killed two Filipino soldiers in clashes near the town of Barangay in Basilan. They then succeeded in killing another 15 Filipino soldiers towards the end of Ramadan in two attacks carried out over the course of two days in the city of Marawi.

Just a few days later, the mujahidin killed another two Filipino soldiers in the town of Togaya, and also destroyed an armored vehicle near the military base in the city of Marawi, killing those inside the vehicle. They would then go on to launch an attack on the Filipino Crusader army with various types of light and medium weapons on the island of Basilan in the southern region of the Philippines. Battles continued into the month of Shawwal with the mujahidin killing several more Filipino Crusaders and capturing strategic points. Another 20 Filipino Crusaders were killed later in the same month in fierce clashes that took place in Basilan.

Jazair Wilayah – On the 8th of Rajab, six soldiers of the murtadd Algerian army were killed and another nine were wounded when the soldiers of the Caliphate detonated an explosive device as the murtaddin passed by on the Mount Wahsh road in the area of Qusantinah. Less than a week later, the soldiers of the Caliphate detonated several explosive devices on Algerian soldiers as they were sweeping the area of Qurush in Jijel in the northeastern region of Jazair.

Ninawa Wilayah – On the 9th of Rajab, six American helicopters backed by two warplanes attempted to carry out a special forces raid at dhuhr in the area of Sabuniyyah on the road between Mosul and Tal'af-ar. The soldiers of the Caliphate succeeded, by Allah's grace, in foiling the operation after targeting the warplanes using antiaircraft guns, driving the Crusaders away in defeat.

Khayr Wilayah – On the 11th of Rajab, the soldiers of the Caliphate, by Allah's grace, succeeded in completely capturing the remaining Nusayri positions in the industrial neighborhood in the city of Khayr after attacking it from several points using various types of weapons. They killed several murtaddin, with the rest fleeing in terror, and the battle moved to the outskirts of the neighborhood of Tahtuh. The mujahidin likewise captured several weapons and various types of ammo* as ghanimah. Less than two weeks later, they launched a surprise attack on Nusayri locations and fortifications separating between the industrial neighborhood and the neighborhood of Tahtuh. This came after one of the mujahidin created openings in the Nusayri line of defense# using a bulldozer, paving the way for Islamic State infantrymen to stealthily advance and carry out a surprise attack. They succeeded in capturing

[*an interesting abbreviation not expected in this document! #American spelling]

270

several points where the murtaddin were entrenched after they fled in defeat. During the course of the same week, they carried out attacks on several Nusayri army locations in the neighborhood of Tahtuh and succeeded in capturing them.

Bengal – On the 15th of Rajab, the soldiers of the Islamic State assassinated a university professor in the city of Rajshahi for calling to atheism.

On the 22nd of Rajab, the soldiers of the Caliphate targeted a Hindu mushrik in the city of Tangail who was known for insulting the Prophet Muhammad and killed him by stabbing him with a knife.

On the 29th of Sha'ban, the soldiers of the Khilafah succeeded in assassinating Sunil Gomes, one of the Christian heads of disbelief*. He was killed in the village of Bonpara in Northwest Bangladesh. On the 2nd of Ramadan, the soldiers of the Caliphate carried out a security operation in which they succeeded in killing a Hindu priest* known as Ananta Gopal Ganguli in the district of Jhenaidah in Western Bangladesh.

On the 5th of Ramadan, the soldiers of the Caliphate assassinated a Hindu mushrik by stabbing him with knives.

On the 27th of Ramadan, five inghimasi soldiers of the Caliphate carried out an attack on the Artisan Restaurant, which is frequented by Crusader foreigners of varying nationalities, in the city of Dhaka. The mujahidin held a number of hostages as they engaged in a gun battle with apostate Bengali police, and succeeded in killing and injuring dozens of disbelievers before attaining shahadah.

[* emphasizes necessity to murder any significant symbol of any other religion!]

Somalia – On the 17th of Rajab, the soldiers of the Caliphate detonated an explosive device on a military vehicle belonging to African Crusader forces in the area of Taridish in the city of Mogadishu, with the blast destroying part of the vehicle.

On the 21st of Shawwal, they targeted three members of the Somali security forces, killing two of them and injuring the third, in an attack in the city of Baidoa.

Hims Wilayah – On the 25th of Rajab, the soldiers of the Caliphate launched a wide scale attack on the Nusayri army in the area of Sha'ir at fajr. They succeeded in capturing three points, and in killing nearly 20 murtaddin and taking a number of light weapons as ghanimah. They then continued their attack, during the course of which an istishhadi operation was carried out, striking the last position in which the murtaddin were entrenched. The mujahidin succeeded in capturing 13 checkpoints, placing the Sha'ir Gas Company within their firing range. A number of Nusayri soldiers were killed in the operation, with the rest fleeing, and the mujahidin captured two tanks, a 23mm heavy machine gun, a 14.5mm heavy machine gun, a number of Konkurs missiles, a mortar cannon with some mortar rounds, several light weapons, and various types of ammo. Two days later, on the morning of the 27th of Rajab, the mujahidin succeeded, by Allah's grace, in completely capturing the Sha'ir Gas Company. This came after they carried out an attack on the main checkpoint, killed several murtaddin, and captured weapons and ammo as ghanimah. On the 29th of Rajab, in continuation of the major battles launched by the soldiers of the Caliphate in the wilayah, the mujahidin carried out an attack on Nusayri locations in the Mahar gas field northwest of Tadmur from several points. They captured half of the gas field following clashes in which several kuffar were killed.

The mujahidin would go on to blow up the Sha'ir Gas Company to deprive the Nusayri regime of a major source of economic benefit, in addition to completely burning the Mahar Gas Company by repeatedly targeting it with artillery shelling.

Egypt – On the 1st of Sha'ban, the soldiers of the Caliphate in Cairo conducted a security operation in which they carried out an attack on a bus carrying 8 murtaddin belonging to the police investigations division in the area of Hilwan in the southern part of Cairo. They fired on the murtaddin and succeeded in killing them all, including Captain Muhammad Hamid, the assistant investigator for the Hilwan police. They also took some light weapons as ghanimah and returned safely back to their locations. The operation came as part of the campaign dubbed "The Battle of Shaykh Abu 'Ali al-Anbari" and in revenge for the oppressed women in the prisons of the murtaddin in Egypt. [It had been reported that rape and beatings had occurred in one/some prison(s)]

On the 2nd of Ramadan, the mujahidin ambushed an Egyptian police patrol unit in the area of Ras al-Birr in Dumyat and succeeded in killing and injuring several murtaddin, including Major General Mustafa Muqbil, the deputy head of security for Dumyat. Meanwhile, following close tracking and surveillance, the mujahidin targeted a vehicle carrying the murtadd, Brigadier General Hisham Salim, head of investigations in Daqahliyyah with a hail of gunfire, killing and injuring those inside.

Hims Wilayah – On the 3rd of Sha'ban, the soldiers of the Caliphate launched a wide scale attack from multiple points on Nusayri army locations near the T4 airbase. They succeeded in capturing the abandoned battalion base as well as two of the checkpoints responsible for protecting the airbase. They killed more than 20 Nusayri soldiers, captured a 57mm cannon, a 23mm autocannon, light and medium weapons, and two vehicles as ghanimah, and also bombarded the airbase with mortar rounds.

Sahil Wilayah – On the 16th of Sha'ban, 10 istishhadi soldiers of the Caliphate set out to target the coastal cities of Tartus and Jablah, which are considered to be among the most important strongholds of the Nusayri army and the Rafidi militias allied to it. Five of the istishhadi attacks were carried out in Tartus and the other five in Jablah. The istishhadi attacks were preceded by two car bombs, one of which targeted the Nusayri bus station in Tartus, with the other targeting the Nusayri bus station in Jablah. This was followed by the istishhadiyyin all detonating their explosive belts on various other groups of Nusayriyyah. The blessed attacks in the two cities resulted in nearly 400 killed and wounded, many of them Nusayri soldiers and officers, including Brigadier General Ayman Qarah Falah, Brigadier General Majd Ahmad 'Abdullah, and Colonel Fuad Ibrahim Isma'il.

'Adan Abyan Wilayah – On the 16th of Sha'ban, the soldiers of the Caliphate carried out an istishhadi operation that succeeded in massacring* dozens of murtaddin. Our brother Abu 'Ali al-'Adani succeeded in reaching the home of the commander of the Badr military base in the area of Khawr Maksur in the middle of 'Adan, which the murtadd Yemeni army uses as a recruitment center. He detonated his explosive belt in the midst of a group of murtaddin, killing more than 30 of them and injuring dozens more. This was followed by an explosive device being detonated at the military base's gate, killing even more of their mushrik soldiers.

[* not a word that any normal army would use/choose to describe an operation!]

274

West Africa Wilayah – On the 28th of Sha'ban, the soldiers of the Caliphate launched a wide scale attack with various types of weapons on a military base in which the murtaddin of both the Niger and the Nigerian armies were mobilizing in the city of Boso in Southeast Niger. They succeeded in killing at least 35 murtaddin and injuring nearly 70 more, in addition to capturing a large quantity of weapons and ammo as ghanimah.

America – On the 7th of Ramadan, our brother Omar Mateen, one of the soldiers of the Caliphate in America, carried out an attack on a nightclub for sodomites in the city of Orlando, Florida. He succeeded in massacring* the filthy Crusaders, killing and injuring more than 100 of them before he was killed. The operation was reported as being the most deadly attack in America since the Manhattan raid 15 years ago.

[* again, strange choice of this word!]

France – On the 9th of Ramadan, a soldier of the Caliphate – our brother Larossi Abdalla – carried out an attack on the assistant police chief for the district of Les Mureaux near Paris. He stabbed him to death in addition to killing his wife, who was also a member of the police, and was then killed.

One month later, on the 9th of Shawwal, a soldier of the Caliphate – our brother Mohamed Lahouaiej-Bouhlel– carried out an attack in the coastal city of Nice in response to the Islamic State's calls to target nations participating in the Crusader coalition fighting the Caliphate. He used a large truck to run down the Crusader citizens in the French city as they were celebrating the French national holiday known as Bastille Day, and succeeded in killing more than 80 people and injuring more than 300 others before being killed by French police.

Less than two weeks later, two soldiers of the Caliphate – Abu Jarir al-Hanafi and Ibn 'Umar – carried out an attack on a church in the area of Normandy in Crusader France in response to the call to target the nations of the Crusader coalition fighting the Muslims. They slaughtered a priest* and wounded a number of others before being killed.

[* in fact, sadly, this was an elderly stand-in priest and not the regular priest!]

Hadramawt Wilayah – On the 22nd of Ramadan, a number of Islamic State soldiers carried out a string of istishhadi operations that struck the dens of the murtaddin, killing more than 50 of them and injuring dozens more. Our brothers Jarrah al-'Adani and Qaswarah al-'Adani detonated their explosive vehicles targeting the counter-terrorism center and the special forces, and succeeded in massacring them. Another four istishhadi soldiers of the Caliphate then entered the counterterrorism center and finished off the murtaddin who were still alive. Meanwhile, our istishhadi brother 'Ammar al-Ansari detonated his explosive jacket on a group of special forces soldiers at the entrance to the area of Khalaf south of the city of Mukalla, while our istishhadi brother Muhsin al-Yamani detonated his explosive jacket on a group of special forces soldiers at the Days point north of the city.

Furat Wilayah – On the 24th of Ramadan, the soldiers of the Caliphate confronted a Sahwah force advancing from the American military bases in Jordan, accompanied by American air cover, towards the Caliphate's territory west of the city of Albu Kamal in Furat Wilayah. They battled them at the Hamdan airport in the area of Hizam, massacring 40 of their fighters and taking another 15 of them prisoner. They also succeeded in capturing 6 4-wheel drive vehicles, 6 trucks loaded with weapons and ammo, and 12 reconnaissance drones. The murtaddin who remained alive retreated through the desert, with the mujahidin pursuing them as they fled.

Sinai Wilayah – On the 25th of Ramadan, an Islamic State covert unit succeeded in assassinating Musa 'Azmi, also known as Rufail, a Christian priest at the Mar Girgis church known for waging war against the Muslims. The priest was targeted and killed using light weapons near his home in the Salam suburbs in the city of 'Arish.

Baghdad Wilayah – On the 28th of Ramadan, our brother Abu Maha al-'Iraqi carried out an istishhadi operation targeting a group of Rafidi mushrikin in Karradah City in the middle of Baghdad. He detonated his explosive vehicle on them, killing more than 200 Rafidi mushrikin and injuring more than 170 others   [.. sending the IS to eternal nowhere!]

North Baghdad Wilayah – On the 3rd of Shawwal, five inghimasi soldiers of the Caliphate carried out an attack on a gathering of Rafidah at one of their pagan sites known as the tomb of Muhammad 'Ibn Ali al-Hadi in the district of Balad south of the city of Samarra. They killed the guards at the tomb as well as a number of mushrikin before engaging in fierce clashes with a patrol that arrived to rescue the tomb and the remaining worshipers. During the course of the clashes, some of the inghimasiyyin detonated their explosive belts on the murtaddin, raising the total number of dead Rafidah to more than 100, with dozens more wounded. The tomb also suffered extensive damage as a result of the operation.

Germany – On the 14th of Shawwal, a soldier of the Caliphate – our brother Muhammad Riyad – carried out an attack in response to the Islamic State's calls to target the citizens of nations participating in the

Crusader coalition fighting the Caliphate. He used an axe to hack the kuffar on a train in the city of Wurzburg, injuring a number of them before being killed by German police. Less than a week later, our brother Muhammad Daleel, carried out an attack targeting a group of Crusaders in the city of Ansbach. He detonated his explosive device, injuring 15 of them, four of whom suffered critical wounds.

Khurasan Wilayah – On the 19th of Shawwal, two soldiers of the Caliphate, Najibullah al-Khurasani and Talhah al-Khurasani , carried out an attack on Rafidi mushrikin in the city of Kabul using hand grenades. They succeeded in killing and injuring a number of them before detonating their explosive jackets on those of them who were still alive, resulting in approximately 87 murtaddin being killed and more than 200 others being wounded. This blessed operation comes in response to their participation in the killing of Ahlus-Sunnah in the Levant and for the purpose of cleansing Khurasan of their shirk, as well as all other usurped lands of the Muslims.

Helter Skelter

We ask Allah to grant the highest levels of Paradise to those who were true to their covenant, to aid those who continue to wage war against His enemies, to continue inspiring those in the lands of the Crusaders to strike them in their most vulnerable places, and to fulfill His promise of victory for those who fight for His cause. Amin."

Some translations:

Caliphate Khilafah	area designated for Muslims only
enemies of Allah	all other persons outside the Caliphate i.e Islamic State - particularly unbelievers or non-Muslims
kufr, kuffar	unbelievers, representatives of any other religion -you an' me bro!
mujahidin	Islamic fighters
shahadah	gain a place in heaven, martyrdom
ghanimah	prize of war
murtadd murtaddin	traitor Muslims
mushrik mushrikin	enemy
istishhadi	suicide soldiers (often with explosive vests)
Rafidi Rafidah	derogative description of Shia Muslims by the Sunni Muslims.. literally: 'those who reject'
Crusaders	those opponents of IS thought to be Christians
apostate	one that has left the religion

Author's Notes: As you can see, all this evil was just a snapshot over a couple of months in 2016. ALL the murderers and especially those that committed suicide have stupidly forfeited their place in the afterlife! Murderers don't get to Paradise!

But there are some telltale aspects that point to one's questioning on how authentic the whole document is! (The author here is not questioning the occurrence of the events.. each described did in fact occur.) For instance, there is a persistent and heavy thrust regarding the destruction of Christian artefacts and Christians themselves. Armies opposing the Khilafah are called 'Crusaders', a term borrowed from the 13th and 14th centuries! If it has been manufactured (the magazine Dabiq that is) by the West or the East purely for propaganda purposes, then it did an excellent job in getting everyone angry and to demonise the Islamic Inquisitors! There are many instances in the various reports that almost ring in the same vein as the communist rhetoric of yesteryear! Further, the terrorist attacks around the world coupled with such propaganda only serve the notion of 'eternal total war' between Muslims and non-Muslims until one or other is completely defeated or worse, annihilated. Again one need ask the most pertinent question:

".. who wants such a war and what is their ultimate objective?"

The Baghdad events as well as some in Egypt were definitely "Sunni Muslims murdering Shia Muslims". Thus we also have another layer where Muslims of one branch of Islam are being encouraged to murder Muslims of another branch. Whom does this benefit?

Besides the one repeatedly given i.e that the Islamic Inquisitors want this total war, there are other alternative answers! The founding dialectic of this book was to explore these possible alternatives. The reader must decide for herself/himself what these might be and what action must follow.

As stated elsewhere we have various factors influencing (either directly or indirectly) this war:

- the necessity of Israel to survive and hence defend itself against its enemies identified or perceived
- empire building or maintenance by the BIG powers of the world (termed the BUGS earlier)
- an attempt to remain eternally as the chief banking empire in the world' economy/economies by a singular entity
- maintenance of armaments manufacture, distribution and usage by large bullyboy corporations in those industries
- a desire to continue the control of oil and gas production and distribution by major corporations in the industry
- a proxy war between players among the BIG powers of the world (again, the BUGS) e.g Russia and America
- very rich Saudi Arabian, Tunisian and other supporters of a Sunni Muslim war against Shia Muslims as well as against all other religions, non-Muslims and atheists
- The artificial creation of al Qaida and Islamic State by BIG MONEY to destroy Islam itself (by creating internal and factional conflict) in order to defend the dominance of the status quo i.e Judeo-Christian Western Civilisation
- a combination of ALL of the above

It's a tangled web of intrigue with MONEY and POWER as the defining forces of perpetual evil that brings misery to millions of humans on the planet. The medical cure for a sick body with an obvious active cancer is to surgically remove the cancerous cells.. so this is what needs to be done!

Reliance on America alone is not the correct road. That great country is not the panacea for all the world's evils. Until it rids itself of the 2nd amendment and severely tightens its gun laws it might be seen by some as part of the problem! This is particularly reinforced by its massive arms sales to foreign countries that then go on to use them to murder civilians (as examples, see: Israel bombing of Gaza; Saudi Arabia bombing of Yemen)

Whilst most people in the West indulge in sports teams, Harry Potter, Star Wars and daily trashy soap operas on TV without a serious analysis of what is developing, we can only expect things to worsen. Each of these is not inherently evil in itself, but act as a cushion and distraction to serious thought. Add to this the surreal of laptops, pods and pads we have a generation of youth with their eyes and heads literally in the cloud! Further add the tens of millions growing up in refugee camps with a daily diet of hatred and confusion; we have a potion of future disaster the envy of that possibly concocted by the Stygian Witches!

The first step of magnificent proportion is to reign in ALL the manufacturers of weapons and armaments and for the UN to bring about tighter international laws on the trading of weapons and armaments. But the world banking system and economic high potentials also need reform. This is a very great challenge as there are exceedingly high walls of defence that these organisations have in place for their own protection and survival. The slow evolution of international law may be the way forward to ensure a true global society where all humans have opportunity and their basic rights are protected. This of course will be anathema and a bitter pill for the mega rich and power brokers that presently spin the planet! Had they done a better job they would be safe, but they have let us down and must now be swept aside. No one will mourn their eventual demise and passing!

[On the subject of weapons and military hardware, it is interesting to note two things regarding Islamic State: (i) they never possessed ICBMs, warplanes, warships, submarines, tanks or any similar hardware and (ii) there has always been scanty mention of **from who and from where they obtained weapons..** we can only surmise on reasons for this absence of information!]

The world has ALWAYS since the beginning of time experienced pogroms and genocide based on ethnicity or religion. After WWI Turkey drove out and was responsible for the death of millions of Armenians. Christian Europe tried to liquidate all its Jews during WWII, exterminating some six million people. The Khmer Rouge murdered more than a million opponents of its brand of communism in Cambodia. In 1994 Rwanda Hutus slaughtered more than half a million Tutsis, mostly by machetes. The Serbs murdered thousands of Muslim men and boys in Srebrenica in the 1990s. The Russians assisted the cruel government in Afghanistan to murder thousands of its opponents in the same period. Chechnya is still under the Bear's yoke! Burma's Rohingya Muslims were driven out of that country with many murdered and their villages burned to the ground. The Kurds of Iraq, Turkey and Iran are still seeking a homeland after centuries of oppression.

Genocide seems to be a human trait conjured up by the herd instinct in difficult times where some scapegoat is required as a sacrificial offering to Satan. It seems that hatred of a group of humans with some identifiable differences to the norm is as easily adopted and slipped into as one might change ones clothes. The human is a gullible and naïve animal that feels safe as part of a herd regardless of the values of the herd. THE VOICES OF PROTEST AND INDIGNATION ARE OFTEN FEW, FEEBLE AND COME TOO LATE! For all the trials and tribulations of the past one hundred years or so, it appears that we have made little progress and we witness a repetition of the mistakes of history. Now, with the pressure of world population and environmental challenges stamped on top of our normal and predictable behaviours, there is little hope for our survival. Perhaps just a lucky few will make it to the end of the 21st century.. and by necessity, having started over!

FOREIGN POLICY OF THE BUGS AND GLOBAL BANKERS

START HERE

```
DEMOCRACY  ◄—  FOREIGN   —►  DICTATORSHIP
               COUNTRY

NOT            FRIENDLY       NOT
FRIENDLY       TO US          FRIENDLY
TO US                         TO US

POOR    LOTS OF   INTERACT IN   LOTS OF    POOR
+ NO    OIL AND   AS PROFITABLE OIL AND    + NO
OIL     MINERAL   A MANNER      MINERAL    OIL
        WEALTH    AS POSSIBLE   WEALTH

IGNORE                                     NO
                                           NUKES
        HAS       HAS NO
KISS    NUKES     NUCLEAR   MASSIVE        NO
THEIR             WEAPONS   FAMINE         CRISIS
ASS...                      OR GOV'T
OR HARASS                   ATROCITY
ECONOMICALLY     FIND PRETEXT               IGNORE
UNTIL            TO INVADE
FRIENDLY                    LOTS
                            OF MEDIA   NO MEDIA
                 INVADE     ATTENTION  ATTENTION
PROVOKE
UPRISING                                   HELP
            INSTALL A
            PUPPET      PROVOKE
SUCCESS  ◄— GOVERNMENT  CIVIL WAR   FAILED STATE
```

[Adapted from original by Andy Singer]

284

Islamic Organisations Listed as Terrorist:

- Abu Sayyaf Group (ASG)
- Al-Murabitun
- Al-Qa'ida (AQ)
- Al-Qa'ida in the Arabian Peninsula (AQAP) Yemen etc.
- Al-Qa'ida in the Indian Subcontinent (AQIS)
- Al-Qa'ida in the Lands of the Islamic Maghreb (AQIM)
- Al-Shabaab
- Ansar al-Islam (formerly known as Ansar al-Sunna)
- Boko Haram
- Hamas' Izz al-Din al-Qassam Brigades
- Hizballah's External Security Organisation (ESO)
- Islamic Movement of Uzbekistan
- Islamic State (formerly listed as Al-Qa'ida in Iraq)
- Islamic State East Asia
- Islamic State in Libya (IS-Libya)
- Islamic State Sinai Province (IS-Sinai)
- Jabhat al-Nusra (alias Jabhat Fatah al-Sham)
- Jaish-e-Mohammed
- Jamiat ul-Ansar (JuA) (formerly known as Harakat Ul-Mujahideen)
- Jemaah Islamiyah (JI)
- Kurdistan Workers' Party (PKK)
- Lashkar-e Jhangvi
- Lashkar-e-Tayyiba
- Palestinian Islamic Jihad

Helter Skelter

References

A Problem from Hell- America and the Age of Genocide, Samantha Power, Flamingo 2002

Boy in Blue Raincoat, Tom Law, Longership Publishing Australia, 2011

China Collection, Tom Law, Longership Publishing Australia, 2014

Collected Works, John Wesley, 32 vols., 1771-1774

Critical Theory Since Plato, Hazard Adams, Harcourt Brace Jovanovich Inc., 1992

DABIQ 1437 Issue 15 pp 40-45, Magazine of Islamic State 2016

Day of the Triffids, John Wyndham, Penguin 2014

Encyclopaedia Britannica, Macropaedia 15th Edition

Filth, Irvine Welsh

Gai-Jin, James Clavell, Hodder & Stoughton 1993

Goeritno, Ir. KGPH, Soeryo, Hitler Mati di Indonesia: Rahasia Yang Terkuak, Indonesia: Titik Media, 2010

Guns Off Cops Guns Off Everyone, Tom Law, Longership Publishing Australia, 2016

Heretic, Ayaan Hirsi Ali, Harper Collins Publishers 2015

History of England, Vol I, vol II, Cassell Special Edn., John K King & Son.

I am Malala, Malala Yousafza with Christine Lamb, Weidenfeld & Nicolson 2013

Islands of Danger, Earnest Beaglehole, Wellington Progressive Publishing Society 1944

Nuclear Islam, Tom Law, Longership Publishing Australia, 2016

On Walden Pond and Civil Disobedience, Henry David Thoreau, Dover Publications, 1995

Practical Self Sufficiency, Dick and James Strawbridge, DK Melbourne 2017

Ratline: Soviet Spies, Nazi Priests, and the Disappearance of Adolf Hitler, Peter Levenda, Ibis Press, Florida USA

Return to Animalia, Tom Law, Longership Publishing Australia, 2015

Six Thinking Hats Edward de Bono, Penguin 1985

Stop the Islamization of America, Geller Pamella

Studies in the Psychology of Sex, Henry Havelock Ellis, seven vols., 1897-1928

Tai Chi, Hinkler Books 2011

The Confessions of William James Chidley, Edited by S McInerney, University of Queensland Press, 1977

The Decline and Fall of the Roman Empire, Edward Gibbon, two vols., The Modern Library Inc., New York

The Door in the Wall, Margurite de Angeli, William Clowes and Sons 1960

The First Fleet, Jonathon King, MacMillan Australia, reprint 1989

The Koran, Penguin

The List, Michael Brissenden,Hachette Australia 2017

The Lord of the Flies, William Golding, Penguin 2016

The Melbourne Age, various 2017

Traitors, Frank Walker, Hachette Australia 2017

What Will Survive, Joan Smith, Arcadia Books 2007

International Organizations to Eliminate Nuclear Weapons:

- The ATOM Project, an International non-profit organisation seeking entry into force of the Nuclear Non-proliferation Treaty and the limitation of all nuclear arsenals
- European Nuclear Disarmament, which held annual conventions in the 1980s involving thousands of anti-nuclear weapons activists mostly from Western Europe but also from Eastern Europe, the United States, and Australia.
- Friends of the Earth International, a network of environmental organizations in 77 countries.
- Global Zero, an international non-partisan group of 300 world leaders dedicated to achieving the elimination of nuclear weapons.
- Global Initiative to Combat Nuclear Terrorism, an international partnership of 83 nations.
- Greenpeace International, a non-governmental environmental organisation with offices in over 41 countries and headquarters in Amsterdam, Netherlands.
- International Campaign to Abolish Nuclear Weapons
- International Network of Engineers and Scientists for Global Responsibility
- International Physicians for the Prevention of Nuclear War, which had affiliates in 41 nations in 1985, representing 135,000 physicians; IPPNW was awarded the UNESCO Peace Education Prize in 1984 and the Nobel Peace Prize in 1985.
- Nuclear Free World Policy
- Nuclear Information and Resource Service
- OPANAL
- Parliamentarians for Nuclear Non-Proliferation and Disarmament, a global network of over 700 parliamentarians from more than 75 countries working to prevent nuclear proliferation.
- Pax Christi International, a Catholic group which takes a sharply anti-nuclear stand.
- Ploughshares Fund
- Pugwash Conferences on Science and World Affairs
- Socialist International, the world body of social democratic parties.
- Sōka Gakkai, a peace-orientated Buddhist organisation, which held anti-nuclear exhibitions in Japanese cities during the late 1970s, and gathered 10 million signatures on petitions calling for the abolition of nuclear weapons.
- The Ribbon International, a United Nations Non-Governmental Organisation promoting nuclear disarmament.

- United Nations Office for Disarmament Affairs
- World Disarmament Campaign
- World Information Service on Energy, based in Amsterdam, The Netherlands
- World Union for Protection of Life

International Campaign to Abolish Nuclear Weapons

The International Campaign to Abolish Nuclear Weapons is a global civil society coalition working to promote adherence to and full implementation of the Treaty on the Prohibition of Nuclear Weapons.

https://icanw.org/au

Other Useful Sites:

https://globalzero.org/

https://cnduk.org/

https://nuclearweaponsfree.org/

https://un.org/disarmament/wmd/nuclear/

https://psr.org/

https://greenpeace.org/Home/What we do

https://concentric.org/films/wpiali-info-resources-anti-nuclear-groups.html

Helter Skelter

Websites to Assist Refugees and Those in Need:

https://amnesty.org.au/DonateToday/PleaseDonateNow

https://anglicare.org.au/directory-category/migrant-refugee-support

https://vinnies.org.au/Refugee-Services

https://refugeecouncil.org.au

https://refugeecouncil.org.au/Charity

https://unrefugees.org.au

https://refugeecouncil.org.au/

https://carad.org.au/

https://asrc.org.au/

https://julianburnside.com.au/asylum-seekers/asylum-seeker-organisations/

https://roads-to-refuge.com.au/refugees-australia/supporting-arrival.html

https://refugeeswelcome.org.au/

https://vinnies.org.au/page/Our_Impact/Asylum_Seekers_Migrants_Refugees/

https://redcross.org.au/migration-support.aspx

https://redcross.org.uk/What we do/Refugee support

https://sanctuaryaustraliafoundation.org.au/

https://riserefugee.org/

https://ssi.org.au/

https://arcrelief.org/

Canada:

https://ccrweb.ca

https://www.nccpeterborough.ca/?page_id=10560

https://www.com-management.org/home/2017/2/11/refugees-citizen-power

https://auraforrefugees.org

https://novascotiaimmigration.com/support-for-refugees/

https://soscanada2000.com/migration/newact/refugee/refasspro.html

https://redcross.ca/how-we-help/migrant-and-refugee-services

Here are some smaller groups to consider helping:

Syrian American Medical Society provides medical treatment on the ground in southern Syria as well as for refugees in Turkey, Lebanon, and Jordan.

Karam Foundation is a Chicago-based charity that operates out of Turkey to raise funds for rebuilding schools in Syria and securing educational opportunities for Syrian children.

Sunrise USA is a U.S.-based non-profit to provide emergency-relief programs to Syrians, both internally displaced and refugees abroad. They deliver food, support education, establish trauma-care facilities, and facilitate orphan sponsorships.

Islamic Relief USA is a larger non-profit; provides food, clothing, housing necessities and medicine for refugees in neighboring countries. To support these efforts, specify "Syrian Humanitarian Aid" on the donation page.

Project Amal Ou Salaam is a grassroots initiative sponsoring schools in Syria, Jordan and Turkey; it also organizes arts, drama, sports and photography workshops for refugees in and outside of Syria.

National Syrian Project for Prosthetic Limbs is a program, operated by UK-based Syria Relief that builds prosthetics and offers physical therapy to Syrians who've lost their limbs in the conflict.

Other Titles by Tom Law:

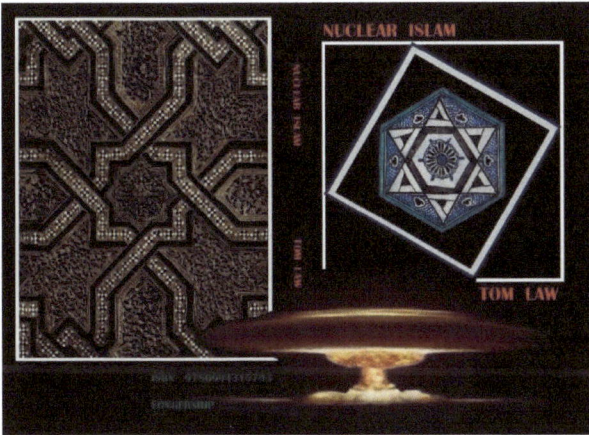

Nuclear Islam   3rd Edition

ISBN   9780994315793

This expose on what our future holds if we continue down the nuclear road looks at the various scenarios from conventional nuclear power plants. Also discusses the causes and outcomes of Islamic terror and how we can heal the divisions between the various religions on the planet. Population expansion is beyond our control- taken together with finite resources, the planet faces some tough times ahead!

Return to Animalia

ISBN 9780994315700

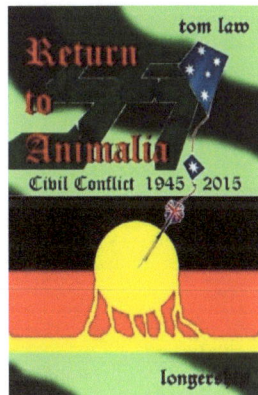

Politics of contemporary Australia as seen through the eyes of perhaps a very British Australian. A disquieting diatribe on many issues with solutions given as possible suggestions. Could easily be construed as unapologetic extremism by some, but sensible remedies by others- depending on one's perspective!

Helter Skelter

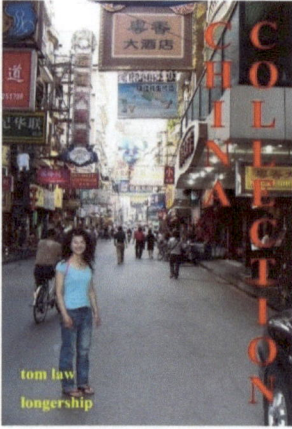

China Collection.

ISBN 9780980725889

This is a collection of four books of poetry by Tom Law on political and environmental observations written over a period of six years whilst working in Jiangsu province, China as a science teacher. It is a commentary on Chinese life, politics with a little romanticism thrown in. There are also references to world events over the period particularly the Middle East conflicts

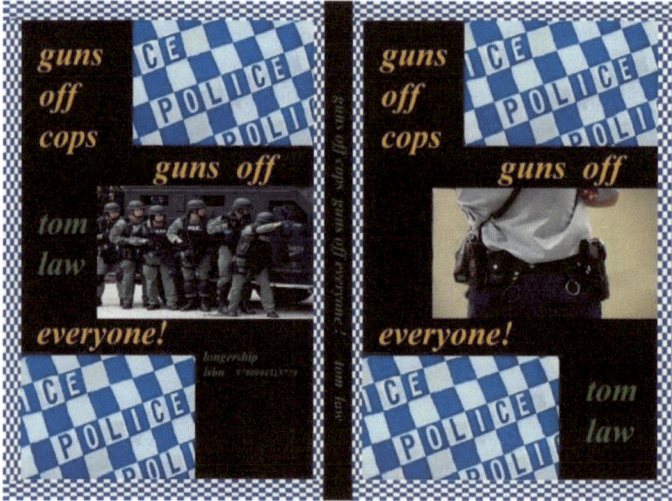

Guns Off Cops Guns Off Everyone!

ISBN   9780994315779

A hard look at US policy on guns and the continual high rate of killings by guns in that country. Also describes the roll of the armaments industries in wars around the world and the development of the new weapons.

Available at: amazon.com   amazon.ca amazon.co.uk   amazon.de amazon.fr amazon.it amazon.es amazon.in amazon.co.jp amazon.cn amazon.id .. also, for other titles by Tom Law please go to: longership.com

Helter Skelter

Radio Star Diana   **words and music by Chas Rose**

Auriga, Spica, Virgo, Vela, Carina
Oh radiant star oh goddess Athena
You live in the heavens, light up the night sky
As gift to this earth your musing harp and voice ply

Your voice to the millions 'cross oceans and deserts
Your countenance brilliant, smile never to leave us
You live in our hearts to a rhythm that's beating
Your distance your closeness touch all the world's people

Radio star Diana, beam down on us forever
Radio star Diana, gentle voice on music quiver
Radio Star, oh radio star, radio star Diana
Radio Star, oh radio star, radio star Diana

You're a comet, a meteor, a satellite and saviour
Planet Venus, silver moon, ethereal spirit of the cosmos
Zodiac new sign, oh constellation
Bringing to mankind a revelation

Radio star Diana, "universal love transmitter"
Radio star Diana, "omnipresent peace transcender"
Radio Star, oh radio star, radio star Diana
Radio Star, oh radio star, radio star Diana

Your subjects that loved you, the sequence of scenes
Paparazzi captured your body for those gloss magazines
At the tip of Apollo your spirit was rising
To tread on the warlords, yoke of the nations
But now they can't touch you, spoil or hurt you
Their fear turns to fever as they slip from their cover
The naked aggressor, the cheap profiteer
The finger accusing, the time it is near

Radio star Diana, winging your way through ether
Radio star Diana, hail messenger of new era
Radio Star, oh radio star, radio star Diana…

Bye bye planet blue I'm so very sad to be leaving you
Bye bye planet blue it's been so long now it's here too soon
Bye bye planet blue this is the end I'm so in love with you
So long planet blue it's just begun, you're almost out of view
https://www.amazon.com/Radio-Star-Diana-Chas-Rose/dp/B075JQVQ6X
https://www.youtube.com/watch?v=sNGR_Vd3KNA

Helter Skelter

About the Author

photo by: Zhang Yumin

Tom Law has lived on and off in East Gippsland, Victoria, Australia for a period of nigh on forty years. Originally from England, he was educated at Melbourne High School and later at Monash University. He describes his academic progress as chequered.. "the problem with education is that it can get in the way of living..." But Tom never lets the dust settle under his feet and seriously views learning as his life-blood along with exploration of everything. As a teacher of Chemistry he has worked in many different countries, Indonesia, China and Australia in particular. The storyline, interspersed with political rambling, is purely fictional but has some elements of personal experiences of a small timber mill community of which he was a part for some twenty years. Building his life and home "among the gum trees" he has developed a deep affinity and love for the natural environment of this unique part of Australia. "Very few places experience the convergence of bird life from such a wide range of habitats.. forest, high plains and coastal dwellers all breeze in and out of this area, depending on the season and prevailing weather. Migratory types such as swallows visit from as far away as China. When I first came here as a young man I could distinguish between a wattle tree and a eucalyptus but that is where it ended. Now I can view a Blackwood and differentiate it from a variety of these trees."

Tom built his first house from natural materials at hand.. stone, timber, slate and whatever could be recycled from earlier building materials left over from the gold era of the mid-nineteenth century. "So many cultures have made an impact on this area in a brief frenetic period of gold mining. They came from China, Europe and North America in search of their fortunes. Some stayed, some died penniless and others returned home after some success. What now takes less than a two hour drive to a large regional town took three days at least by wagon and horse. The local cemetery tells tales of woe and grief from a bygone age of hardship and struggle difficult to comprehend in modern times."

Tom has two adult sons from his first marriage plus a daughter and son from his second marriage to an Indonesian lady.

Helter Skelter

English and French depart Genoa to attack Barbary Corsairs   1390

From Froissart MS, British Museum.

Helter Skelter

Helter Skelter

Helter Skelter

Helter Skelter

Helter Skelter